Rich, timely, wide ranging, provocative, and wise, Miller's *The Grand Design* is a book to be read slowly, pondered, and discussed. Even those who may disagree with a point or two will be immeasurably enriched by the huge wealth of insights here.

OS GUINNESS
Author of *The Magna Carta of Humanity*

Darrow Miller has worked in sexist cultures where women are devalued, treated as little more than servants for men. And he has worked in Western feminist cultures, where women are often expected to function like men; their uniqueness as women is still devalued. In *The Grand Design*, Darrow offers a healing biblical vision where men and women reflect the relationship within the Trinity: unity without uniformity and diversity without superiority.

NANCY PEARCEY
Professor and scholar in residence at Houston Christian University, author of *Love Thy Body* and *The Toxic War on Masculinity*

This brave book reminds us that women can do everything a man can do and one thing a man can't do. A woman's childbearing ability means men should step up and take on obligations to free women to be all they can be, both in the general economy and the home economy. We need to make room for exceptions, but *The Grand Design* shows the overall pattern that God intends and we can enter, for His glory and our good.

DR. MARVIN OLASKY
Chairman, Zenger House

Other Books by Darrow Miller

Servanthood: The Vocation of All Christians

Discipling Nations: The Power of Truth to Transform Cultures, with Stan Guthrie

God's Remarkable Plan for the Nations, with Scott Allen and Bob Moffitt

God's Unshakable Kingdom, with Scott Allen and Bob Moffitt

The Worldview of the Kingdom of God, with Scott Allen and Bob Moffitt

Against All Hope: Hope for Africa, with Scott Allen and the African Working Group of Samaritan Strategy Africa

On Earth as It Is in Heaven: Making It Happen, with Bob Moffitt

The Forest in the Seed, with Scott Allen

Nurturing the Nations: Reclaiming the Dignity of Women in Building Healthy Cultures, with Stan Guthrie

LifeWork: A Biblical Theology for What you Do Every Day, with Marit Newton

My Place in HIStory: Discover Your Calling

LifeWork: Developing a Biblical Theology of Vocation

Emancipating the World: A Christian Response to Radical Islam and Fundamentalist Atheism

Recovering Our Mission: Making the Invisible Kingdom Visible

Wisdom: The Way to Human Flourishing, with Gary Brumbelow

A Toxic New Religion: Understanding the Postmodern, Neo-Marxist Faith that Seeks to Destroy the Judeo-Christian Culture of the West, with Scott Allen

Don't Let Schooling Stand in the Way of Education: A Biblical Response to the Crisis in Public Education, With contributions by Scott and Kimberly Allen, Thomas A. Bloomer, Vishal Mangalwadi, Darrow L. Miller, Christian Overman, and Elizabeth L. Youmans

A Call for Balladeers: Pursuing Art and Beauty for the Discipling of Nations, with Stan Guthrie

THE
GRAND
DESIGN

THE
GRAND
DESIGN

Rediscovering Male and Female as the Image of God

DARROW MILLER
WITH STAN GUTHRIE

credo
house publishers

Published in the United States of America by Credo House Publishers,
a division of Credo Communications LLC, Grand Rapids, Michigan
credohousepublishers.com

ISBN: 978-1-62586-265-5

Cover design by Joshua Hernandez
Interior design by Jonathan Lewis
Editing by Vanessa Carroll

Printed in the United States of America
First Edition

To Marilyn—The Bride of My Youth

My wife for fifty-seven years (and counting)

The mother of our four children:

Nathan

David

Jonathan

Maryrose

The grandmother of fourteen precious grandchildren

The Queen of the Manor!

Contents

So God created man in his own image,
in the image of God he created him;
male and female he created them.

GENESIS 1:27

If man is not made in the image of God, nothing then
stands in the way of inhumanity. There is no good
reason why mankind should be perceived as special.
Human life is cheapened. We can see this in many of
the major issues being debated in our society today.

FRANCIS SCHAEFFER

Prologue

I HAVE SEEN broken families and broken nations. I have seen children abandoned by their fathers and women exploited, abused, and discarded by the men in their lives. As I have traveled the world for forty years working for international nonprofit organizations that seek to address hunger and poverty, my heart has been broken by the hurt in people who have not known who they are, why they are here, and for what they have been made.

Over these years, I have been confronted with two inescapable truths:

First, one of the greatest causes of poverty in the world is a lie: "Men are superior to women!" This lie is virtually universal and goes back in time to near the beginning of creation.

Second, from the beginning of time, the family was designed to be the bedrock of a nation. If the family is broken, the nation will be broken!

With the deplorable philosophical relegation of spiritual reality into subjectivism, Western cultures today view the world exclusively through a materialistic lens. We define our problems in materialistic terms and believe that money alone will solve poverty. But money will not solve the problems of broken and impoverished families, communities, and nations. These have deeper roots, roots that are at the level of culture and belief systems. To begin to substantially help hurting families and communities, we must begin at the level of worldview and mindset.

Even though we remain primarily a materialistic society, we can't escape the natural spiritual longings that God places in our hearts. As Saint Augustine said, "You have made us for yourself, O Lord, and our heart is restless until it rests in you."[1] Tragically, instead of satiating our thirst with living water, we continue to dig dry wells of pagan spirituality.

In the early decades of this century, a wave of irrationality and denial of reality began sweeping the world at warp speed via social media. This wave asserts without evidence that individuals are "god," they are the center of the universe, and they have the power to define reality. It denies that we live in a moral universe, the universe is real, and we are born biologically either male or female. As we now know all too well, people are seeking to deny the reality of their own biology and change their sexual nature with chemicals, surgery, and language.

Binary male and female sexuality is being deconstructed through a new ideology that manifests *linguistically*, *physically*, and *legally*. Because ideas have consequences, and terrifying ideas have terrifying consequences, the sexes are being eliminated through a militant ideology that denies reality, reason, and biology, and enthrones human emotions at the center of the universe.

The erasure of woman takes place *linguistically* with the redefinition or elimination of the words "woman" and "mother" from our vocabulary. At the confirmation hearings of Judge Ketanji Brown Jackson to join the U.S. Supreme Court, Sen. Marsha Blackburn asked the nominee, "What is a woman?" Brown Jackson, a Harvard graduate, lawyer and judge, woman, wife, and mother of two, declined to answer, saying she was not a scientist.

Simply saying the obvious, that a woman is a "female human being," would have undermined the sexual deconstruction narrative of so many of her supporters. It's easy to see that the language of reality is being replaced with a whole new vocabulary born in delusion: "transgender," "gender affirmation," "pregnant person," and LGBTQIA+.

The destruction is done *physically* by denying the reality of motherhood. This happens by emptying the womb of life through abortion. It continues by surgically removing sexual organs and breasts so that a woman cannot get pregnant or nurture the next generation. What was known for years around the world as the evil of female genital mutilation has gone mainstream and is now a multibillion-dollar industry.

Finally, the onslaught is *legal*. Laws are changing to allow, protect, and promote these once illegal procedures, to permit and encourage biological men to compete in women's sports, and to mandate the use of the new vocabulary—including punishments for those who choose to affirm the language of reality.

This irrationality—really, a toxic new religion—is being promoted in schools to children as young as four or five. School boards, local, state, and national governments, universities, and nonprofits are on board. Whole industries are making billions of dollars off this ideology, including hospitals, "big pharma," medical technology, and banking. What was once unheard of or dismissed as evil, is now promoted as the new normal, "the good."

The destruction sure to follow will bring immense pain to individuals and nations and will not be solved with money. The root of the problem is in the realm of ideas. So what is the idea that has sparked all this insanity?

It is the big lie, mentioned above and believed by sexists, feminists, and many transgender people, that male is superior to female. Thus, we will need a better set of ideas—articulated and incarnated into life and institutions—to replace the big lie.

The truths we must articulate and live are these: We do not live in a lifeless and silent universe without God. We are not gods. Trying to define our own existence is perilous. Doing so amid the fixedness of the universe inevitably leads to trouble! Women are *not* inferior to men and are not to be treated as objects. They are, like men, the very *imago Dei* (image of God) and thus possess inherent dignity and are worthy of respect. Although someone might seek to deny his or her biological sex, defying reality usually brings great pain.

What is the solution to the deep issues of sexism and "transgenderism"? We must understand the Grand Design, see the divine pattern for our existence, and discover why we have been made the way we have. We must understand the purpose of our existence. The solution to our problems is not found in money, material things, chemicals, or surgery. It is instead rooted in the *teleonomic* character of living organisms. That is to acknowledge that in their structure and performance human beings, in fact all living things, were designed to realize and pursue a purpose. If you examine your body, you can understand the purpose of your existence. The argument from design is our strongest apologetic for this critical issue. We will examine it thoroughly in *The Grand Design*.

This book is my attempt to speak Truth to the lie that has dominated history and is now running roughshod through this toxic new religion. *The Grand Design* stands on the following presuppositions:

> We live in a personal and moral universe. God exists, and He is not only eternal and all-powerful, but also personal and moral.

> God is the Designer and Creator of the universe. He has made it with transcendent patterns that reflect His existence and nature.

Because there is a Grand Designer, there is a Grand Design. We are made biologically male and female in the image of God—the *imago Dei* for a purpose. Behind our biology is a transcendent nature (think architectural design): masculine and feminine (or paternal and maternal).

From where did this design come? The very heart of God! God the Father has both a paternal and maternal heart.

I trust that this book will be life-affirming for you. Enjoy this journey of discovery!

The Deadliest Lie

WHEN SHE WAS twelve, Chloe Cole told her parents she wanted to be a boy. At thirteen, Chloe began taking puberty blockers and testosterone to begin the transition. Also at the age of thirteen, Chloe chose to take the next radical step and had her perfectly healthy female breasts surgically removed.

At seventeen, Chloe awakened to the possibility that one day she might desire to have her own children, but now a successful pregnancy might be impossible. And if she could somehow conceive and give birth, she would never be able to breastfeed those precious babies. In a recent television interview, Chloe stated that:

> As an adult, I will never be able to breastfeed whatever children I will have. I don't even know if, because I was put on puberty blockers and testosterone at only thirteen years old, . . . I'll be able to conceive a child naturally. I made an adult decision as a child.[2]

Chloe's choices, based on teenage feelings, were almost completely irreversible. She gave doctors permission to mutilate her body and change her physical makeup permanently in pursuit of an idea. Ideas have consequences!

The idea that destroyed Chloe's life is almost as old as time; it is the sexist lie that *men are superior to women*. This deadly lie is perhaps the greatest lie in the world, bringing immense poverty and personal and family destruction. Chloe is simply one young woman whose life has been shattered by

1

this lie. In the first chapter of the book, you are likely to be overwhelmed by the horror and poverty this lie has brought to our global family.

The latest iteration of this lie comes from the newest movement of feminism, in which the distinctives between male and female are obliterated. Chloe is one of the millions of people who now believe that they can choose their biological sex. They deny that they are given a sex by God from conception and instead believe that they can write their own narrative. They believe they can create the world they want. They alone determine their identity in every way. In many ways they want to usurp God's role and *be* gods themselves.

How did we get here?

This lie has deep roots that can be traced back to the Enlightenment's rejection of the "old order" established by the Creator and embrace of a "new order" with man at the center. In seventeenth-century Europe, the so-called Age of Reason began to replace premodern Judeo-Christian theism with the modern notions that God does not exist, man is the center of the universe, and that through the study of the natural world, mankind can discover truth and create a perfected future. As the worship of God was replaced with the worship of man, culture and language changed. All that was downstream from culture—politics, economics, and social institutions—was "de-formed." Half the universe—the transcendent—simply disappeared.

Men and women were no longer considered to be the *imago Dei* but were reduced to highly evolved animals. Human freedom founded within the framework of a moral universe was replaced by a "silent universe" in which people had license to live however they wanted, without moral constraints. Like other animals, human beings were now free to function sexually on instinct and impulse. The transcendent nature of masculine and feminine was eradicated, reducing people to biological and sexually binary male and female.

The Enlightenment was the ideological starting point of the modern world. Eventually it gave birth to the sexual revolution. Biologist Charles Darwin argued that men were mere animals who had sex out of instinct, not moral or metaphysical purpose. Philosopher Friedrich Nietzsche pronounced God as effectively dead and sexual license as the name of the game. Psychoanalyst Sigmund Freud argued that sexual repression stemmed from Judeo-Christian moral virtues. Eugenicist Margaret Sanger argued that evolution needed to be sped up to cull those deplorables unfit for life. To perfect the human species she founded what became Planned Parenthood, the largest abortion provider in the world. Physician and advocate Mary Calderone saw the public schools as the platform for indoctrinating children into comprehensive sex education.

Modern feminism brought many deceptions that have led to our current chaos. Out of reaction against misogyny, or macho culture, women tried to prove that they could do just what men do. In rebellion against the ubiquitous lie that men are better than women, women ironically started living out that lie *by trying to become men.* They abandoned their distinct feminine qualities and crusaded for interchangeability. These feminists have argued that men and women are *equal* and therefore, they are the *same.*

Modern feminists rejected the legacy of first-wave maternal feminists, who argued that despite men and women's essential differences, they had equal dignity and value. They also asserted that the woman's maternal role was of equal importance to the health and flourishing of a nation. In contrast, the modern feminist denied the unique contribution of the feminine nature and the maternal heart, insisting that equality would only be achieved by women seeking to be like men. The lie of male superiority survived the feminist challenge.

This is the sexual legacy of modernism. But how did we move from the modern world, where biology still means something, to the postmodern world of gender identity and so-called "transgenderism"? This thread begins in 1923 with the Frankfurt School, aka Institute for Social Research, and some influential German academics who sought to reshape Marxism through cultural rather than economic categories. In 1935 the Institute moved to the United States where the movement of Cultural Marxism slowly spread, giving birth to Critical Theory.

The Postmoderns in the movement not only rejected the Bible as a source of truth; they rejected science (reality) and reason (philosophy) as sources of truth. While the Moderns eliminated the ideas of a transcendent masculine and feminine, the Postmoderns eliminated biology—male and female. They moved from the word "sex," which was related to biology, to the social-construct word "gender." While sex is physical and binary (male and female), "gender" is fluid.

With the death of modern culture, a postmodern culture has emerged that denies reason and reality and has created a toxic environment of confusion for people of all ages, especially for young people. With input from institutions and social media, young Chloe Cole determined that she wanted to be a man so badly that she would deny her biological reality, taking testosterone and receiving a double mastectomy.

While some groups seek to eliminate female genital mutilation globally, there is a new multi-billion dollar "medical" industry that seeks to mutilate the bodies of boys and girls, men and women for enormous profits through "gender-affirming surgery." Let's call this what it is, an all-out war against and mutilation of men and women alike. This is the latest set of evil ideas aiming to deform humanity made in the *imago Dei*.

This is insanity. It seems that the whole postmodern manifestation of the same lie is destroying a new generation of children, adults, and families. As we have abandoned the Creator and His creation, we have lost our way. We no longer know:

- who we are as individuals,
- what it means to be human,
- what it means to be male and female, or
- what human sexuality is.

As we have turned from the living God, we have worshiped and served images made to look like man or created things. As we have returned to pagan worship, we have reverted to pagan sexuality.

In our quest to determine our own realities, lives are being torn apart. We live in a post-truth, post-moral, post-family, and post-maternal world. Modern and postmodern worldviews have led to sexual license (unbridled sexual freedom or sex without responsibility). Sexual license has led to sexual addiction and, on a global scale, a horrendous sex trade.

We need to rediscover the Grand Design, and what it means to be male and female made in the image of God. As we do so, let's remember that we live in a broken world full of shattered lives. *The Grand Design* is meant to convey a vision of what God has imagined for the human family, a beautiful standard to be aimed for—not a standard to break ourselves against.

There is hope in our broken world. God exists and He has designed us, in His image, for a wonderful purpose. There is hope for the family of faith to understand the depth and beauty of the biblical narrative and the sheer wonder and significance of our being made male and female.

There is hope for today's generation of young people who are confused about their identity. Let me say to them: *Your life is unique. There is no one in the world like you. Your biology is one of the markers that help you discover your uniqueness. You were made by God for a God-given purpose. The adventure of life is to discover that purpose and to walk in its calling. You can find your true identity in the One who created you, Jesus Christ.*

The Grand Design will be helpful for anyone who is interested and open to honest discussions on the nature of human sexuality and the importance of family formation. I have written this book for several audiences:

- first, for all who are looking for a beautiful, wonderful, reality-bound expression of human sexuality and family formation;
- second, for globally minded, thoughtful Christians;
- third, for men and women who have struggled with their identity in today's sexually chaotic environment and who are interested in what it means to be male and female; and
- fourth, for leaders working in compassion ministries, missions, youth ministry, and in training church and civic leaders.

I have created study questions after each chapter to encourage personal reflection, to use as a starting point for discussion with friends, or as the basis for a study group.

Now enjoy the journey of rediscovering the Grand Design—of being male and female in the image of God.

——— STUDY GUIDE ———

1. What is your response to Chloe's story?
2. Where do you see the gender identity movement growing in your culture?
3. What is the lie that marks one of the greatest causes of poverty and destruction in the world?
4. What two fundamental things does postmodern culture deny? Why is that significant?
5. From what does pagan sexuality derive? Do you agree or disagree? Why?
6. Where can we find hope for the poverty and brokenness derived from the lie that men are superior to women?

Section 1

PART 1

Sexism vs. Husbandry

CHAPTER 1

The War Against Women

[WARNING: Chapter One, "The War Against Women," reveals the darkness of reality in a fallen world that has denied the Designer and the Grand Design. Many people reading about the breadth and depth of this manifestation of evil can feel overwhelmed. If this reality is too heavy for you, please skip ahead to Chapter Two.]

DR. AMARTYA SEN, a Harvard economist and Nobel Prize laureate, shocked the world in 1990 with this statement: "More than 100 million women are simply not there."[3] Sen coined the term "missing women," those who should be alive but are not. Baby girls in the womb and out of the womb have been systematically murdered simply because they are female.

A war is being waged against women. It's rooted in misogyny, the hatred of women (*miso*, hatred, and *gyny*, women). Today, it is estimated that there are 200 million fewer women alive in the world than there should be—nearly equal to Brazil's population. India and China systematically kill more baby girls each year than are born in the United States. Imagine what wonder, beauty, creativity, and lives those 200 million women would have contributed to the community.

Sadly, they no longer exist. These beautiful lives, filled with vibrancy, creativity, music, children . . . are gone. It's gendercide. This slaughter of women is largely invisible, something we ignore. And this is just part of the war against women.

Down through history, no culture in the world has treated women with the same integrity as men. Some treat women better than others, but no culture recognizes women as having the absolute moral integrity of a male. We act as if we live in a man's world rather than in God's world. Because of this tragic failure, we live with a continuous *zeitgeist* of male superiority, and female inferiority.

"Wherever brute force of the warrior is counted God-like," Lydia Sigourney said, "woman is appreciated only as she approximates to sterner natures."[4] Our fallen world regards power and sternness as godlike. This is how things are seen in a man's world. Women do not cut it; they are seen as inferior to men. Thus the modern feminist movement, wanting women to be equal to men, makes women like men. The nurturing nature of female is undervalued in a male world.

Throughout much of the world, the female child is often unwanted and aborted at birth, or simply murdered after she is born. Very often, if she survives birth, she is neglected and malnourished. She is fed last, denied an education, often denied health care. She's placed in childhood labor. In many households, she is there to serve her brothers. She may be sold into prostitution or married off at a young age. Often, she is molested and raped by family members: A father rapes his daughter, a brother his sister, an uncle his niece. Then, this may be covered up by the mother.[5]

As an adult, the female is raped—often while pregnant. In many cultures, the adult male eats first, then male children, and only then the female, whether mother or child, if anything is left. Females are frequently overworked and under-recognized. They're treated violently, humiliated by their husbands and other men. They're often murdered by husbands, or fathers, or other men in the community. Very often widows are abandoned. And often the church—which historically was the first institution in the classical world to recognize the dignity of women and speak for them—is silent.

Historian Lilian Calles Barger, who immigrated to the United States from Argentina, has written a provocative book titled *Eve's Revenge* in which she states, "It appears that, universally, the physical vulnerability of women and deep-seated ideas about the meaning of womanhood incite domination in men and self-loathing in women."[6] Barger's reflection echoes the curse on the relationship between the man and the woman in Genesis 3:16 after the Fall. While Genesis 1 and 2 speak of God's good, life-affirming intention for the relationship between male and female, Genesis 3 shows the deadly post-Fall conflict: "Your desire shall be contrary to your husband, but he shall rule over you" (Genesis 3:16b).

The word for *desire—teshuqah*—occurring just three times in the Old Testament—is translated "longing," "desire," or "craving." Psychologist Mary Stewart Van-Leeuwen points out two equally dysfunctional interpretations of this passage.

Interpretation # 1: The woman grovels before her husband, utterly dependent upon him.

> "The man's fallen propensity to dominate the woman, seems compulsively matched by the woman's fallen, destructive 'desire' for the man—for securing relationships, even unhealthy ones, no matter what the cost."

Interpretation # 2: The woman has a combative desire to usurp the husband's authority. She is aggressively hostile toward his authority.[7]

In either case, the woman is likely responding to sexism, a displacement of loving, serving headship. The woman becomes either slavishly dependent on the abusive man on the one hand, or tries to seize authority, on the other.

Here are some examples of how different Bible translations and paraphrases describe this dysfunctional, fallen relationship between the man and the woman described in Genesis 3:16.

"You'll want to please your husband, but he'll lord it over you." The Message

"You will want to control your husband, but he will dominate you." NET

"You will greatly desire your husband, but he will rule over you." NCV

"Still your desire will be for your husband, but he will be your master." BBE

> "The man's fallen propensity to dominate the woman, seems compulsively matched by the woman's fallen, destructive 'desire' for the man—for securing relationships, even unhealthy ones, no matter what the cost."

Since the Fall, male tyranny along with family and sexual dysfunction have only grown. This disaster has led to the continual, unbroken domination and crushing of women.

In our day, I have observed that sexist culture manifests itself in four key ways through dysfunctional male-female relationships: (1) in the destruction of the family, (2) in trafficking, (3) in reproduction, and (4) in the murder of women. All of these in one way or another relate to the objectifying of women, in treating them as less than the human beings they are. Let's look at examples of each.

Family Destruction
Family destruction includes three major categories: domestic violence, rape, and divorce.

- *Domestic violence* is a universal phenomenon, transcending race and ethnic boundaries, education and economic levels, and religion. It is mostly men abusing and hurting women. Men abuse their wives or girlfriends to exercise power and control over them. Worldwide, perhaps 35 percent of women have been victims of domestic violence. In some countries it may be as high as 70 percent.[8] Shockingly, domestic violence and spousal abuse are most often viewed as "a family matter" in which people see no need for civil authorities to become involved. Domestic violence against women comes in five categories:
  - » *Coercive sex.* A boyfriend, husband, or "partner" intimidates or bullies a woman to have sex against her will, with himself or another man, or as an unwilling partner in a polyamorous relationship. It can also include violent sex, or sadomasochism—that is, sexual activity that inflicts emotional or physical pain on another person.
  - » *Psychological abuse.* This includes using demeaning language, intimidation, harassment, emotional abandonment, and smothering until the woman or girl has no place to be herself. The opposite of smothering is detachment, when a woman living in the same household as a man has been emotionally abandoned.
  - » *Spiritual abuse.* The husband or man berates her faith or prevents her from engaging with her faith community.
  - » *Economic abuse.* This involves neglecting the wife's basic needs, living off her income, refusing to work, or squandering the family income on gambling or other selfish pursuits. Or it may involve creating a spirit of economic dependency in the woman, making her utterly dependent and desperate to please

him because she has no alternative means of support for herself or her children. Often in the West, women are flaunted
in commercials and objectified in order to sell material things.

» *Physical abuse.* This includes beatings and worse. In some
cultures, it is not unusual for a man who fears that his wife's
beauty will attract other men to throw acid in her face to
make her unattractive.

- *Rape* happens when a man, known or unknown to the woman,
physically overpowers or manipulates and then violates her. It
has many variations, including statutory rape, acquaintance rape,
date rape, and gang rape. In England, young English girls have
been gang raped, then groomed to become the wives of Muslim
men. Such bride "preparation" has been done to thousands of
English females as young as eleven while police and city officials
have turned a blind eye to avoid being labeled racist.[9] This is one
of the consequences of moral and cultural relativism.

- Perhaps even more horrific is a young girl or woman raped by
a family member—a father, brother, uncle, or cousin. An early
study featured by the U.S. Department of Justice reviewed Australian and American surveys, and research revealed that: "About
80 percent of sex crimes committed against children occur within
the family, and 50 percent of the offenders are fathers."[10]

- *Taharrush* is an Arabic expression that translates to "collective
assault" and refers to a cultural practice of gang rape. In war,
Political Islamists use forced marriage and rape as instruments of
war and to produce Muslim babies. In April 2014, 276 female
students were kidnapped by Boko Haram from a secondary
school in Chibok, Borno State, Nigeria. Many were sexually
assaulted and forced into marriages with their abductors.[11]

- Rape is not merely physical; it's an assault on the soul, an attack
on a woman's personhood, dignity, her very identity. In fact, the
emotional and spiritual effects are profound. They can include
depression, the inability to give oneself to a husband, fear of men
in general, even suicide. Recently I was in Peru and a group of
teen girls approached me. Eight out of the nine had been raped
by a family member. This abuse from trusted people left them
with a distrust and hatred of all men.

- *Divorce.* It almost seems archaic to include divorce in this list. In our post-familial age, the problem has decreased somewhat because so few people get married. Nevertheless, the statistics for divorce are horrendous: 42 to 45 percent of first marriages, 60 percent of second marriages, and 73 percent of third marriages end in divorce.[12] The United States has the third-highest divorce rate in the world.[13] Divorce represents the ultimate level of family destruction.

Trafficking

Trafficking comes in five major categories: pornography, prostitution, sex trafficking, sex tourism, and trafficking in baby body parts.

- *Pornography* is trafficking in images. This applies to soft-core pornography, the stuff of bathroom jokes, posters, *Playboy* magazines, television and magazines ads, as well as violent and dark hardcore pornography. With the development of the internet, porn has gone viral. When Poland was freed from the Soviet Union, the first industry from the outside was pornography. The United States is the largest producer and consumer of porn in the world. A June 20, 2018, article published by *Quartz* estimated the value of porn from $6 billion to $15 billion a year. Globally, porn is a $97 billion "industry."[14]

- *Prostitution.* Tragically, in many societies, prostitution is a career choice. Certain factions in the U.S. government have promoted this. Chuck Colson points out that the pro-abortion movement has caused people to see a woman's decision to keep or abort her child as a right. The natural outflow of this is that she can do whatever she would like with her body, including selling sex.[15]

- *Sex trafficking* is a form of modern slavery. This includes trafficking in children as well as bride trafficking. The law of unintended consequences plays a role in trafficking. China, for instance, enforced a one-child policy for decades, believing the lie of over-population. Typically, if a couple could have only one child, they wanted a male. As a result, over the course of thirty or more years, female babies were routinely aborted in the womb or abandoned after birth. Today China has 35 million men of marriageable age without prospective brides. This vacuum is being filled by traffickers taking young girls into China from bordering countries.[16]

  Meanwhile, Chinese men are being exported to other countries so their rulers in Beijing can address the huge imbalance of men over women. I witnessed this kind of reverse trafficking in Kenya in 2019. Way out in the bush, I noticed some curious buildings up on a hill and asked, "What's that up in the hills?" I was told, "That's where the Chinese live."

China is building infrastructure—roads, bridges, dams, and harbors—all over Africa. The regime requires the use of Chinese labor. Chinese officials are sending some of the 35 million men mentioned above to Africa and other parts of Asia so that they can find brides.[17] Unfortunately, the strategy is a dismal failure. Many of these Chinese laborers have sexual relations with African women and return to China, leaving the woman and her children behind.[18] Elsewhere, people outside China are kidnapping young women and selling them as brides in China.

The latest global estimates indicate that 50 million people were living in modern slavery in 2021. Of these people, 28 million were in forced labor and 22 million were trapped in forced marriage. Unfortunately, the number of people in modern slavery has risen significantly in the last five years. An estimated four million women and girls in the world are victims of sex trafficking.[19]

- *Sex tourism.* It's extremely easy for a man to google "sex tourism" and access a package tour to Thailand or some other exotic destination. These tours include airfare, ground transportation, a hotel room, and a tour "companion" of his choice. His escort will show him the sights and then accompany him to dinner and to bed. Such tourists are generally older men from the United States and Europe. They want to avoid the social stigma of hiring prostitutes back home. They seek out young girls, expecting to avoid sexually transmitted disease.

- *Trafficking in baby body parts.* Globally there is an industry in the trafficking of human body parts, with a major subset in baby body parts. Perhaps the leading country in the world for this grizzly, immoral and evil practice is the United States. The memorandum opinion filed in the U.S. District Court for the District of Columbia on March 11, 2021, reveals the collaboration between Planned Parenthood and the federal government of the United States in harvesting baby body parts for a profit.[20]

In the U.S., abortion provider Planned Parenthood has generated a significant revenue stream from abortion by harvesting baby body parts and selling them to labs for research.[21] Also, research on the Department of Health and Human Services in the United States reveals that "nearly $3 million in federal funds were spent on the University of Pittsburgh's quest to become a 'Tissue Hub' for human fetal tissue ranging from 6 to 42 weeks."[22]

Reproduction

Reproduction issues come in three categories: forced sterilization, abortion, and female genital mutilation. They are based on the hard but real truth that an empty womb allows a woman to function like an unencumbered man.

- *Forced sterilization.* Margaret Sanger was a Social Darwinist, a leader of the American eugenics movement, and founder of Planned Parenthood. Her book *The Pivot of Civilization* argues that sex and hunger are linked. To end hunger, the poor must be prevented from having children. One way to do this is via forced sterilization. In Vietnam, more than 31,000 women suffered quinine sterilizations between 1989 and 1993. Peru began a public health sterilization program using quinine in 1995; in 1997, 110,000 women were sterilized.[23] Between 1965 and 1971, one million women in Brazil were sterilized. During the 1970s an estimated 25 percent to 40 percent of American Indian women were sterilized without their informed consent.[24]

- *Abortion.* A woman's womb was designed by God to be one of the safest places in the world, the place of compassion. Instead, in a world that denies God, the womb has become one of the world's most dangerous places.

  From 2015 to 2019, the pro-abortion Guttmacher Institute estimates that 73 million abortions occurred each year around the globe.[25] This is up from an estimated 50 million abortions per year between 1990 and 1994.[26]

  Abortion on demand, rather than children loved and cared for, is the fruit of modern feminism. Feminism is not about the feminine, and it's not a celebration of the female. It's a reaction to the lamentable and persistent abuse of women by sexist culture. It asks the question, "How can a woman become most like a man?" The answer: By being free to have sex whenever she wants and not be pregnant—either via birth control or abortion. According to modern feminism, the ideal human is an unencumbered male available twenty-four hours a day, seven days a week. So, becoming unpregnant instantaneously gives a woman the power to be like a man.

Abortion is a capitulation to a male-dominated value system that does not value females. Suzanne Venker, a maternal feminist (that is, from an earlier era in which women *as women* were still valued), wrote a book called *The Flip Side of Feminism*, in which she says that "feminists are determined to keep abortion as the number-one woman's right. And force taxpayers, to pay for as many abortions as they can."[27] Abortion

> **"How can a woman become most like a man?" The answer: By being free to have sex whenever she wants and not be pregnant—either via birth control or abortion.**

becomes a woman's right because it allows a woman to be most like a man.

- *Female genital mutilation (FGM)*. Over two million girls each year (6,000 every day) are genitally mutilated. Overall, 200 million girls have suffered genital mutilation. It is practiced in 40 countries, including America.[28] The World Health Organization recognizes several types of FGM:

> *Circumcision*: "Excision of the prepuce, with or without excision of part or all of the clitoris." Known as Sunna circumcision in Muslim counties, it is analogous to male circumcision.
>
> *Excision*: "Excision of the clitoris with partial or total excision of the labia minora."
>
> *Infibulation*: "Excision of part or all of the external genitalia and stitching/narrowing of the vaginal opening." This practice is known as Pharaonic circumcision in Muslim countries. It is the most severe form of FGM, practiced on 20 percent of all affected women.

Seventy-five percent of all cases of FGM are found in Egypt, Ethiopia, Kenya, Nigeria, Somalia, and Sudan. It is most prevalent in Muslim populations.[29] While FGM is illegal in the USA, it is still being performed. Equity Now, a global legal advocacy group writes: "In the US, approximately 513,000 women and girls have undergone or are at risk of female genital mutilation (FGM). Women and girls who were born in the US may be subjected to FGM here or even during vacations to their families' countries of origin—a practice known as 'vacation cutting.'"[30]

The irony is that, as of this writing, there is a full-on promotion of FGM and male genital mutilation in the transgender movement, euphemistically called "gender-affirming care." This new industry of sex reassignment surgery is being developed and promoted for *mutilating* perfectly healthy females and males. A Market Analysis Report states: "The U.S. sex reassignment surgery market size was valued at USD 1.9 billion in 2021 and is expected to expand at a compound annual growth rate (CAGR) of 11.23% from 2022 to 2030."[31]

Female genital mutilation has been seen by the Western world as a barbaric and immoral practice. What was considered evil is now becoming culturally popular. Sexual Reassignment Surgery is expected to grow globally into a multi-billion industry to rival the global abortion industry.

Murder

Both males and females are victims of murder, of course, but women and girls face four unique vulnerabilities: female feticide and infanticide, honor killing, dowry death, and gendercide.

Female feticide and infanticide. Feticide is the abortion or killing of a baby in the womb. Infanticide is the killing of a child within one year of its birth. In both cases, girls are much more likely to be victims.

- *Female Feticide* is the abortion of babies simply because they are female. In India, in 2021, 108 boys were born for every 100 girls.[32] In the past, abortion clinics have advertised: "It is better to spend $38 now to terminate a female fetus [baby] than $3,800 later on her dowry."[33] The Invisible Girl Project estimates the occurrence of 700,000 sex selection abortions per year in India. "On average, one girl is aborted in India, every minute just because she is a girl."[34]

- China's situation is similar to India's. China released a national census in May 2002 that reveals "more than 116 male births for every 100 female births."[35] Some Chinese experts claim that there are already as many as 70 million more males than females in the country. As R.J. Rummel, author of *Death by Government,* writes, "The imbalance between the sexes is now so distorted that there are 111 million men in China—more than three times the population of Canada—who will not be able to find a wife."[36]

- Because of this, there are entire villages in parts of the world with virtually no women available for men to marry, just one of the horrible social consequences of trafficking of young girls to be brides.

- *Infanticide.* This is the murder of babies simply because they are female. Again, India and China lead the way. In China, baby girls are known as "maggots in the rice." In China and India, an estimated 2 million baby girls go "missing" each year.[37] Shockingly, in 1995, *The Dying Rooms,* a British documentary film, shone a spotlight on the practice at Chinese state orphanages of simply leaving newborn girls to die.

- India's customary dowry and marriage costs overwhelm poor families. The cruel solution: Simply bury a baby girl alive or abandon her to die by starvation.[38]

- *Honor killing.* In some cultures, a girl can be murdered for being raped, while the rapist goes free. This happens most often in Muslim societies. Such unspeakable, horrible injustice is rooted in the culture's view of a woman. Shahid Khan, a professor at Aga Khan University in Pakistan, states:

> Women are considered the property of the males in their family irrespective of their class, ethnic or religious group. The owner of the property has the right to decide its fate. The concept of ownership has turned women into a commodity which can be exchanged, bought and sold.[39]

Because a woman is considered the property of men, she is a reflection on the family's honor. A young girl is taught to remain a virgin until married, taught to never bring shame (*eib*) but always honor (*sharaf*) to the family. "A woman is like a cup;

if someone drinks from it, no one will want it. . . . A woman is like a sheet of glass; once it is broken it can never be fixed."[40] If a girl or woman shames her family, a male must often restore the family honor by killing her.

- *Dowry death.* In some cultures, if the woman brings an inadequate dowry to the marriage, the groom kills her and then marries another girl. In India, more than 7,000 women are murdered each year because of inadequate dowries.[41]

- *Gendercide* is the systematic murder of females because they are females. Because of gendercide, the world is missing 140 million women.[42] Think of the lost lives, dreams, and potential. For a documentary exposé on gendercide, see Evan Grae Davis's *It's A Girl.*[43]

Crushed and Eliminated

In the modern world, a single, unfettered male is the ideal. This leads to the crushing of women. Now, in the postmodern world, we're witnessing the death of the very concept of male and female, leading to the disappearance of women.

Sexism and the radical response of feminism both deny the dignity of women and the maternal. In *Eve's Revenge,* Barger says, "By entering the public sphere at the expense of the private, a woman legitimates the male world and rejects her own."[44]

Each of us has a choice. We can heed the lie of the culture and give up the battle. That's what women do when they see themselves as inferior to men; it's what men do when they see themselves superior to women.

Or we can listen to God's Word as it affirms both male and female as made in the image of God. There is a moral, metaphysical equivalence between men and women. You can celebrate and enjoy your nature as masculine or feminine and enjoy the person next to you of the opposite sex. You can choose to fight back, to stand against the injustice of sexist, radical feminist and transgender ideology starting right now.

—————————— **STUDY GUIDE** ——————————

1. What is your reaction to the fact that there are as many 200,000,000 fewer women in the world than there should be?

2. How are women viewed when the "brute force of the warrior is counted godlike" as stated by Lydia Sigourney?

3. What are the two possible interpretations of the woman's "desire" for her husband in God's curse in Genesis 3:16? Where have you seen these patterns of behavior play out in real life? What is the pre-fall pattern for male and female as you understand it?

4. In what four key ways does sexist culture manifest itself? What is the opposite of each of these four dysfunctions?

5. Pick four examples from those listed in this chapter that you have seen manifest in your culture. How have you responded to them?

6. How does the reality that we are made female and male in the image of God lay a foundation for our fight against sexism and radical feminism?

CHAPTER 2

The Spiritual Root of Sexist Culture

VIRTUALLY EVERY CULTURE around the world believes, at one level or another, that men are superior to women. This lie has historical roots in every nation. The historical roots of this lie vary for each culture, but all sexist cultures share a spiritual root.

Christian apologist Mardi Keyes has observed that the Old Testament traces three strands relative to women's dignity or lack thereof: a dark strand, a brighter strand, and the brightest strand.[45]

The *dark strand* is seen in the worship of Baal and the rise of sexism. The *brighter* strand appears in the Hebrew distinctives of the ancient world—they treated women better than their animistic neighbors. The *brightest* strand comes at the end of the Old Testament in the prophecy of Hosea with the return of *ish* (אִישׁ).

In Romans 1:21–25, Paul argues that humans have made a disastrous trade, what you might call a Great Exchange.

> For although they knew God, they did not honor him as God or give thanks to him, but they became futile in their thinking, and their foolish hearts were darkened. Claiming to be wise, they became fools, and exchanged the glory of the immortal God for images resembling mortal man and birds and animals and creeping things.

> Therefore God gave them up in the lusts of their hearts to
> impurity, to the dishonoring of their bodies among them-
> selves, because they exchanged the truth about God for a lie
> and worshiped and served the creature rather than the Cre-
> ator, who is blessed forever! Amen.

After rebelling against their Creator, people exchanged righteous behavior for wicked:

> The LORD saw that the wickedness of man was great in the
> earth, and that every intention of the thoughts of his heart
> was only evil continually. And the LORD regretted that he
> had made man on the earth, and it grieved him to his heart.
> (Genesis 6:5–6)

This behavior was rooted in their exchange of the truth for a lie. They
exchanged the worship of God for the worship of created things (Romans
1:23, 2526). In the Great Exchange, the worship of the glorious God is
exchanged for the worship and service of two counterfeits: pagan human-
ism ("like mortal man") and pagan animism (created things, that is, birds,
animals, reptiles). In the context of the Old Testament, the Hebrew people
returned to pagan animism.

This exchange of the heart and mind led to a change in behavior. Paul
records this shift from the thoughts and emotions of the inner man to the
outside behavior and vice of the external man, Romans 1:24–27:

> Therefore God gave them up in the lusts of their hearts to
> impurity, to the dishonoring of their bodies among them-
> selves, because they exchanged the truth about God for a lie
> and worshiped and served the creature rather than the Cre-
> ator, who is blessed forever! Amen.

> For this reason God gave them up to dishonorable passions.
> For their women exchanged natural relations for those that
> are contrary to nature; and the men likewise gave up natural
> relations with women and were consumed with passion for
> one another, men committing shameless acts with men and
> receiving in themselves the due penalty for their error.

Paul is making the principled argument that ideas have consequences. As the graphic shows, Paul argues that the exchange in belief systems leads to a change in values, and that in turn leads to a change in behavior. Notice as well that this pattern is so important to understand that Paul repeats the pattern three times in these few verses.

THE GREAT EXCHANGE
Romans 1:18-32

Exchanging belief systems	23		25		28
A change in values	24		26-27		28b-31
Wicked behavior	24		26-27		28b-31
Summary					32

The scripture says they exchanged the glory of God for images resembling mortal men. The object of their worship shifted, resulting in a myriad of terrible lifestyle changes. Eventually this led to a society where the behaviors were approved and celebrated (Romans 1:18–32):

> And since they did not see fit to acknowledge God, God gave them up to a debased mind to do what ought not to be done. They were filled with all manner of unrighteousness, evil, covetousness, malice. They are full of envy, murder, strife, deceit, maliciousness. They are gossips, slanderers, haters of God, insolent, haughty, boastful, inventors of evil, disobedient to parents, foolish, faithless, heartless, ruthless. Though they know God's righteous decree that those who practice such things deserve to die, they not only do them but give approval to those who practice them (v. 26–32).

To put it simply, the worship of pagan gods leads to pagan sexuality. The worship of the living God leads to virtue, but the worship of pagan gods leads to vice.

A major biblical concept is identified by the word *sin!* The word sin means to "miss the mark" of God's good intentions for us. As a result of the exchange of the glorious God for idolatry—the worship of man and nature—the word *sin* has almost disappeared from the English vocabulary and Western thought.

Now what does this have to do with the sexist lie that men are better than women? Only everything! Your concept of "man" and "husband" is determined by the kind of god you worship! The God (or god) you worship will determine what you think it means to be a man, a woman, a husband, a wife. The cultures we create and the way we live our lives in community is determined by the object of our worship. To put it simply, culture is derived from worship or cult. In some places, the word cult has a negative connotation as it has been used to identify a particular group with unusual beliefs and practices, but at its root cult can be applied to any system of religious worship. Paul's point is that we build cultures that reflect the nature, character, and qualities of the God or gods we worship.

We build cultures that reflect the nature, character, and qualities of the God or gods we worship.

In the Old Testament, the word for husband is *ish*. We will look through Scripture in this chapter about how God himself is *Ish*, a husband. In fact he is the archetype of what it means to be a husband. He is the loving and self-sacrificing head of the human family, of Israel. Christ is head of the church. And this headship of God provides a model for a husband.

So the transcendent root of *ish* is God Himself. God's very nature is to *husband* (as a verb this means to conserve and care for). The Scriptures reveal God's love for His people in the Old Testament and Jesus' love for the church in the New Testament. In Adam and Eve, God created the first earthly model of the transcendent nature of God's love for His people. And subsequently, God's intention has been for the human *ish* to lovingly and self-sacrificially provide leadership for his wife and family.

The Old Testament introduces the concept of covenantal marriage, a relationship between a man and a woman before God. In a sense, marriage is a tripartite arrangement. The man makes a promise to the woman, the woman to the man, and these pledges are spoken before the God who designed us for a binary relationship.

In Exodus 19–24, Israel enters a covenantal marriage with God (Exodus

24:3) but soon commits "adultery" with a god of her own making. While Moses is on the mountain, the people make a golden calf and worship it (Exodus 32). They break the covenantal relationship with their husband, *Ish*. Moses describes this calamity as committing adultery with another god.

Yet God the loving Husband accepts Israel's repentance and renews the covenant (Exodus 33–34). But because of their unfaithfulness, they will wander in the wilderness forty years (Numbers 14:33).

Note the sexual language used in the context of Israel's relationship to Yahweh. Israel "prostituted herself." God is the loving "husband" (*ish*). She "committed adultery" by betraying Him. He extends self-sacrificial love, accepts Israel's repentance, and renews the covenant with her. During these forty years, God warns Israel against prostituting herself again when she enters the Promised Land. We see this in Exodus 34:12–17:

> Take care, lest you make a covenant with the inhabitants of the land to which you go, lest it become a snare in your midst. You shall tear down their altars and break their pillars and cut down their Asherim (for you shall worship no other god, for the LORD, whose name is Jealous, is a jealous God), lest you make a covenant with the inhabitants of the land, and when they whore after their gods and sacrifice to their gods and you are invited, you eat of his sacrifice, and you take of their daughters for your sons, and their daughters whore after their gods and make your sons whore after their gods. You shall not make for yourself any gods of cast metal.

The land of promise was home to local, tribal, animistic deities, including Baal, a deity in Moab and the land of the Philistines. Baal was credited with providing water, leading to fertility, and thus gained ownership of a place. Baal means *owner*, *master*, and is also translated *husband*.

When I was writing an earlier book, *Nurturing the Nations*, I studied the biblical concept of *husband*. I was shocked to find in the Hebrew lexicon that most occurrences of "husband" in the Old Testament translated the word "baal." I struggled with this. I asked God to help me understand this. Why does the Hebrew Bible use *baal—owner* or *master—*for *husband*?

After six months, I began to understand. The worship of Baal involved sacred sexual practices of men with temple prostitutes. This is why God equates idol worship with adultery. Pagan worship leads to a corrupt understanding of what it means to be a man and a woman and the nature of human sexuality. The Israelites rejected *Ish* and worshiped the Baal—the owner or master. That worship included sexual activity.

As used in the Bible, baal was a general term for local animistic deities. At the end of their forty years of wandering in the desert, the Hebrews were on Mount Peor in Moab. This was the site of the temple to the Baal of Peor. From the high ground on Mount Peor, where this Baal was worshiped, God showed Moses the Promised Land and said, "You will not enter, but this generation will enter in the promised land" (see Deuteronomy 32:51–52).

" LORD OF THE HOLE

- Baal-peor

- Mt. Peor in Moab place of worship

- Another name Molech (Jer. 19:5)

- Name means "Lord of the Hole" – body orifices

The name Baal of Peor literally means "lord of the hole, the lord of bodily orifices." The Hebrews were worshiping the god of bodily orifices. In Numbers 25:1–3 we read:

> While Israel lived in Shittim, the people began to whore with the daughters of Moab. These invited the people to the sacrifices of their gods, and the people ate and bowed down to their gods. So Israel yoked himself to Baal of Peor.

The Hebrew people had enjoyed a covenantal marriage with God. But when they entered the Moabites' land, they turned their backs on that covenant to prostitute themselves before the local animistic deities and engage in sex with temple prostitutes. They broke their wedding vows to God and worshiped a pagan, animistic god instead: "At Horeb they made a calf and worshiped an idol cast from metal. They exchanged their glorious

God for an image of a bull, which eats grass" (Psalm 106:19–20). Again, pagan worship led to pagan sexuality.

Notice again the language of the Great Exchange. The Psalmist restates this tragic memory of what the Hebrew people had done: "They yoked themselves to the Baal of Peor and ate sacrifices offered to lifeless gods; they aroused the LORD's anger by their wicked deeds" (Psalm 106:28 NIV).

Pagan worship led to pagan sexuality.

Once again, the change in worship produced wicked deeds. This is the human pattern. When we worship the living God in spirit and in truth, our attitudes and behavior are to reflect His character. When we exchange worship of the living God for worship of pagan deities, however, our attitudes and behaviors will degrade. Pagan worship leads to pagan attitudes and practices—including pagan sexuality. And to state it in the reverse, pagan practices and sexuality lead to pagan values and thinking.

> They served their idols, which became a snare to them. They sacrificed their sons and their daughters to the demons; they poured out innocent blood, the blood of their sons and daugh-ters, whom they sacrificed to the idols of Canaan, and the land was polluted with blood. Thus they became unclean by their acts, and played the whore in their deeds. (Psalm 106:36–39).

We form cultures in the likeness of the god or gods we worship, because culture is a product of *cult* or worship. As Israel worshiped the lord of the hole, her culture followed suit. These are the marks of pagan animistic culture. Consider how they may manifest themselves in your culture.

- Sensuality
- Self-indulgence
- Sexual immorality
- Unfaithfulness in marriage
- Human sacrifice (low view of human life)
- Fatalism
- Corruption (bribery of the gods)

As Israel abandoned *Ish*, its culture and language changed. This is why the Hebrew word often used for husband is baal. The people exchanged the loving, self-sacrificing headship of their *Ish*, and worshiped Baal, characterized as owner and master.

The word "husband" changed, the language changed, and the concept of marriage changed. Baal became the husband, the tyrant. The wife was no longer understood as the co-equal counterpart of the husband and vice-regent of creation. She became his property, to be treated as he willed. She moved from being a person to an object or tool. She lost her voice and became mere chattel. This is the dark strand in the Old Testament concept of the woman.

While the brightest strand is yet to come, let us examine the second strand of the relationship between men and women in the Old Testament. Believe it or not, the dark consequences of Israel's adultery were not as bad as in most other ancient societies. While too often treated poorly, women in Israel were not treated as poorly as they were in other cultures. God's Word curbed some of the worst abuses of men against women.

First, the narrative of creation reveals that women, not just men, were made in the *imago Dei*, and thus women were equal with men in the mandates to fill the earth and govern creation (Genesis 1:26–28). As Old Testament scholar Nahum M. Sarna observes, "Curiously, the extant literature of the ancient Near East has preserved no other account of the creation of primordial woman."[46]

While a distant memory, the creation narrative was not forgotten entirely. In addition, the Hebrew laws offered significant protections for women: God, hating divorce, called husbands to faithfulness (the seventh commandment); the first year of marriage preempted military or civic duty (Deuteronomy 24:5); and a daughter had a right to inheritance (Numbers 27:1–11).

Throughout, we see that woman is the image of God, equal in being and an equal partner in the Creation Mandate. The God of the universe sees Hagar, a lowly servant girl and calls her by name (Genesis 16:8). Old Testament scholar Bruce Waltke captures the extraordinary nature of this divine action: "This is the only instance in all of the many thousands of ancient Near Eastern texts where a deity, or his messenger, calls a woman by name and thereby invests her with exalted dignity."[47]

Women are prominent in Scripture, mentioned 400 times. Mothers are mentioned 300 times, wives 400 times, daughters 200 times. In an era when women were seldom recognized by name, the Bible records the names of 200 women, many of them of humble stature, like Hagar.

Two books are named after heroines: Ruth and Esther. In Scripture we see women as public figures: queens (Esther and the queen of Sheba) and a judge (Deborah). We see prophetesses (who spoke authoritatively on behalf of God): Deborah (Judges 4:4), Miriam (Exodus 15:20), Huldah (2 Kings 22:13–14), Isaiah's wife (Isaiah 8:3), and the false prophetess Noadiah (Nehemiah 6:14).

The Hebrew Bible also presents the model of a godly woman, more precious than rubies, in Proverbs 31. She is a vital part of an extended community, the maker of a home, the master of the manor, the queen of the forest, and a vice-regent of creation. Here is no autonomous feminist, self-focused individualist, housewife who is chained in the kitchen, barefoot and pregnant. Instead, she is the maker of a home, with her husband a co-creator of culture, a developer of creation, a builder of a nation. Her fullness of life is her being. Here is a woman practicing womanhood and a mother practicing motherhood. Her domain begins in her home and extends to the world. She welcomes the world to her domain and sends her influence into the larger society. She is a steward of what has been entrusted to her.

John Angell James speaks to women about the women of Scripture:

> . . . there she is seen enlivening the sacred page with her narrative—adorning it with her beauty; sometimes darkening it with her crimes, at others, brightening it with her virtues; now calling us to weep with her in her sorrows, then to rejoice with her in her joys. In short, woman is everywhere to be found wrought into the details of God's Scriptures, a beacon to warn us, or a rule to guide us. And, as written by the inspiration of the Holy Spirit, it is to be considered as his testimony to the excellence and importance of your sex, and the influence it is intended and destined to exert upon the welfare of mankind.[48]

Thank God, some of the gloom of sexist culture is broken in the larger Old Testament narrative. But the brightest strand appears near the end of the Old Testament in the Book of Hosea, called by some the God-sized love story. After six months of struggling to understand why baal is used for "husband" in much of the Old Testament, I found the blessed answer here.

How did God, *Ish*, respond to Israel's adultery? He raised up a prophet to speak to the nation that she might be redeemed. The narrative begins to unfold in Hosea 1:2–3.

> When the LORD first spoke through Hosea, the LORD said to Hosea, "Go, take to yourself a wife of whoredom and have children of whoredom, for the land commits great whoredom by forsaking the LORD." So he went and took Gomer, the daughter of Diblaim, and she conceived and bore him a son.

Men, if you were in Hosea's shoes, seeking to be a godly man, and during your time of prayer and reflection in the morning you heard God call you by name and say, "I want you to marry a prostitute," what would you do? What would you think?

Perhaps Hosea wondered, "Is that really You, Lord? How can You ask me to do something like this?" We don't know his thoughts, but, in the end, Hosea did as God said. He married Gomer.

But why would God ask a righteous man to marry a prostitute? In Hosea 3:1–3 we begin to understand the answer.

> And the LORD said to me, "Go again, love a woman who is loved by another man and is an adulteress, even as the LORD loves the children of Israel, though they turn to other gods and love cakes of raisins." So I bought her for fifteen shekels of silver and a homer and a lethech of barley. And I said to her, "You must dwell as mine for many days. You shall not play the whore, or belong to another man; so will I also be to you."

God sent Hosea to marry a prostitute as a living metaphor to manifest to Israel through a human being the nature of God's love. Hosea demonstrated the nature of *Ish*'s–a husband's–love, so Israel could see that even though she had broken the covenant, even when she had prostituted herself before a pagan deity, God still loved her. God is *Ish*, faithful to His promises even when Israel is unfaithful and when *we* are unfaithful. His response is based on His character, not on the flawed character of His wife, Israel.

How did Hosea model God's self-sacrificing love? "So I bought her for fifteen shekels of silver and a homer and a lethech of barley" (v. 2).

Why did Hosea need to do this? To picture what God had done for Israel. Because Gomer was the "property" of her owner, Hosea had to pay the price to redeem her, to set her free. Hosea was manifesting in human form God's love and self-sacrificing service. He was leading Israel from slavery to freedom, from despair to hope. Hosea is the dawn at the end of the darkness of the Old Testament narrative concerning male-female relationships. His life is the prologue of the rising of the Son in His glory at the beginning of the New Testament.

Paul uses this word picture from Hosea 3 in Ephesians 1:7.

> In him we have redemption through his blood, the forgiveness of our trespasses, according to the riches of his grace.

The Greek word for redemption is *apolytrōsis* and means deliverance, redemption, a ransom, a release. Paul is alluding to the Roman slave markets, that people in his era would be all too familiar with. Scholars estimate as much as 20 percent of the Roman empire's population was enslaved, accounting for as many as 10 million people. A man would go to the slave market and buy a slave, a human being, maybe to cook his meals, or clean his house, or tend his fields. People were property.

As Hosea bought back Gomer from slavery, he was pointing toward the coming of Jesus, who would go to the slave market to redeem us. Jesus paid *the corresponding price* for our freedom. What was that price? It was the shedding of His own blood. This is the biblical language of redemption. Jesus said, in effect, "You are worth the price of my life."

Hosea is pointing ahead to the One who would pay the ultimate price to set us free. God called Hosea to show Israel what *ish* means, what it means to be a husband. Hosea paid the price to buy Gomer and take her back. Think of that for a moment. What price did Judas Iscariot get paid by the Romans to betray Jesus? Or what value did the Romans place on Jesus' head? Thirty pieces of silver. Some say that was less than the price of a cheap slave. In contrast, what price did God say you were worth? The price of the life of His Son. Please think deeply about this for a moment.

In Hosea 2:14–23 we come to what Pastor John Piper calls "the love song of God." He describes it as "one of the most tender and most beautiful love songs in the Bible."

In Hosea 2:14, Ish says of Israel: "Therefore, behold, I will allure her, and bring her into the wilderness, and speak tenderly to her." This sounds like a man courting the woman with whom he is in love. Note the gentle language used here. Who speaks this language? Who would speak in this way to an adulterous wife?

And there I will give her her vineyards and make the Valley of Achor a door of hope. And there she shall answer as in the days of her youth, as at the time when she came out of the land of Egypt. (Hosea 2:15)

Although "Valley of Achor" means "valley of trouble," God was going to provide a "door of hope." The hope Israel experienced when she was freed from Egypt will be experienced again when she is freed from Baal. Israel was a prostitute, but God will restore her to a state of innocence.

> "And in that day, declares the LORD, you will call me 'My Husband,' and no longer will you call me 'My Baal.'

Now we come to the beautiful and powerful turning point in the whole Old Testament narrative regarding the relationship between man and woman, husband and wife. "And in that day, declares the LORD, you will call me 'My Husband,' and no longer will you call me 'My Baal.' For I will remove the names of the Baals from her mouth, and they shall be remembered by name no more" (Hosea 2:16–17).

Here is the heart of the Book of Hosea, perhaps the pivoting point of the Scripture's nuptial narrative. Between the glorious Eve and the glorious Bride of Christ, Israel fell to her lowest point, but here is the promise of restoration. God is not baal; he is *Ish*. The pattern for a godly husband is the loving, self-sacrificing head, *Ish*, not the tyrannical, brutal owner, baal. Hosea will demonstrate *Ish* to Gomer so she may be restored. This restoration pictures the coming of Christ to redeem His people.

Next, in Hosea 2:19–20, we see the character of this faithful husband.

I will betroth you to me forever. I will betroth you to me in righteousness and in justice, in steadfast love and in mercy. I will betroth you to me in faithfulness. And you shall know [*yada*, intimately know] the LORD.

This is a remarkable reminder. When the Hebrew people broke the original covenant with God, as recorded in the Book of Exodus, Moses went up Mount Sinai the second time to renew the covenant. As part of this process, God tells Moses His name, the longest name of God in the Bible. Why did He do this? So that His bride would know who He is and the nature of His character. Here is the name that God told Moses to tell the people (Exodus 34:5–7):

> The LORD descended in the cloud and stood with him there, and proclaimed the name of the LORD. The LORD passed before him and proclaimed, "The LORD, the LORD, a God merciful and gracious, slow to anger, and abounding in steadfast love and faithfulness, keeping steadfast love for thousands, forgiving iniquity and transgression and sin, but who will by no means clear the guilty, visiting the iniquity of the fathers on the children and the children's children, to the third and the fourth generation."

When God brought the Hebrews out of slavery in Egypt and gave them the marriage covenant, He also gave them His name. When He took them out of slavery in the Valley of Trouble, He described His husbandly character again. Notice the similarities: God's name reflects His character. We will unpack the Hebrew original to understand the nuances of meaning[49] He is:

Merciful (*ră·ḥûm*—to have compassion, also translated "womb")

Gracious (*ḥăn·nûn*—compassionate, merciful to the needy and repentant)

Slow to anger (*'ā·rēḵ 'ăp̄*—patient, long suffering)

Steadfast in love (*chesed*—unfailing love, loyal love)

Faithful (*'ĕmĕṯ*—truthful, trustworthy, full of integrity, true to His word)

Forgiving (*nā·śā(')*—to remove incurred guilt and its penalty, to forgive sin)

Just (*nā·qā(h)*—by no means clears the guilty—there is ultimate justice)

This is absolutely beautiful. This is stunning! It gives me a chill in my spine and tears in my eyes just to reflect on these things and write these words. What kind of a God do we worship? What does it mean that He is the archetypical nature of a husband?

What does it mean to be a husband? In a machismo, sexist culture, the husband is the owner and master, while the woman is a slave. This is a lie, and it destroys men and women. To the married men reading this, what kind of a husband are you? Do you reflect the character of *Ish* or baal?

To those young men wanting to marry someday, consider what it means to be a godly husband. Are you willing and ready to be *Ish*, a man who loves and sacrifices himself to lead his wife? Don't dwell on the question, "What kind of a woman do I want to marry?" Rather, reflect on the question "What kind of a husband do I want to be?"

——————— STUDY GUIDE ———————

1. How would you describe the Great Exchange that takes place in the events of Exodus 19–24 and that Paul describes in Romans 1:18–32?

2. Reflect on Paul's writing about the relationship between belief systems, values and behavior (see the graphic The Great Exchange). What principle is he articulating? Why do you think he repeats this three times? What is the significance of this for your life?

3. What are some aspects of idolatry found in your own life?

4. What words does God use to describe the people's rebellion against God? How is the Great Exchange related to sexism?

5. There are two Hebrew words that are translated "husband." The first is *ish;* the second is *baal.* Describe the nature of each of the deities behind these names. Which God honors women and which dishonors? Why?

6. List the seven manifestations of pagan animistic culture? Which of these do you see in your culture? What are the implications of this?

7. What is the significance of Hosea buying back his prostitute wife from Baal? How does this relate to the significance of Paul's words in Ephesians 1:7?

8. What is the significance of God telling Israel "You will no longer call me master but husband" (Hosea 2:16, my paraphrase) for the husband-wife relationship?

CHAPTER 3

Servanthood: The Divine Pattern of Leadership

TWO TERMS, *SERVE* and *submit*, are dirty words in the modern world. Modern secularism and feminism see subordination and equality as contradictions. To be under authority is to be inferior; equality necessitates autonomy. "No one's going to tell me what to do" is the mantra of modern culture. In postmodern culture the mantra is "I'll do me, you do you!" To obey God or any human authority is to restrict freedom.

In today's world, the freedom that many people seek is synonymous with license. But freedom and license are not the same. True freedom is found within the framework of God's order. Personal responsibility is a huge part of freedom. License, on the other hand, does not acknowledge responsibility; it functions outside any moral order. Doing whatever we want, whenever we want, is license, not freedom.

Modern and postmodern secularists and feminists promote license. Freedom, however, requires structure and boundaries. License without restraint is held to be a virtue, but it leads to slavery, which is not virtuous at all. Sexist culture equates leadership with tyranny. We should reject authoritarianism, but we should not reject leadership. On the other hand, in reaction to the aberrations of sexist culture, modern feminists tend to deny the significance of authority. Authority exists for building up, not for tearing down.

Form (structure and boundaries) and freedom go together! Tyranny is form without freedom. Anarchy is freedom without form. To be truly free, we need to live within the framework of God's laws and ordinances. We see this in the Great Commission when Jesus says, "Teaching them [the nations] to obey everything I have commanded you" (Matthew 28:20 NIV).

We are most free when we govern ourselves. Government isn't just something "out there" in a distant capital city. Government begins in each person's heart. Freedom demands internal self-government based on God's laws and ordinances. When we govern ourselves this way, we are most free. When we rebel against God's laws and His order of creation, however, we end up impoverished and enslaved.

Tyranny is form without freedom. Anarchy is freedom without form.

The Trinitarian nature of God challenges modern man's pride. Modern man despises service, humility, and self-sacrifice, and honors power, self-fulfillment, and pride. On the other hand, God honors humility, self-sacrifice, and submission because such virtues reflect the nature of God.

The Apostle Paul wrote these world-shaking words in Philippians 2:5–11:

> Have this mind among yourselves, which is yours in Christ Jesus, who, though he was in the form of God, did not count equality with God a thing to be grasped, but emptied himself, by taking the form of a servant, being born in the likeness of men. And being found in human form, he humbled himself by becoming obedient to the point of death, even death on a cross. Therefore God has highly exalted him and bestowed on him the name that is above every name, so that at the name of Jesus every knee should bow, in heaven and on earth and under the earth, and every tongue confess that Jesus Christ is Lord, to the glory of God the Father.

Why was Jesus glorified by God? Because He humbled himself. Though He was God, Jesus was a servant. Paul says, "Have this mind in you, the mind of Christ. He who was God but did not count equality with God a thing to be grasped" (v. 5–6, my paraphrase).

Agape love—the kind of love of God gives to the undeserving—is humble, self-sacrificing, selfless. It considers others first, and it serves others first. Agape is the love most fully expressed by the death of Christ on the cross.

Today, much of Christendom preaches, "You're a child of God. God wants you to be comfortable. He wants to lavish all sorts of things on you." That's what we hear repeatedly. Did Christ come in that spirit? No. He came "to serve, and to give his life as a ransom for many" (Mark 10:45). This is agape love.

My friend Dr. Bob Moffitt, co-founder of the Disciple Nations Alliance, has said,

> It was because Jesus was voluntarily and sacrificially willing to be a servant, that God exalted him with the ultimate expression of glory. He has been given the highest position that could be given. He has been given a name that supersedes every name. Every tongue will confess that this servant is Lord. This is exaltation greater than any being has had or will have.
>
> Therefore, God honored Jesus in this exalted manner because Jesus fully reflected what God intended when he created man. When God created man, he created beings who were other-focused, not self-focused. Jesus fully expressed the highest expression of God's image—voluntary and sacrificial servanthood. This is the highest expression of the image of God.[50]

What will define your life—the modern, narcissistic focus on self, or a glorious focus on the example of Jesus Christ? In becoming human, Jesus fully expressed God's image. God is a servant and Jesus modeled that servanthood. Jonathan Edwards captured this in his sermon, "The Excellency of Christ":

> Infinite highness and infinite condescension. Infinite justice and infinite grace. Infinite glory and lowest humility. Infinite majesty and transcendent meekness. Deepest reverence towards God and equality with God. Infinite worthiness of good and the greatest patience under suffering of evil. An exceeding spirit of obedience with supreme dominion over

heaven and earth. Absolute sovereignty and perfect resigna-
tion. Self-sufficiency and an entire trust and reliance on God.[51]

The cross is an affront to the modern values of power, pride, and
self-fulfillment as we see Christ humble Himself even on this remorseless
instrument of Roman torture. Of course, the theme of God's breathtaking
humility is seen even in the earliest pages of the Bible. In the creation
account we see three major manifestations of God's humility:

1. The freedom to choose, captured in the tree of the knowledge of
   good and evil in Eden. And the LORD God commanded the man,
   saying, "You may surely eat of every tree of the garden, but of the
   tree of the knowledge of good and evil you shall not eat, for in
   the day that you eat of it you shall surely die." (Genesis 2:16–17)

   The tree of the knowledge of good and evil establishes human
   freedom. We make real choices, choices that affect our lives and
   the lives of others. This is true freedom, the freedom to say no to
   God—the God of the universe who created us wanted us to be
   free! God gave us this freedom because of the value He places on
   love. Only in freedom can we truly love. He planted this tree to
   give us the freedom to love.

2. Naming the animals.

   Now out of the ground the LORD God had formed every beast
   of the field and every bird of the heavens and brought them to
   the man to see what he would call them. And whatever the man
   called every living creature, that was its name. (Genesis 2:19)

   God made the animals. He envisioned, designed, and created
   them. He alone knew all there was to know about them. It stands
   to reason that God was the right one to name them. But He did
   not. God gave Adam the authority to name the animals, and
   then God used Adam's names for them!

3. The phrase "suitable helper" (Genesis 2:18 NIV).

   The LORD God said, "It is not good for the man to be alone. I
   will make a helper suitable for him." . . . So the man gave names to
   all the livestock, the birds in the sky and all the wild animals. But
   for Adam no suitable helper was found. (Genesis 2:18, 20 NIV)

   Most cultures consider a helper as someone who serves you,
   someone who does what you are not willing to do yourself, some-

one inferior to you. In Eden, God designates the woman as Adam's "suitable helper." Many Bible readers interpret this as an inferior position.

Suitable here means "corresponding to" or "counterpart." The concept of the complementary nature of male and female and natural marriage is rooted in this word. Not interchangeable, not identical, not the same as. In Genesis 1, God makes us in His image, male and female, to let *them* rule. The female is suitable to the male, and the male suitable to the female. They are equal and different, fitting together, corresponding to one another.

The word "helper" in Genesis 2:20 is the Hebrew word *ezer*, which means one who assists and serves another with what is needed. It's variously translated *help, succour, assist, support, comfort*. This word is used twenty-one times in the Old Testament. Twice it refers to Eve, the suitable helper for Adam. Three times it speaks of those who give aid to the needy. And sixteen times, the word *ezer* is used of God Himself! God is the *Ezer*. God is our helper.

> **The cross is an affront to the modern values of power, pride, and self-fulfillment**

To ask if God is inferior to man, of course, is to risk blasphemy. God is infinitely superior to man in every way! Yet, even in His divine, perfect, infinite nature, God is our *Ezer*. When we consider a helper our inferior, we have not bothered to understand the true meaning of the word. God Himself is a helper.

In fact, there is submission within the Godhead. Professor Henry Krabbendam from Covenant College writes, "In the Trinity, the parties are there not for themselves but for the other in a radical and total manner."[52]

This is another way to say that self-sacrificing love binds the Trinity together. The persons of the Trinity are there not for themselves, but for the others, radically and completely. Love is a radical focusing on the needs of the other.

The unity of the Trinity is expressed in the Greek word *agapaó*. The Apostle John records Jesus' words of prayer to the Father: "You loved (*agapaó*) me before the foundation of the world" (John 17:24). Self-sacrificing love existed in the community of the Trinity before the universe was conceived. We might assume that submission and service began with the

Fall, but they didn't. Nor did they begin at creation. They existed eternally in the character and nature of God.

Again, Bob Moffitt says,

> God does not command sacrificial service for its own sake. He invites it because it results in the demonstration of his greatest attribute, love. True love always results in the action of sacrificial serving. Loving service heals brokenness. It restores, it redeems. This is God's agenda and when it is fulfilled, those who serve are honored and he is glorified.[53]

In Mark 10:33–34, Jesus tells the disciples He's going to die. Afterward, two of them approach with a request: "Jesus, when you enter into your glory, we want to be at your right and left hand" (v. 37, my paraphrase). Jesus has just told them He's going to die, but all they can think about is that He's going to be king. He's going to ride into Jerusalem carrying a sword. He will throw out the occupying Roman army and set up a political kingdom, and they want to reign with Him in power, at His right and left hand. They want to be the secretary of state and the secretary of war. They want *power*.

They had been with Jesus three years, watched His life, seen How he treats people, heard what He teaches, and still they don't understand. They think the kingdom is about power. They think that's where glory is found. The other disciples are indignant at this posturing: James and John had beaten them to the punch.

Then Jesus brings the disciples together and says,

> "You know that those who are considered rulers of the Gentiles lord it over them, and their great ones exercise authority over them. But it shall not be so among you. But whoever would be great among you must be your servant, and whoever would be first among you must be slave of all. For even the Son of Man came not to be served but to serve, and to give his life as a ransom for many." (Mark 10:42–45)

Jesus contrasts the world and the kingdom. The world regards the person with power and authority as great. Greatness, according to the world, is measured by how many servants you have. But Jesus says the Kingdom of God has a value system that's upside down from this. Actually, the Kingdom of God is right-side up; it is the *world's* value system that is upside down.

The biblical principle, the kingdom pattern, is servanthood. "Even the Son of Man came not to be served, but to serve" (v. 45a). He could have come to the emperor's palace in Rome and demanded the service of everyone in the empire. But the Lord didn't come for power or worldly authority. He came "to serve, and to give his life as a ransom for many" (v. 45b). The King of kings, the Lord of lords is servant of all. Why? Because He is God! When did servanthood begin? It did not begin; it is grounded in the very nature of God. Servanthood is rooted from eternity in the character of the living God.

The world and the kingdom of God represent two value systems. The world sees the person with the most servants as great. "I want to be the president of the country," or "president of the biggest corporation," or "I want to have a large church." God help us! We worship prestige and power, but Jesus says, "Not so with you" (v. 43 NIV).

> **Servanthood is not a prerequisite for greatness, something you do to *become* great. Servanthood is the very standard of greatness.**

In the kingdom, the one who serves is greatest. Just before the last supper, their last time together, shortly after Jesus had taught about servanthood, a fight breaks out between two of the disciples. What's the fight about? "A dispute also arose among them as to which of them was considered to be greatest" (Luke 22:24).

At this point, Jesus had just performed a powerful lesson in service. He had stripped off His clothes, wrapped a towel around His waist, and used a bowl of water to wash the disciples' feet. He will soon be arrested. He's going to be crucified, and this is the last thing He's going to share with them. "Guys, get this. I'm not just verbalizing it. I am modeling it for you. I am your Lord. I am your Savior and what am I doing? I am washing your feet."

DIFFERING VALUE SYSTEMS

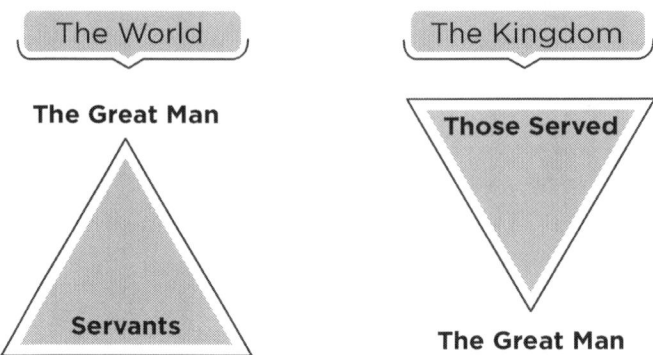

Servanthood is not a prerequisite for greatness, something you do to *become* great. Servanthood is the very *standard* of greatness. God's concept of greatness is the opposite of the world's standard. Serving and leading are two sides of the same coin. A leader serves and a servant leads. Service is defined as leadership, not groveling.

Just as serving was essential to Christ's identity as God, it is essential to the identity of every one of us as human beings made in God's image. The Genesis mandate to have dominion is for both male and female servants of the living God, vice-regents of creation. We are to submit to one another as sons of Adam and daughters of Eve. Both male and female are called to be servant leaders. Why? Because God himself is *Ezer*.

STUDY GUIDE

1. Why are the words *serve* and *submit* "dirty words" in the modern and postmodern world? How has this cultural norm impacted your life?
2. What is the difference between freedom and license?
3. How do God's Trinitarian nature and Christ's humility during His incarnation challenge our cultural concepts of freedom, leadership, and success?
4. Is Genesis' description of the woman as man's "helper" an indication of her inferiority? Why or why not?

5. Why does God command sacrificial service? What are some practical ways you could demonstrate this quality in your own life today?
6. Reflect on the Differing Value System graphic. Describe in your own words how serving and leading relate in the world's context and the Kingdom's context.

CHAPTER 4

Servant-Leadership Modeled in Marriage

IN OUR BROKEN world, adultery, divorce, and cohabitation are now considered normal. Sex is recreational, a form of entertainment. Homosexuality and lesbianism are common, and even celebrated. Gender identity and transgender surgery are moving toward acceptable practice. Pedophilia is beginning to be promoted under the euphemism "Minor Attracted People" (MAP) and there is movement from the American Psychiatric Association and academia toward the legalizing of pedophilia in the U.S.[54] In addition bestiality, or Zoophilia, is practiced in the dark underworld in places around the world, even in Western Europe and the United States.[55]

But this sexual brokenness was never God's intention. It is a result of man's rebellion against God and the moral order of the universe. Instead, God's intention is expressed in Genesis 2:24, which states: "Therefore a man shall leave his father and his mother and hold fast to his wife, and they shall become one flesh." This is strange math. One plus one equals one! And in this partnership, something new is formed: a family. Often a baby is begotten—a brand new, one-of-a-kind human being who will live forever and leave his or her mark on eternity.

And marriage as God intended brings us closer to even deeper realities. Both testaments in the Bible foreshadow marriage: God's faithful love to Israel, and Christ's self-sacrificing headship of the church. Human marriage, small and fragile as it is, points to the future, ultimate marriage of the Lamb of God. The Scriptures begin and end with a wedding. Male and female. Husband and wife. The first marriage—Adam and Eve—and the ultimate wedding—Christ and the church. Marriage comprises a beautiful, binary relationship that models this marriage that will last for all eternity.

Paul picks up this thread in Ephesians 5:31–32.

> "Therefore a man shall leave his father and mother and hold fast to his wife, and the two shall become one flesh." This mystery is profound, and I am saying that it refers to Christ and the church.

The marriage of a man and a woman is a profound mystery. And part of that mystery is what marriage reveals to the world about Christ and His church.

These verses come near the end of a paragraph that begins in verse 22 with: "Wives, submit to your own husbands, as to the Lord." That imperative springs directly from verse 21, "submitting to one another out of reverence for Christ." Here is the entire passage:

> [21] submitting to one another out of reverence for Christ.

> [22] Wives, submit to your own husbands, as to the Lord. [23] For the husband is the head of the wife even as Christ is the head of the church, his body, and is himself its Savior. [24] Now as the church submits to Christ, so also wives should submit in everything to their husbands.

> [25] Husbands, love your wives, as Christ loved the church and gave himself up for her, [26] that he might sanctify her, having cleansed her by the washing of water with the word, [27] so that he might present the church to himself in splendor, without spot or wrinkle or any such thing, that she might be holy and without blemish. [28] In the same way husbands should love their wives as their own bodies. He who loves his wife loves himself. [29] For no one ever hated his own flesh, but nourishes and cherishes it, just as Christ does the church, [30] because we are members of his body. [31] "Therefore a man shall leave his father and mother and hold fast to his wife, and the two shall become one flesh." [32] This mystery is profound, and I am

saying that it refers to Christ and the church. [33] However, let each one of you love his wife as himself, and let the wife see that she respects her husband.

Most Bibles put a break between 21 and 22. Verse 21 closes a passage about the body of Christ; 22 begins a passage about marriage. But these paragraphs are related and ought not to be separated artificially by a header. Mutual submission between brothers and sisters in the larger body of Christ provides an important context for the next texts that deal with male and female relationships within marriage.

God knows we are born completely obsessed with the self. As we grow, that changes (it is fervently to be hoped!). If we are to have good marriages, it *must* change. S. Michael Craven, vice president of the Colson Center for Christian Worldview, has said, "Marriage is . . . the one relationship that effectively prepares and conditions us for living in community with others. By restraining self-centeredness and promoting love of another, [it] then becomes the foundation for social order."[56]

Ephesians 5:22–30 addresses both wife and husband, but Paul has a different message for each. We are equally human, equally valuable, equal in our diversity, of equal importance, and we are to submit to one another equally as human beings. Yet within marriage we find a distinction in roles.

When I was a student pastor at a university, I provided pre-marriage and marriage counseling. I took couples to Ephesians 5 and was intrigued by what the man heard and what the woman heard, especially a husband and wife who were struggling. I would read the passage and the wife would say, "See? You are to love me." The man would listen and say, "See? You are to submit to me." Neither was listening to the part of the text directed to *them*. They were listening to the part meant for the other.

So I changed my approach. After reading verse 21, I'd say to the man, "Now this is for you," and to the woman, "This part is not for you" and then read verses 25–32. And vice versa before verse 24.

The challenge focused on the husband is probably the more difficult, especially in that the Apostle Paul calls the husband to love his wife as Christ "gave himself up" for the church. What might this look like in a marriage today?

[25] Husbands, love your wives, as Christ loved the church and gave himself up for her, [26] that he might sanctify her, having

cleansed her by the washing of water with the word, [27] so that he might present the church to himself in splendor, without spot or wrinkle or any such thing, that she might be holy and without blemish. [28] In the same way husbands should love their wives as their own bodies. He who loves his wife loves himself. [29] For no one ever hated his own flesh, but nourishes and cherishes it, just as Christ does the church, [30] because we are members of his body. [31] "Therefore a man shall leave his father and mother and hold fast to his wife, and the two shall become one flesh." [32] This mystery is profound, and I am saying that it refers to Christ and the church.

Pastor John Piper has said,

> Therefore, headship is not a right to command and control. It's a responsibility to love like Christ, to lay down your life for your wife in servant leadership. Headship is the divine calling of a husband to take primary responsibility for Christ-like servant leadership, protection, and provision in the home. The husband does not need to know that he is the head of his wife.[57]

The part of the text that says the husband is the head of his wife is addressed to the woman, not to the man. The man doesn't need to be told that he is the head of his wife. He needs to know *how* to express that headship, how to lead his wife.

The text does not say that the man is the head of all women. He is the head of only one woman, his wife.

How is the husband the head?

- v. 23 "as Christ is"
- v. 25 "as Christ"
- v. 28 "In the same way"
- v. 29 "just as Christ does"

The pattern for a man's headship is Jesus Christ's headship of the church. While the word "head" means a position of authority, the nature of that authority is defined by Christ's example, not by sexist culture. Headship is built on the relationship between God and Israel, not merely on authority. As we have seen, Israel rebelled against God, prostituting herself before other gods. And what did God, *Ish* (the husband), do? He continued to love. He continued to serve. He continued to give Himself to His bride, who had become an adulteress.

And it's the pattern of Christ to His church. It's the pattern of the head to the body. It's the pattern of the husband toward his wife. And the operative word in these texts is *love*. If you look at this text, you will find the word *love* six times:

- twice in v. 25
- three times in v. 28
- once in v. 33

How is Christ the head of the church? He loves her. The self-sacrificing love that binds the Trinity together is the same love that binds husband and wife together. The word for "love" that appears six times in the text is not *eros*, intimate sexual love. Is there to be sexual intimacy within marriage? Of course, and it is to be enjoyed and celebrated. It's one of the greatest gifts God has given human beings. But that's not the love being described.

> **Therefore, headship is not a right to command and control. It's a responsibility to love like Christ, to lay down your life for your wife in servant leadership.**
> **John Piper**

Neither is it *phileo*, the love of friends. My wife is my best friend. I love her. I *phileo* her. So, yes, just as there is *eros* in the relationship between a husband and wife, there is *phileo*.

But the word here is *agape*, self-sacrificing love. You sacrifice yourself for the other. You put the other before yourself. The culture teaches us, "It's about me." But Ephesians says, "No, it's about the other." *Agape* love defines headship. *Agape* love sent Christ to the cross. He thought more of us than of himself. The husband is to exhibit such love toward his wife.

In a profound book, *The Four Loves*, C.S. Lewis describes *agape*:

> This headship, then, is most fully embodied, not in the husband we should all wish to be, but in him whose marriage is

most like a crucifixion; whose wife receives most and gives least, is most unworthy of him, is—in her own mere nature—least lovable. For the church has no beauty, but what the Bride-groom gives her; he does not find, but makes her, lovely.[58]

This is the love of Hosea for his unlovely wife. Despite his repeated sacrifices, she kept prostituting herself. So ultimately he went to the slave market and bought her back. Christ went to the ultimate slave market, the cross, to redeem us. That's why headship is most fully embodied in the husband whose marriage is most like a crucifixion!

Agape love defines headship. *Agape* love sent Christ to the cross. He thought more of us than of himself. The husband is to exhibit such love toward his wife.

This is sanctifying love, a love that creates a space for his bride to flourish, to become all that she is intended to be. It's a love that means "to feed and care for." It's not the sexist concept of headship. It's self-sacrificing headship, giving all that you are to your wife.

We began with the difficult assignment for husbands; now let's look at the difficult assignment for the wife in verses 22–24.

> Wives, submit to your own husbands, as to the Lord. For the husband is the head of the wife even as Christ is the head of the church, his body, and is himself its Savior. Now as the church submits to Christ, so also wives should submit in everything to their husbands.

Submission is offensive to the modern world. We want nothing to do with it. This, it goes without saying, is a tough pill to swallow in our culture, even in the church. But it helps to know that we are not to apply a sexist mentality to this difficult assignment of submission. As Piper explains,

> Submission is not slavish or coerced or cowering. That is not the way Christ wants the church to respond to his leadership. He wants it to be free and willing and glad and refining and strengthening. Submission is the divine calling of a wife to

honor and affirm her husband's leadership and help carry it through according to her gifts.[59]

The wife is called to be the *ezer* of her husband, to use her gifts to be his helper. As God is our helper—*Ezer.* The Greek word for submission, *hupotasso* is found three times in these verses. It is often translated "submit yourself." This submission is not coerced, but willing. The wife, a free moral agent, submits herself, willfully putting herself in submission to, her husband. The Bible considers this kind of submission sacred. Think of Mary's attitude and free volition when she says to the angel, Gabriel, "Behold, I am the servant of the Lord; let it be to me according to your word" (Luke 1:38).

In Ephesians 5, verse 22 is incredibly important: "to your own husband." A woman is called to submit to *her own husband*, not to all men. The sexist view, by contrast, makes every man the head of every woman. This is not headship, but tyranny. There is no warrant for it in Scripture.

Verse 23 brings us to a word that has been misunderstood by many: "head." "For the husband is the head of the wife even as Christ is the head of the church, his body, and is himself its Savior." Again, The Message enhances our understanding of the word "head" in verse 23: "The husband provides leadership to his wife the way Christ does to his church, not by domineering but by cherishing."

Husbands and tyrants all over the world have abused the word "head." They have interpreted it as "master" and "owner." Because the concept of headship has been so warped by fallen cultures, we need to understand what this term really means.

"Head" is the English translation of the Greek *kephale*, used three times in this passage. In its literal sense, it is the head of a human being. Metaphorically, *kephale* is "anything supreme, chief, prominent . . . of a husband in relation to his wife; of Christ: the Lord the husband of the Church; of things: the cornerstone."[60] As a cornerstone, *kephale* refers to the foundation stone that anchors and aligns a structure. As the head, it refers to governing authority.

Author and theologian Dr. Wayne Grudem says of *kephale*:

> I once looked up over 2,300 examples of the word "head" (*kephale*) in ancient Greek. In these texts, the word *kephale* is applied to many people in authority, but none without

governing authority. In the Greek-speaking world, to be the head of a group of people always meant to have authority over those people.[61]

A governing structure, of course, is part of the nature of the Godhead. Its very context is loving, other-serving relationships. It is part of the unfallen order of creation and thus is not evil in itself. As we have seen, the Godhead and human relationships have unity without uniformity, diversity without superiority. The Father has authority over the Son, but is not superior to the Son. Likewise, the husband has "governing" authority over his wife, but he is in no way superior to her.

However, human authority structures have been impacted by the Fall. Daily we witness twisted and deformed forms of governance. We see tyrannical governments and uncritically compliant citizens. We see tyrannical husbands and rebellious or servile wives. We have seen that sexism relishes the authority structure to the extent that it denies a woman's worth. Feminism denies any authority structure, deeming the structure intrinsically evil.

Authority structure and loving, self-sacrificing leadership apply in four spheres: the individual, the family, the church, and civil society. Let's look at each of these briefly.

FOUR SPHERES OF GOVERNMENT

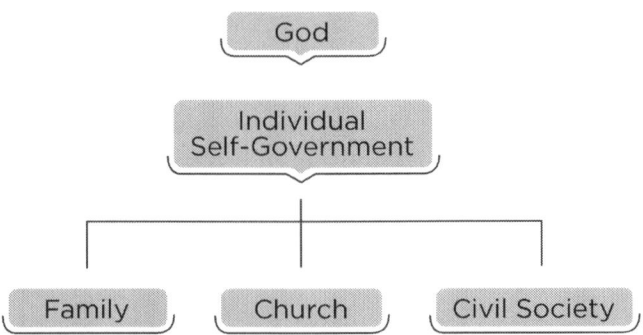

Successful governance in all societies begins first with individual, self-governance. Each person, female and male, is an agent equipped by God to govern in a way that stewards creation and glorifies God. Women and men are volitional beings and are called to govern their own lives well. All people, male and female, live before the face of God and must govern their lives according to biblical principles and personal conscience. Each individual stands under God's governing authority and is responsible for his or her role in governing the family, church, and civil society.

The second level of governance essential for a flourishing society comes in the family—God's agent for raising children and producing the next generation of nation-leaders. Parents are responsible, more than the state, to educate their children.

God has delegated to the husband servant leadership as the king of the family, the *prime* (aka first) *minister*. He is to be the head of his wife and family—to provide for, protect, and give godly and wise direction. To the wife, God has delegated servant-leadership as the queen of the family. She has an integral role in the family's mission and success. She is the nurturer of her children and plays an essential role in their education. She provides comfort and support for her husband and hospitality to the guests in her home. Again, the pattern for the husband's headship is Christ's loving, serving headship of the church. The wife is responsible to her own husband, not to all men.

The third space where loving, self-sacrificing leadership is necessary is in the church. The church is to be God's agent for redemption and the advancement of the kingdom through the preaching, teaching, and manifesting of the Word of God. Because of the priesthood of believers, all Christians are called into full-time ministry. Maleness is not a requirement for ministry in the church, nor is it required for all forms of leadership. Men and women are free to responsibly use all their natural and spiritual gifts.

The church is the embassy of the kingdom of God. Individual congregants are ambassadors of the King. We are to love the world and serve the brokenness in our community and beyond. Women and men have millions of opportunities to lead and minister over their lifetimes, inside and outside the church. The only limitation placed on most men and all women is the office of *episkope*: "Oversight: overseership, office, charge, the office of an elder; the overseer or presiding officers of a Christian church."[62] Just as God delegates to men the authority under Christ to govern the family, so Jesus Christ, the Chief Elder, delegates the *episcope* to male leaders, operating under His authority. We will explore the important issue of women in leadership later in this book.

The fourth sphere for governance comes within civil society, where leaders ensure justice and social order. There are no gender restrictions on work, ministry, and leadership. All women and all men have the freedom to pursue servant-leadership in any sphere of society.

Why did Jesus die on the cross? One reason is clearly stated in Colossians 1:20: "and through him to reconcile to himself all things, whether on earth or in heaven, making peace by the blood of his cross." Part of that reconciliation is to take place in the area of governing structures.

Authority structures are not abolished by the cross, as if they are perpetually evil. They are redeemed by the cross and are to be reformed by the followers of Christ, neither expanded nor contracted beyond what Scripture establishes. This truth moves human authority from fallen authoritarianism to loving, self-sacrificing relationships.

We see this in Jesus, the King of Kings and Lord of Lords (Revelation 17:14; 19:16), who yet is a servant (Mark 10:45). Jesus' servant nature does not contradict His Lordship or kingly rule. Servant leadership defines His authority. His leadership is defined by service, His headship by self-sacrifice.

Before a supper in New Testament times, the lowest servant would wrap a towel around his waist and wash the feet of those present. But at the last supper of our Lord, the King of the universe conferred dignity upon the menial. He modeled for all husbands what it means to be the head of his wife. Godly headship moves husbands to serve their wives by washing their feet—or the dishes.

Besides Paul's instruction in Ephesians 5:22–24 on the nature of servant-leadership, the text also addresses motivation and imitation. The wife is to submit to her husband just as she would to Jesus Christ. She is motivated by Christ to do this and in doing this imitates her submission to Christ. So "as to the Lord" (v. 22) addresses both motivation and imitation.

We find here a symmetry between the husband's call and the wife's call. The husband loves his wife as Christ loves the church. The wife submits to her husband as the church submits to Christ. Then the text says "in everything" (v. 24), which comes from the simple Greek word *pas*. We find it twice in the Great Commission—"all nations," and "all that I have commanded" (Matthew 18:18–20).

To obey in "all things" does not mean the wife is to disobey God in order to obey her husband. Her final authority is God. As all *imago Dei*, the wife is to think and ask questions. Too often many men and women fail to use the cognitive gifts God has given them. God has given us minds, and we are to love God with our minds. Women should be encouraged to think, to ask questions, to reason. The wise husband will solicit his wife's counsel and opinion, and she will do well to express them. She is given to him as his helper.

As we read this passage, we need to abandon a sexist mentality: "You stay home. You're here to have kids. You're here to take care of me." This is not the concept portrayed here. The wife is every bit the equal of her husband in worth and dignity. She is to respect her husband, to reverence him, to give him deference. In an ideal world, he is her loving, self-sacrificing head.

Do we revere Jesus Christ for who He is and what He has done? Yes, we're grateful. And in the same way wives are to respect their husbands. The wife is called to proactively respect her own husband. Is this always easy? No. No man is worthy, and some men are jerks. They think more of themselves than of their wives. But just as the husband is called to sacrifice himself for his wife, to think more of her than he does of himself, the wife is to respect her husband.

Listen to what theologian Dr. Susan Foh has to say in her wonderful book, *Women and the Word of God*:

> God's commands concerning marriage involve self-denial for both husband and wife, but of different sorts. The wife's submission establishes the God ordained headship of her husband. And the husband's love ensures the wife's best interest, her treatment as a person. Each one's obedience helps the other to fulfill his or her duty.[63]

When we think of the other person first, we show our pagan world, our sexist world, our feminist world God's design for marriage. Sexism and feminism put self at the center; the Trinitarian order puts the *other* at the center. The relationship is bound by self-sacrificing love.

Men and women are equal in marriage, but they have different roles and responsibilities. And those roles and responsibilities are toward the other, not toward the self. This servant-leadership so well modeled in marriage is a vital part of the Grand Design, and leads us back into what Paul calls the "mystery" of marriage.

A good friend who was my pastor for ten years is also a psychologist. He met his wife when he was four years old and she was three. They grew up together and attended the same school. When they became adults, they got married. They're in their eighties now and have known each other for almost eighty years. One day Pastor Ramon said to me, "You know, Darrow, I'm going to write a book someday and I know the title, *The Stranger in My*

Bed." Ramon knew his wife since he was four years old, and they're deeply in love, but there's still a mystery.

Celebrate the mystery, because it points to the end of history and the thrilling coming of Jesus Christ for His bride.

STUDY GUIDE

1. What deeper reality does the Bible say marriage is intended to portray? What roles do husband and wife play in this portrayal?
2. Ephesians 5:21 is the context for the description of marriage that Paul gives in the rest of Ephesians 5. Before we are husband and wife, what are we? Why is the brother to serve his sister and why is the sister to serve her brother?
3. Identify a non-family brother or sister and do something specific to serve them today.
4. What is the operative word in the Ephesians 5 passage on the husband's headship? Why did C.S. Lewis say that headship is most fully embodied in a marriage in which a husband receives the least in return?
5. What qualities characterize biblical submission? In the Bible, what woman do you think best exemplifies submission? Why?
6. In what four spheres of life do we find a God-ordained authority structure and a call to self-sacrificial leadership?
7. In what way is the Trinitarian order for life fundamentally different from both sexism and feminism?

PART 2

Unity and Diversity

CHAPTER 5

The Trinity: A Pattern for Humankind

THE SHEPHERD KING, David, spent many nights in the Judean hills watching the heavens as he protected the flock. He recorded his beautiful reflections in Psalm 19:

> The heavens declare the glory of God,
>   and the sky above proclaims his handiwork.
> Day to day pours out speech,
>   and night to night reveals knowledge.
> There is no speech, nor are there words,
>   whose voice is not heard.
> Their voice goes out through all the earth,
>   and their words to the end of the world. (Psalm 19:1–4)

David realized that the heavens God made declare his glory. Indeed, the creation reflects God's imagination in space and time. Much as the arresting *Pietà* sculpture communicates something about the genius of the Renaissance artist Michelangelo, the universe, in its unity and diversity, communicates truth about God. Christians understand God as both unity and diversity, the one God who exists eternally as three Persons. Not surprisingly, he created a universe that captures something both of his unity (*uni*) and diversity (*verse*).

The immense diversity of the universe reflects something true about the one God's divine nature. His creation comprises millions of billions of diverse elements. At the inanimate level, we see the universe with its billions of galaxies and their untold stars, moons, elements, gases, particles, and so on. Then there is the living universe, animated life found in a myriad of plants, animals, angels, and human beings. The unity of diversity appears at every hand: the doggie-ness of the dog, the rose-ness of the rose, the entire human family, billions of individuals, unique human beings all of "one blood" (Acts 17:26, NKJV).

Since ancient times, humans have contemplated a dichotomy referred to by philosophers as "the one and the many." Is reality best captured by the concept of one or by the concept of many? Is the universe single or multiple? Does unity characterize our experience or diversity? Universals or particulars? Simplicity or complexity? The question has social implications at the level of race, tribe, caste, and human sexuality.

Another question humankind has pondered, especially in recent centuries, is whether the universe is purposeful or purposeless. Does life have meaning, or did Shakespeare's *Macbeth* have it right?

> Life's but a walking shadow, a poor player
> That struts and frets his hour upon the stage,
> And then is heard no more. It is a tale
> Told by an idiot, full of sound and fury,
> Signifying nothing.[64]

Contrary to modern culture's view, God's grand story tells us that we are not cosmic accidents, unintentional intruders in the universe. We are here for a God-given purpose—to discover our Grand Design and live out the adventure of our calling. Our existence is not insignificant, but a truth of wonder and power, rooted in eternity—a truth rooted in God Himself. As King David exulted:

> When I look at your heavens, the work of your fingers,
>   the moon and the stars, which you have set in place,
> what is man that you are mindful of him,
>   and the son of man that you care for him?
> Yet you have made him a little lower than the heavenly
> beings
>   and crowned him with glory and honor.

You have given him dominion over the works of your hands;
  you have put all things under his feet,
all sheep and oxen,
  and also the beasts of the field,
the birds of the heavens, and the fish of the sea,
  whatever passes along the paths of the seas. (Psalm 8:3–8)

Human nature is part of a Grand Design from before the foundation of the world. We are rooted in the Trinitarian pattern of God Himself. Our design and function reveal who we are and the purpose for which we were made: God's divine calling on our lives.

While the heavens indeed declare the glory of God, the Scriptures speak of God's unity and diversity. Several Old Testament passages reveal God's **oneness**:

- Deuteronomy 6:4: "Hear, O Israel: The LORD our God, the LORD is one."
- Isaiah 44:6: "Thus says the LORD, the King of Israel
    and his Redeemer, the LORD of hosts:
  'I am the first and I am the last;
    besides me there is no god.'"
- Isaiah 44:8: "Fear not, nor be afraid;
    have I not told you from of old and declared it?
  And you are my witnesses!
    Is there a God besides me?
    There is no Rock; I know not any."

Several New Testament passages indicate the same:

- Romans 3:29–30: "Is he not the God of Gentiles also? Yes, of Gentiles also, since God is one—who will justify the circumcised by faith and the uncircumcised through faith."
- 1 Corinthians 8:4: "Therefore, as to the eating of food offered to idols, we know that 'an idol has no real existence,' and that 'there is no God but one.'"
- Galatians 3:20: "Now an intermediary implies more than one, but God is one."

- 1 Timothy 2:5: "For there is one God, and there is one mediator between God and men, the man Christ Jesus"
- James 2:19: "You believe that God is one; you do well. Even the demons believe—and shudder!"

Other texts reveal God as **community**.

- Genesis 1:26–27: "Then God said, 'Let us make man in our image, after our likeness. And let them have dominion over the fish of the sea and over the birds of the heavens and over the livestock and over all the earth and over every creeping thing that creeps on the earth.' So God created man in his own image, in the image of God he created him; male and female he created them."
- Genesis 3:22: "Then the Lord God said, 'Behold, the man has become like one of us in knowing good and evil.'"
- Genesis 11:7: "'Come, let us go down and there confuse their language, so that they may not understand one another's speech.'"
- Isaiah 6:8: "And I heard the voice of the Lord saying, 'Whom shall I send, and who will go for us?' Then I said, 'Here I am! Send me.'"

In the Scriptures, God reveals His nature with plural pronouns—*we, us, our,* and *ours,* as well as singular pronouns such as *I, me, myself,* and *mine.* The very beginning of the biblical narrative, Genesis 1:1, reveals God by the Hebrew word *Elohim,* the plural form of the word *El,* the "Mighty One."

While most languages have only a single word for "one," the Hebrew has two. *Yachid* is the "single," "absolute," or "indivisible" one, captured by the equation 1 = 1. *Echad,* on the other hand, is the "united," "compound," or "bound together" one, as in 1+1+1 = 1.[65]

We see *echad* in Genesis 2:24, "a man shall leave his father and his mother and hold fast to his wife, and they shall become one (*echad*) flesh." Deuteronomy 6:4 records the Shema, "Hear, O Israel, the Lord our God, the Lord is one (*echad*)." *Yachid* is the one, the single one, the absolute, indivisible one. *Echad* is the united compound or bound-together one. One plus one equals one. *Echad* equipped the Hebrews to grasp the one and many.

UNITED ONE
THE MEANING OF ONE ECHAD OR YACHID

- **TEXTS:** Genesis 2:24; Deuteronomy 6:4-5

- **HEBREWS HAD TWO WORDS FOR "ONE"**

  - **One Yachid** – "single," "absolute," or "indivisible" one; (1=1)

  - **One Echad** – "united," "compound," or "bound together" one; (1+1+1 = 1)

The New Testament, likewise, reveals the community nature of the one true God. Scripture reveals that God is Trinity, the combined-one Lord. We see this revealed in:

- The baptism of Jesus with the voice of the Father and the descent of the Spirit:
  - » Matthew 3:16–17: "And when Jesus was baptized, immediately he went up from the water, and behold, the heavens were opened to him, and he saw the Spirit of God descending like a dove and coming to rest on him; and behold, a voice from heaven said, 'This is my beloved Son, with whom I am well pleased.'"
  - » Mark 1:9–11: "In those days Jesus came from Nazareth of Galilee and was baptized by John in the Jordan. And when he came up out of the water, immediately he saw the heavens being torn open and the Spirit descending on him like a dove. And a voice came from heaven, 'You are my beloved Son; with you I am well pleased.'"
  - » Luke 3:21–22: "Now when all the people were baptized, and when Jesus also had been baptized and was praying, the heavens were opened, and the Holy Spirit descended on him in bodily form, like a dove; and a voice came from heaven, 'You are my beloved Son; with you I am well pleased.'"

- In John 14:16–19, Jesus speaks of the Father and the work of the Spirit: "And I will ask the Father, and he will give you another Helper, to be with you forever, even the Spirit of truth, whom the world cannot receive, because it neither sees him nor knows him. You know him, for he dwells with you and will be in you. I will not leave you as orphans; I will come to you. Yet a little while and the world will see me no more, but you will see me. Because I live, you also will live."
- Believers' baptism in Matthew 28:19: "Go therefore and make disciples of all nations, baptizing them in the name of the Father and of the Son and of the Holy Spirit."
- Paul's prayer in Ephesians 3:16–17: "that according to the riches of his glory he may grant you to be strengthened with power through his Spirit in your inner being, so that Christ may dwell in your hearts through faith—that you, being rooted and grounded in love."
- Paul's benedictions:
  » 2 Corinthians 13:14: "The grace of the Lord Jesus Christ and the love of God and the fellowship of the Holy Spirit be with you all."
  » Ephesians 4:4–6: "There is one body and one Spirit—just as you were called to the one hope that belongs to your call— one Lord, one faith, one baptism, one God and Father of all, who is over all and through all and in all."
- Peter's prologue in 1 Peter 1:2: "according to the foreknowledge of God the Father, in the sanctification of the Spirit, for obedience to Jesus Christ and for sprinkling with his blood."
- John's doxology in Revelation 1:4–5: "Grace to you and peace from him who is and who was and who is to come, and from the seven spirits who are before his throne, and from Jesus Christ the faithful witness, the firstborn of the dead, and the ruler of kings on earth."

The early church fathers, of course, wrestled with the New Testament data revealing the Father as God, the Son as God, and the Holy Spirit as God—even as they knew there is only one God. Finally, the early church councils articulated the doctrine of the three in one: Father, Son, and Holy Spirit, one God in three persons. Tertullian, about 210 A.D., first used the Latin word *Trinity* (literally "triad" or "threefold") to articulate the orthodox understanding that God is three in one, all the members of the Godhead being co-eternal and of the same nature or essence. Orthodox theology knows the three members of the Trinity as distinct persons in divine community.

GOD IS TRINITY
(UNITY & DIVERSITY)

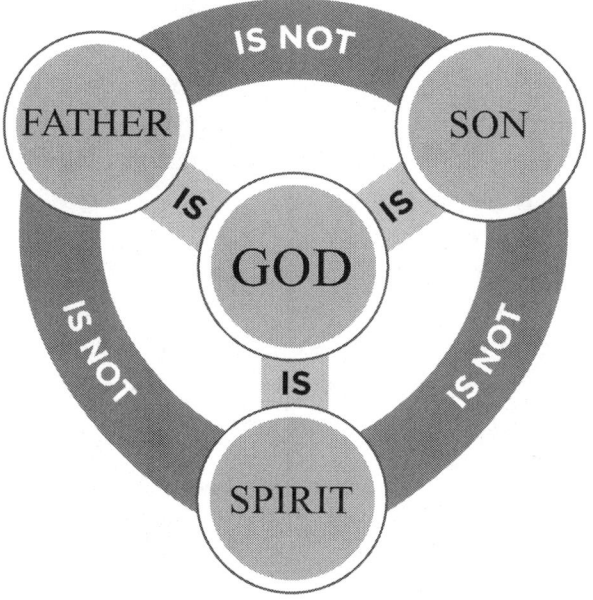

But the modern mind, bound by the concept of a single, undivided one, struggles with this philosophical framework. Thus Arthur Koestler, writing in *The Ghost in the Machine*, proposes the word *holon*, from the Greek *holos*, "whole," which signifies the whole and the part existing simultaneously.

The Trinitarian doctrine, one God in three persons, stands in contrast to (1) philosophic and religious monism, which holds that everything is one without significant diversity, and (2) atomism, in which everything is diverse, without ultimate unity.

The Trinitarian concept provides the foundation for resolving the perennial tension between the one and the many. It reveals God as both a single and a community at the same time. Each member of the Trinity possesses the fullness of the Divine nature. They are one in being, in substance, in nature, in glory, in majesty, in power, and in eternity. The Athanasian Creed holds "that we worship one God in Trinity, and Trinity in Unity; neither confounding the Persons, nor dividing the Essence. For there is one Person of the Father; another of the Son; and another of the Holy Ghost. But the Godhead of the Father, of the Son, and of the Holy Ghost, is all one; the Glory equal, the Majesty coeternal."

This plurality contrasts with the monotheism of Jews and Muslims on one hand, and with polytheism (many gods) and atheism (no God) on the other. The one God known in the Christian faith reveals Himself as a community of three distinct persons: Father, Son, and Holy Spirit.

Each member of the Trinity is a unique person, identified by name, with a particular role and function. The Father is not the Son. The Son is not the Spirit. They are bound together by love, yet each manifests His own personhood. Just as in a human family each member has his or her own individuality, so it is in the Trinity.

We see this in creation. In Genesis 1:1, God the Father creates. God the Son is the agent of creation (John 1:3; Colossians 1:15–17). And the Spirit of God hovers over the creation (Genesis 1:2).

We see it also in salvation. The Father is the author who planned salvation. The Son is the executer of the plan who becomes incarnate and dies to fulfill the plan. The Holy Spirit seals the plan, regenerating the sinner. Each person of the Trinity has a particular role or function in the plan of salvation.

Another differentiation is controversial in the modern world, but nonetheless it's how God has revealed himself within the Trinity: a subordination of function. The Father has authority over the Son (John 6:38). The Father and Son have authority over the Holy Spirit (John 14:26, 15:26).

One God, three persons. Different roles, different functions, equally God. The Scriptures teach that God is one in being and in essence, who has existed eternally in three distinct and coequal persons. He is the *One and the Many*—God.

Perfect love in the Godhead provides unity. In John's Gospel, Jesus says to the Father, "You loved me before the foundation of the world" (John 17:24). Love existed before the universe came to be. Father, Son, and Spirit, the one and many God, existed before the universe, bound together by *agape* love.

This is unity without uniformity and diversity without superiority.

These two principles—unity without uniformity and diversity without superiority—are rooted in the nature of the Godhead. They are also very practical principles for all social relationships, including those in marriage, business, and government. Why are these distinctions important? Because our answer to the one and the many question carries social implications. Ideas have consequences.

For generations people have suffered under systems of racism, tribalism, sexism, casteism, communism, fascism, etc. We never seem to get to the end of all this suffering. Why? Because we are sinners, yes, but the problem is not merely moral. It is a metaphysical problem, related to the concept of the one and the many.

> **This is unity without uniformity and diversity without superiority.**

Atomism and its child, sexism, represent diversity without unity, that is, diversity with superiority. Sexist culture says men and women are different, and men are superior to women. This leads to the crushing of women. Society's response to that problem is monism, the opposite of atomism. All is one. Aristotle said, "Everything is diverse, there is no ultimate unity." Radical feminism responded to sexism by erasing distinctions, promoting unity without diversity. This implies uniformity or interchangeability—in this case, the interchangeability of role and function, which leads to the disappearance of women. Radical feminism erases the distinctiveness of the woman; the woman's goal is to be like a man. And now in postmodernism, even the biological distinctives are being erased. For some confused women, the goal is to *be* a man.

Atomism and monism have other social implications. With respect to race, atomism manifests as racism. Historically whiteness has been seen as superior to blackness. My country, the US, was infected with racism, perhaps dominated by it at times. South Africa was dominated by racism. In Latin America, light-skinned people have for generations been seen as superior to dark-skinned indigenous people. This is diversity without sufficient unity to bind the two together.

Another manifestation is tribalism: "My tribe is better than your tribe." Tribalism has led to massive, bloody conflicts throughout Africa. During three months in 1994 in Rwanda, the conflict between the Tutsis and the Hutus ended with the slaughter of 500,000 to 1 million people. We see tremendous ethnic conflict today in Nigeria, which has a population of 211 million people with over 250 different ethnic groups and over 400 spoken languages and dialects.[66]

Yet tribalism is not only a problem in places like Africa. America is seeing increasing levels of tribalism, be it political, social, or economic. Critical Race Theory and intersectionality are tools for dividing races and creating a neo-tribalism. We have kept the *E pluribus* ("out of many") in our national motto and discarded the *unum* ("one").

India has its caste system, which says, "My caste is higher than your caste." The mistreatment of lower castes by higher castes has gone on for centuries and continues today, despite the ideal of equality expressed in the Indian Constitution. It even thrives in the Indian Diaspora in high-tech areas such as Silicon Valley.[67]

Regarding sexism, Confucian culture exhibits a social hierarchy. People in China and Korea say "men are high, women are low; men are honored and women despised"—"namjon-yeobi." In my travels, I have been confronted many times with language that demeans women or even erases their existence. Some languages refer to women as tools, slaves, or demon witches.

Atomism sacrifices unity to diversity. Such cultures pit one thing against another. "This is higher, this is better than the other." Monism, on the other hand, sacrifices diversity to unity.

In Mao's China, everyone was required to be the same. Everyone read Mao's Little Red Book, had to think the same thoughts, had to wear the same uniforms, including the same haircut and cap. If you did not conform, you would be killed. An estimated 100 million or more people were killed in Mao's China to affirm unity without diversity. Millions died of the same "disease" in Stalin's Soviet Union, Pol Pot's Cambodia, the Kims' North Korea, and other communist countries, in an effort to produce the monistic social paradise of equality. What they got instead was a foretaste of hell.

The Western world has also witnessed movement toward monism. We did not go directly from the reality of biology to undifferentiated gender identity. At one time, most women wore dresses and men wore pants. Often in today's professional world, women and men alike wear pants, jackets, and even ties. Men's and women's college dorms transitioned to men's and women's floors; now men and women use the same bathrooms. This shift accompanied the breakdown of biblical theism in the culture. Now we are awash in full-blown confusion about gender identity. This is a cultural application of the philosophy of monism, with its ultimate, the transgender movement, blurring all distinctions.

The very biology of male and female is denied. People define themselves without any consideration for obvious, objective reality. Women expecting babies are taking hormones, growing beards, and claiming to be pregnant men. Males, such as swimmer Lia Thomas, are declaring themselves female and competing in women's sports. As they decimate their biological female competitors, with few critics willing to speak up, these males are largely cheered as transgender heroes. Theologian Carl R. Trueman describes this denial of reality as "expressive individualism." He writes, "Essentially, the expressive individualist intuits that the true self is that which we are inside, the inner emotions and psychological feelings that we experience."[68]

When we speak of unity, it is imperative to distinguish between uniformity and correspondence. Uniformity is conformity. It's the mirror image. The identical. Unity in this sense destroys diversity. Uniformity is a pair of gloves or pair of earrings.. They are indistinguishable from one another.

UNIFORMITY   CORRESPONDENCE

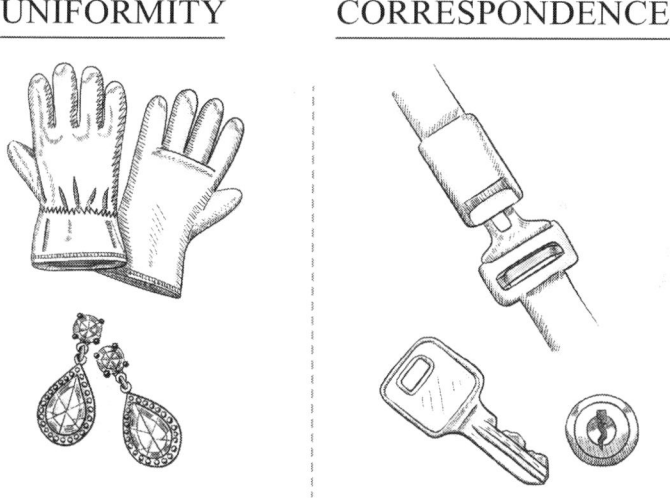

Correspondence, on the other hand, is a lock and a key, or the two ends of a belt, a buckle on one end and holes on the other; not the same, but made to fit together. If both ends were buckles, the belt would not function. The belt works because of a corresponding relationship. The two are made for each other.

We need to champion the kind of unity that fulfills all things in a complementary relationship rather than one thing by the elimination of the other—uniformity. Unity is healthy when it is a compatibility, a connection between two distinct things, the compound oneness of the two. This is a unity of diversity, or, to use the Hebrew, *echad*. This pattern comes from God Himself, one God in three persons who complement each other and make the whole.

A lesbian or homosexual "wedding" manifests uniformity—two of the same, they don't fit together. A man and a woman marrying is correspondence—they are different, but like a lock and a key, they were designed to fit and function together. The very anatomy of male and female demonstrate they were designed to fit together both physically and physiologically for a purpose to have children and form families and to fulfill the Cultural Mandate.

The social significance of the Trinitarian faith is huge. Just as the members of the Trinity are equal in their divinity, we see that men and women are equal in their humanity. Humans, like the members of the Trinity, are diverse and equally valuable. Our fallen world, tragically, has historically been a man's world. Sexism and radical feminism have the same ultimate effect: the superiority of the male.

- Egalitarianism, espoused by radical feminism, says that a woman is equal by becoming like a man, functioning like a man. Perversely, this reaffirms the superiority of maleness to femaleness.
- Sexism, valued by macho culture and attitudes, values maleness over femaleness. It says that men and women are different in function, and the male is superior to the female.

The Trinitarian framework, however, creates a better way, which sees men and women as diverse but equally valuable, equal in being while different in function. Males and females bring different gifts and abilities to the world. This complementary diversity makes a glorious whole. In the Trinity there is unity without uniformity, diversity without superiority. God as one and many, Father, Son, and Holy Spirit, provides a model for the relationship of men and women and the flourishing of humankind and creation.

STUDY GUIDE

1. How do the two Hebrew words for "one" differ in meaning? Where in Scripture do we see examples of the divine *"echad"*?

2. Describe in your own words the meaning and significance of the twin principles, "There is unity without uniformity and diversity without superiority!"

3. How does this understanding of God's Trinitarian nature impact our understanding of the human family? In male-female relationships?

4. Do the persons of the Trinity have identical roles? Are there relationships of authority within the Godhead? What are the implications of this for us?

5. Describe in your own words the difference between "uniformity" and "correspondence." How do sexism and egalitarianism each denigrate womanhood? How does the Trinity model a way forward?

CHAPTER 6

The Framework: Examining the Assumptions Behind Our View of Male and Female

BEFORE WE EMERGE from the womb, we are learning of our mother's tastes in food, the sound of her voice, the music she listens to, and the rhythms that order her life. We exit the womb with wonder. Our parents are blown away by this new baby, beautifully and wonderfully made, a unique human being fashioned from the mystic combination of two DNA sets. And the same wonder overwhelms the baby as she moves from the darkness of the womb into the light of the universe.

The child has seemingly endless questions, verbalized or not, from early childhood and on. What is this? Do I put it in my mouth? Is it part of me or separate from me? Who am I? What am I? Why am I here? To whom do I belong? Where is my community? For what am I made? How is the opposite sex different from me? What do we have in common? Are we made for each other? For what purpose? Are we equal and different? Do our differences make us unequal? Because we are equal, are we the same?

These questions and many more beg for answers. And the replies the baby receives will be determined by our own framework for understanding the world. We answer questions from what is most reasonable from the voice of our own worldview and understanding.

Regarding male and female, sexists, as we have seen, are rooted in an atomistic framework that deems men and women different, and men as superior to women. Modern feminists respond from a monistic faith: Men and women are equal and therefore the same, without distinction. A Trinitarian framework, however, acknowledges women and men as equal in being and uniquely and gloriously different in function. This means we must be alert to challenges from both extremes.

Francis Schaeffer, the founder of L'Abri Fellowship and a man who mentored me in my twenties, told me, "In this fallen world, things constantly swing like a pendulum from being wrong in one extreme way to being wrong in another extreme. The devil never gives us the luxury of fighting on only one front. This will always be the case." We Christians usually need to fight on two fronts. If we're only fighting on one, we're probably missing the heat of the battle.

WORLD'S CONCEPT OF TRUTH

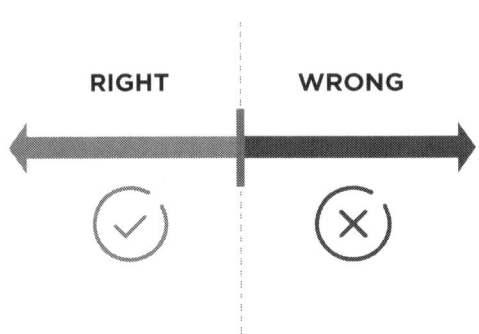

Once when I was at a dinner table with Dr. Schaeffer, he drew a line and put a point on it. One side of the point he labeled "right," the other side he labeled "wrong." To my knowledge he never wrote or spoke publicly about what he shared with us that night. But this was the beginning of one of the profound observations that shaped my life when I was living in his home in Switzerland.

We Christians tend to divide life between right and wrong. We want to be right. In fact, if we are very conscientious, we want to stay as far away as possible from wrong. But when we see life this way, we often separate what was not meant to be separated. In many cases, institutions are split over these divisions. We put grace on one side and law on the other. Some churches focus on grace, some on law. We forget how easily we are influenced by denominational emphases or personal choices.

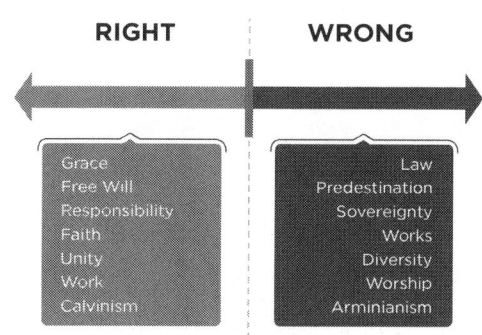

Some divide free will and predestination, responsibility and sovereignty, faith and works, unity and diversity, feminism and sexism. We separate what should not be separated. People often reason that if you're on one side, you're right, and on the other side you're wrong.

Schaeffer drew another diagram with *two* points on the line to represent that the Scriptures speak of God's sovereignty *and* man's free will, of faith

and works. When we separate them, we develop whole denominations who divide unnecessarily from other Christians. When I was younger, I spent endless, wasted hours debating with fellow Christians. Schaeffer's drawing helped me reconcile many tensions. By using two points, Schaeffer was saying a person can be wrong on either side. We need to live within the tension of these two points.

G.K. Chesterton is often called "the Prince of Paradox." In his profound book *Orthodoxy*, he charges us to hold seemingly contradictory points in tension. Chesterton treats seeming contradictions in the Bible, not by framing one text as true and the other false, but by showing the genius of the biblical message:

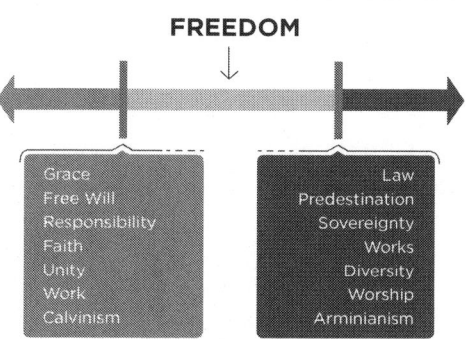

"... in short, Christianity got over the difficulty of combining furious opposites, by keeping them both, and keeping them both furious. The Church was positive on both points."[69]

One of the most striking examples is the concept that Jesus could be fully God and fully man. Yet this is what we understand in the Incarnation, God taking on human form.

> In the beginning was the Word, and the Word was with God, and the Word was God. He was with God in the beginning. Through him all things were made; without him nothing was made that has been made. In him was life, and that life was the light of all mankind. . . . The Word became flesh and made his dwelling among us. We have seen his glory, the glory of the one and only Son, who came from the Father, full of grace and truth. (John 1:1–4, 14 NIV)

Is Christ God or man? Chesterton writes:

> For orthodox theology has specially insisted that Christ was not a being apart from God and man, like an elf, nor yet a being half human and half not, like a centaur, but both things at once and both things thoroughly, very man and very God.[70]

The reality is that Christ was the God-Man, fully God and fully man. We are meant to bow in the face of this wonder.

Another example is the cross. God is the source of both righteousness and love. His righteousness demands the punishment of sin; His love moves Him to take that punishment on Himself. At the cross, God's love and justice meet. Psalm 85:10 is a prelude to the cross: "Steadfast love and faithfulness meet; righteousness and peace kiss each other."

Chesterton captures this when he writes that life demands maintaining a tension between God's righteousness and His love. Each is a bright color that needs to be manifest in all its glory. And the ultimate glory is the cross. Chesterton powerfully writes:

> [The church] has kept [seeming paradoxes] side by side like two strong colours, red and white, like the red and white upon the shield of St. George. It has always had a healthy

hatred of pink. It hates that combination of two colours which is the feeble expedient of the philosophers. It hates that evolution of black into white which is tantamount to a dirty grey. . . . All that I am urging here can be expressed by saying that Christianity sought in most of these cases to keep two colours co-existent but pure. It is not a mixture like russet or purple; it is rather like a shot silk, for a shot silk is always at right angles, and is in the pattern of the cross.[71]

Shot silk, also known as taffeta, is silk fabric made of two colors woven together to create an iridescent appearance.

Another paradox that Chesterton identifies is man as both the highest creature (Genesis 1:26–27) and the greatest sinner (Romans 3:23):

In one way Man was to be haughtier than he had ever been before; in another way he was to be humbler than he had ever been before. In so far as I am Man I am the chief of creatures. In so far as I am a man I am the chief of sinners.[72]

Romans 12:3 affords Chesterton an example:

For by the grace given to me I say to everyone among you not to think of himself more highly than he ought to think, but to think with sober judgment, each according to the measure of faith that God has assigned.

Finally, three more of Chesterton's favorite paradoxes:

One can hardly think too little of one's self. One can hardly think too much of one's soul.[73]

Charity—Charity is a paradox, like modesty and courage. Stated baldly, charity certainly means one of two things—pardoning unpardonable acts, or loving unlovable people.[74]

The sin and the sinner—Christianity came in here as before. It came in startlingly with a sword, and clove one thing from another. It divided the crime from the criminal. The criminal we must forgive unto seventy times seven. The crime we must not forgive at all. . . . We must be much more angry with theft than before, and yet much kinder to thieves than before. There was room for wrath and love to run wild. And the more I considered Christianity, the more I found that while it had established a rule and order, the chief aim of that order was to give room for good things to run wild.[75]

Perhaps this insight can help us to deal with so many doctrinal divisions—between law and grace, free will and predestination, and so on. The Bible teaches both. Let's follow Chesterton and live in the glorious tension. Too many theologians emphasize one side at the expense of the other. It's not one or the other; it's both / and. We are to live creatively within that tension.

WORLD'S CONCEPT OF TRUTH

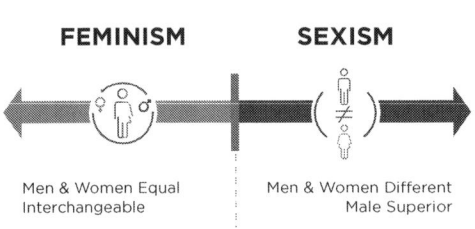

FEMINISM　　**SEXISM**

Men & Women Equal
Interchangeable

Men & Women Different
Male Superior

In terms of the Grand Design, God has made male and female equal but not the same. Both male and female are active reflections of the image of God and yet are gloriously different. As with the seeming paradox of the Trinity—God as the One and the Many—so with male and female, equal in being, equal in intrinsic identity, and different by design and function. Together they make the glorious complementary whole. To go outside either boundary is to err. Sexism focuses on our differences and concludes men are superior to women. Modern feminism errs on the other side by saying that men and women are equal and therefore the same—interchangeable, without distinction. Postmoderns go so far as to deny reality and thus deny the wonder of male and female sexuality.

In Arizona, we get to enjoy a unique place called Monument Valley, which has pinnacles rising out of the desert. From the top of a pinnacle, you can fall off on more than one side. If you move too far from the cliff, you'll fall off the other side. Schaeffer said this captures the concept of truth; it's like a pinnacle—you can fall off on either side if you don't live in the tension of the middle.

Monism is an extreme: no distinction, everything is interchangeable. Reality is a unified whole. Atomism is also an extreme. Everything is different, some things are more important or higher than others. We must avoid both cliffs, monism and atomism. If we don't keep both in view, we will certainly fall off one of them.

Think of a child's mobile over a crib. What makes it so intriguing? It hangs in balance, gently moving. But if you remove a tiny part of the mobile, the whole thing collapses and becomes static. The point: Truth, like a child's mobile, is finely balanced. If you disconnect one part, it becomes lifeless.

Men and women are equal in their being. They have equal worth, equal dignity. Yet they are gloriously different in function, which is a cause not for consternation but for celebration. God framed male and female for a purpose in the created order. In so doing, he created them with a complementary nature. This is part of a larger pattern in creation.

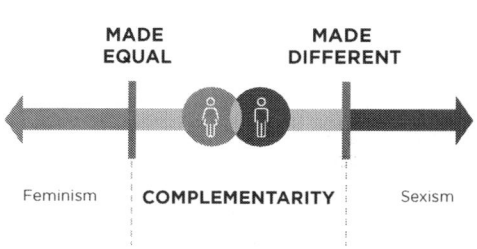

BIBLICAL CONCEPT OF TRUTH

We see complementary pairs in Genesis.

- 1:1, heaven and earth,
- 1:4, light and dark,
- 1:5, day and night,
- 1:7, the waters above and the waters beneath,
- 1:10, the sea and the dry land,
- 1:16, the greater light, the lesser light.
- 1:17, binary male and female—complementary, made for each other in the Grand Design.

N.T. Wright says this sequence points to heterosexual marriage at the climax: "It's all about male and female."[76] Seven pairs of binary realities end with male and female, complementary binary pairs, designed to work together. Each part derives its full significance from its connection to the other.

Dennis Prager, the Hebrew scholar and social/cultural commentator, writes of the significance of binary:

The human-animal distinction is one of the many distinctions the Torah

[The Five Books of Moses] makes and upon which higher civilization is based. The contemporary age, in its rejection of the Bible and its values, is undoing distinctions. Examples, as noted in Genesis 1:2, include good and evil, male and female, God and man, holy and profane.[77]

Note the immense importance of distinctions. It is the human-animal distinction that leads to the rise of Western civilization. Rejecting such a basic distinction will mark a return to the pagan world. Confusing the distinction between man and animals does not raise the stature of animals. It merely reduces man to an animal. The wonder of binary male and female transcends nature. God's Word speaks of male and female, and His work shows this complementary nature.

Early in the 19th century, Lydia Sigourney saw far ahead when she wrote, "But still wherever the brute force of the warrior is counted godlike, woman is appreciated only as she approximates to sterner natures."[78] If brute force is the primary value, women are destined to be deemed inferior.

Professor Ivy George of Gordon College has said, "When woman's work of caring is rendered invisible by societal arrangements and structures, a kind of social femicide is in process."[79] Eventually we will kill the very idea of female. Why? Because feminine and female are organically connected. Neither is valued in a sexist world.

In the early 19th century, most men and women embraced what I call *maternal* feminism, though they didn't use those words. They understood that women were equal to men and significant in their being and in their function. Modern feminism came along in the 1960s, however, and began to turn the world upside down.

In the 1970s, the debate in feminist circles was between "equality feminists" and "difference feminists." The former are now known as egalitarian feminists, or modern feminists. The difference feminists were essential feminists. They affirmed the truth that men and women are essentially different.

Egalitarians focused on the similarities between male and female. Their goal was "equality," by which they meant interchangeability of men and women in all spheres of life. Women must go out of the home because a career trumps motherhood. Essential feminists, on the other hand, affirmed real biological and physiological differences between men and women. The two sexes have equal value and are to be celebrated. Tragically, in the debate between egalitarians and difference feminists, the former won. They determined the nature of second-wave feminism.

In the 1980s, the church began to engage in this debate. Tragically, it failed to lead the discussion from the perspective of the Grand Design and the Judeo-Christian worldview. In 1984, an organization was formed in England called "Men, Women and God." This group of evangelicals supported the egalitarian position, igniting a movement within the evangelical and charismatic churches in both England and the United States.

Three years later, in the United States, an organization was begun called "Christians for Biblical Equality." This group sought to consciously function from a Judeo-Christian worldview. Its position was similar to difference feminism: Men and women are biologically different and equal in dignity and honor.

Sadly, the battle continues within the church. Whole denominations and churches have been divided over this issue. When the church fails to fulfill the Great Commission to disciple the nations (Matthew 28:18–20), she gets discipled by the dominant culture, as manifested in modern feminism.

Modern feminism infecting the church is simply a new manifestation of syncretism, in which an unbiblical worldview is grafted onto a biblical worldview, resulting in an ungodly mix that obscures the truth and leads people astray. Syncretism with modern feminism, or monism, manifests in the church as egalitarianism, the downplaying of differences, the belief that men and women are interchangeable.

On the other extreme, we have a syncretism with sexism or atomism. This is chauvinism. Tragically, much chauvinism remains in a church that has embraced sexist culture. This dynamic has often led to the crushing of women.

But there is a middle ground, if we will take it. Paul writes, in Romans 12:2, "be not conformed to this world." Whether it is a sexist world or a feminist world, "be not conformed to this world, but be transformed by the renewing of your mind." The renewing of the mind begins with the Trinitarian principle: God is the one and the many.

This is the foundation for a proper biblical understanding of male and female: equal in value, different in role and function. Let's celebrate the dignity of women as women, and men as men. This is the answer God calls us to provide to the questions of every inquiring child.

—— STUDY GUIDE ——

1. What did Francis Schaeffer mean by this statement: "The devil never gives us the luxury of fighting on only one front"? Are there ways in which the church of our own day is committing this error?

2. What examples does G.K. Chesterton give of the church "getting over the difficulty of combining furious opposites, by keeping both and keeping both furious"? What would have been lost if the church had conceded either side of these paradoxes?

3. What two opposite truths do Christians need to affirm with regard to men and women? What would be lost if the church were to concede either one?

4. What is the difference between equality and interchangeability? Which understanding has prevailed in modern feminism (and in many evangelical churches)?

5. In what ways do you see syncretism with sexism or feminism in your church or community?

CHAPTER 7

Transcendent Sexuality: The Root of Our Biological Differences

JORDAN PETERSON, THE outspoken Canadian psychologist, stated provocatively in a recent debate, "There's only two reasons that men and women differ. One is cultural, and the other is biological. If you minimize the cultural differences [by giving women freedom to choose what they want to do], you maximize the biological differences. . . 'the finding that gender differences maximize as egalitarian policies are developed is one of the most solidly grounded findings ever produced by social scientists.'"[80]

What does this mean? If women have freedom to choose, most will choose to honor their biology, their sex, their maternal nature. Elisabeth Elliot would agree: "Our sexual differences are the terms of our life, and to obscure them in any way is to weaken the very fabric of life itself."[81]

One's metaphysical assumptions establish one's understanding of the physical world, including one's sex. If one begins from a secular, materialist viewpoint, there is no transcendent reality. According to this worldview, biology is all there is! The only distinction between men and women is the "plumbing." Sexual behavioral differences are learned through a process of socialization. In the Darwinian vision of reality, the stronger survive. Life tends to be played out against a backdrop of "maleness." Generally, men are bigger and stronger than women and thus are thought to be better than women.

In the postmodern world, however, we are insanely abandoning even the concept of biological function. In its place we are promoting the ideology of gender identity. All this is rooted in the rejection of transcendent reality. Masculinity and femininity are, however, the architectural pattern for the biology of male and female. There is a transcendent pattern behind our physical bodies.

> "Our sexual differences are the terms of our life, and to obscure them in any way is to weaken the very fabric of life itself."
> Elisabeth Elliot

We must know the Designer and His design. Elliot writes, "In order to learn what it means to be a woman, we must start with the one who made her."[82] And we *can* know the one who made woman! God has revealed Himself through His Word and also through what He has made.

> Because that which may be known of God is manifest in them, for God hath shewed it unto them. For the invisible things of him from the creation of the world are clearly seen, being understood by the things that are made, even his eternal power and Godhead; so that they are without excuse. (Romans 1:19–20, KJV)

The bottom line? In addition to His Word (the written Scriptures and the living Word, Jesus Christ), God has revealed Himself through His works, the creation. Paul is arguing that this revelation is so clear that people have no excuse for denying the Creator.

Jacques Monod was a French biologist who in 1965 received the Nobel Prize for medicine. He was the director of the Pasteur Institute in Paris and involved in some of the initial DNA research. In his book *Chance and Necessity*, a classic in its day, Monod writes that "one of the fundamental characteristics common to all living beings without exception [is] that of being objects endowed with a purpose or project, which at the same time they exhibit in their structure and carry out through their performances."[83]

Although Monod was a naturalist, he recognized that all living things reveal the purpose for which they were "endowed." Their structure and function communicate their purpose. Monod unwittingly confirms what the Scripture says: creation communicates. Any rational and objective observer would conclude from abundant evidence that the universe has a Designer.

But Monod professes to be an atheist. As such, he cannot live with this conclusion. So how does he deal with this inconsistency? Here is his stunning confession:

> Objectivity nevertheless obliges us to recognize the teleonomic character of living organisms, to admit that in their structure and performance they act projectively—realize and pursue a purpose. Here therefore, at least in appearance, lies a profound epistemological contradiction. In fact the central problem of biology lies with this very contradiction, which, if it is only apparent, must be resolved; or else proven to be utterly insoluble, if that should turn out indeed to be the case.[84]

Monod sees an inconsistency in modern biology: The scientist must categorically assume what science cannot demonstrate, that there is no God. At the same time, the scientist cannot deny—indeed, he must *affirm*—the design of living things. In their structure and performance, he observes that they are purposeful.

What is a woman's fundamental purpose? What is a man's? Isn't it obvious? They were made male and female to fit together, to complement one another to bring forth new life. That design not only reveals purpose, it also reveals something of the glory of nature and character of the Living God.

Creation, quite apart from the Bible, shows that we are made for a purpose. God is the Designer. God has an imagination and has made us with an imagination. He imagined the universe. You could say, looking at the universe—all its diversity, grandeur, and beauty—that God's imagination ran wild. The glory, beauty, and detail of creation all bear witness to His existence, His character, and His imagination. *Male and female are God's idea.*

God's imagination envisioned and then spoke into existence a beautiful and orderly universe. His intention was to create human beings in His own image, and thus we possess eternal significance. He made us for community, as a human manifestation of the Eternal Community—the Trinity.

He made us to be families—basic human communities whose purpose is to develop what He had made.

Since creation, our sexuality has stemmed from the transcendent architectural design to reflect and pursue a purpose. *This is the Grand Design!* God built into our male and female bodies a design and a purpose. We are female and male in our biological and physiological makeup. Our structures, our functions, our performance all fulfill their design and purpose.

In the modern and postmodern world, however, we deny the Designer and the transcendent design. We even ignore our biology, as the trans movement shows us all too well. In other words, we often live contrary to who we really are. Because of our denial of and rebellion against God, we contradict our very nature. Simple observation yields an understanding of our reason for existence. But because we deny God, we don't look objectively at who we are. We believe a lie and warp our lives to fit that lie, diminishing ourselves.

Since creation, our sexuality has stemmed from the transcendent architectural design to reflect and pursue a purpose. *This is the Grand Design!*

In *If the Foundations Are Destroyed*, Alan Snyder writes, "The biblical concept of individuality can be stated succinctly. God has created all things distinct and unique for a specific purpose. He has given an identity to all parts of His creation, whether material objects, animals or human beings."[85]

Amid all creation, humans are unique. Men and women share the same human nature, made in the image of God. And yet have been differentiated for complementary purposes, different functions, and different purposes for the binary whole. This is our glory! Our differences are not a curse. A man cannot exist without a woman's gestation and nurture, a mother who bore him. A woman could not exist without her mother being inseminated by a man! But when you separate the physical from the transcendent—spiritual reality—the physical loses its meaning. We no longer fully understand what the physical is, or its purpose.

Does one's sexuality mean anything? While the differences between females and males are obvious to the average observer, how many people ask, "Why?" There are several answers given to this question.

- Accidental differences, differences established by chance

- Incidental differences, differences in "plumbing"
- Superficial, no connection to the transcendent
- Transcendental difference, differences based on design

In an interview with *New Covenant* magazine, Elisabeth Elliot said, "I think it's dangerous and destructive to treat sexuality as if it were meaningless. Much of the church, which is being strongly influenced by the world's ideologies, is ignoring the fact that sexuality means something."[86]

The fundamental revelation regarding this truth is Genesis 1:27: "So God created man in his own image, in the image of God he created him; male and female he created them." This is repeated in Genesis 5:1–2: "This is the written account of Adam's family line. When God created mankind, he made them in the likeness of God. He created them male and female and blessed them. And he named them 'Mankind' when they were created" (NIV). Dennis Prager has written:

> [T]here are two types of human beings—male and female. Not one and not more than two. The male-female distinction is the only built-in human distinction that matters. Race doesn't matter, nor does ethnicity or nationality. Only the sex distinction does. Attempts to undo this division of human beings fundamentally tamper with the divine order as presented in the Torah.[87]

The fundamental difference in the line of Adam and Eve is not race, ethnicity, nationality, or any other distinctive. In our humanity, we are first brothers and sisters, from the same blood line. We are of infinite significance and intrinsic worth, male and female, precisely because we are made *imago Dei*.

It takes "male and female" to fully reflect the unity of being and diversity of function found in the Trinity. The diverse function is a reflection of the polarity—the dissimilarity of men and women. The unity of being is a reflection of the complementariness—the perfect fit of the diverse functions. There is a complementary convergence of the divergence of male and female that mimics the unity and diversity of the Trinity. Just as God is beautiful, the complementariness of transcendent masculine and feminine nature as manifest in female and male sexual-ness is one of the most beautiful aspects of all creation.

Karl Stern, writing in *The Flight from Woman*, says, "The sex organs and the sex cells manifest a polarity and complementariness in morphology and in function. In the act of sexual union the male organ is convex and penetrating and the female organ is concave and receptive. . . . That this polarity and complementariness should not be confined to the physical but also be reflected in the character of man and woman, is a view as old as history."[88]

Now let us examine the similarities and dissimilarities between men and women.

First, the similarities. We are made from the same DNA (Eve was taken from Adam's rib). We are of one blood. Acts 17:26 says, "And hath made of one blood all nations of men" (KJV). All humans have transcendent qualities. In creation, we are the image of God (Genesis 1:26–27). All are "created equal" and are thus endowed with certain inalienable rights that include the right to life, liberty, justice, and the pursuit of their God-given purpose. In the Fall, we are equally sinners (Genesis 3:7; Romans 3:23). In redemption, we are equally recipients of God's grace (Galatians 3:28). And at the consummation, we will all be raised to the same glory if we are in Christ. Both (men and women) represent God. We are vice-regents: male and female vice-regents; king and queen vice-regents; stewards of creation.

And God gave us, both men and women, the full responsibility of the Creation Mandate to form families, to populate the earth, and to develop the creation. We have a body. We have a brain. We have a nervous system to perceive the world. Both men and women have eyes to see, ears to hear, mouths to chew and taste, noses to smell, skin to feel and touch. We have intelligence. We have creativity to think, emotions to feel. We have a will to establish our moral volition, and we have the responsibility to make moral choices that not only shape our lives but the world around us. All of these things and more we have in common because we are human beings.

Second, the dissimilarities between men and women. Modern and postmodern feminists say, "We are equal, therefore we are the same; we are interchangeable." This thinking tragically has permeated the church. Men and women are actually more alike than different, and yet it is equally obvious that men and women are very different. The male and female bodies differ in complementary fashion. Women and men have physical, emotional, psychological, and biochemical differences that complement one another.

MIT Professor of Biology Dr. David Page has said, "We can all recite the mantra that we are 99% identical . . . but the reality is that the genetic differences between male and female absolutely dwarf all other differences in the human genome."[89] While men and women are very much alike, the differences between the sexes are far greater than the differences between races and ethnic groups.

At the Weismann Institute's Molecular Genetics Department in Israel, two researchers, Moran Gershoni and Shmuel Pietrokovski, studied about 20,000 protein-coding genes, sorting them by sex and searching for differences in expression in each tissue. They eventually identified around 6,500 genes with activity that was biased toward one sex or the other in at least one tissue. For example, they found genes that were highly expressed in the skin of men relative to that in women's skin, and they realized that these were related to the growth of body hair. Gene expression for muscle building was higher in men; that for fat storage was higher in women. Surgery or hormone treatments only change the appearance. The reality? Six thousand, five hundred gene markers declare female or male. Biologists Colin Wright and Emma Hilton say that all biological forms have only two complementary sexes. The postmodern concept of a sexual "spectrum" does not exist.

> Moran Gershoni and Shmuel Pietrokovski, studied about 20,000 protein-coding genes, sorting them by sex and searching for differences in expression in each tissue. They eventually identified around 6,500 genes with activity that was biased toward one sex or the other in at least one tissue.

In humans, as in most animals or plants, an organism's biological sex corresponds to one of two distinct types of reproductive anatomy that develops for the production of small or large sex cells—sperm and eggs, respectively—and associated biological functions in sexual reproduction.

In humans, reproductive anatomy is unambiguously male or female at birth more than 99.98% of the time . . . . The evolutionary function of these two anatomies is to aid in reproduction via the fusion of sperm and ova. No third type of sex cell exists in humans, and therefore there is no sex "spectrum" or additional sexes beyond male and female. Sex is binary.

> The existence of only two sexes does not mean sex is never ambiguous. But intersex individuals are extremely rare, and they are neither a third sex nor proof that sex is a "spectrum" or a "social construct." Not everyone needs to be discretely assignable to one or the other sex in order for biological sex to be functionally binary. To assume otherwise—to confuse secondary sexual traits with biological sex itself—is a category error." [90]

Those genetic markers for male and female manifest themselves in differing body systems and structures. There are hormonal differences. Men have more testosterone, women more estrogen. Testosterone injections may produce whiskers on a woman's face, but they do not make her a male.

Males tend to have denser, stronger bones, tendons, and ligaments, which allow for heavier work. Women have a thicker layer of subcutaneous fat that acts as insulation and energy reserve. It gives women more endurance over the long haul than men.

Another difference appears in the peripheral nervous system. Women on average have a more acute sense of touch. Females, likewise, have a more acute sense of hearing, smell, and taste. When our children were young, if one of them cried during the night, my wife, Marilyn, would hear the cry, while I remained oblivious. After she'd get up three or four times, finally she would punch me and say, "Don't you hear the baby crying? It's your turn." No, I didn't. Why? Because we are built differently. The woman has a more acute sense of hearing, smell, and taste. It has been argued that females are generally more perceptive and aware of the context of what is going on around them. Such a system would give women an advantage in childcare and social interaction.

This is God's design. If we deny it, we deny who we are. We contradict our own nature. Our eyes, our ears, many physical functions, and the nervous system that runs them are different in men and women.

Then you have a mother's nurturing nature. This includes a physiological dimension, manifested in the powerful hormone oxytocin. Social psychologist Erica Komisar, in her groundbreaking book *Being There*, writes: "The more a mother engages with her baby, the more oxytocin she produces; the more oxytocin she produces, the more she bonds with her child; in other words, the more you love your baby, the more you can love your baby." [91] Oxytocin is the biological manifestation of a woman's nurturing nature. This is why it is so important for the mother to be present during the first thousand days of a baby's life.

OXYTOCIN - THE BIOLOGICAL MANIFESTATION OF NURTURING

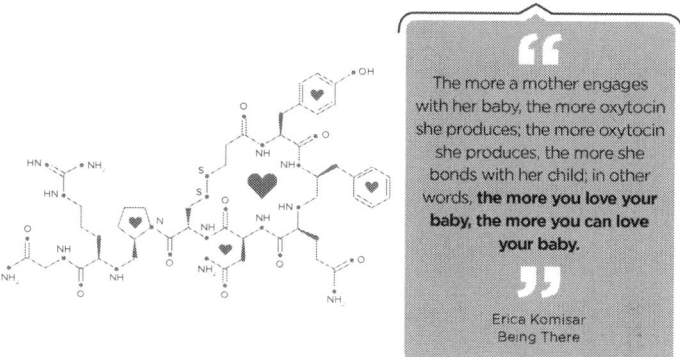

> The more a mother engages with her baby, the more oxytocin she produces; the more oxytocin she produces, the more she bonds with her child; in other words, **the more you love your baby, the more you can love your baby.**
>
> Erica Komisar
> *Being There*

And here is a wonderful mystery. Anthropologist Anna Machin, in her book *The Life of Dad: The Making of the Modern Father*, states: "Recent research has shown that fathers and mothers who live together during pregnancy exhibit similar levels of circulating oxytocin within the blood."[92]

Here again we see the Grand Design. Built into human biology is a picture of the transcendent nature. Similar to the love bond of the members of the Trinity, what binds the relationship between a mother, father, and their child? It is love! Only here, by design, there is a biological component: oxytocin. When a man husbands his wife and fathers his children, the love bond grows.

The limbic systems in the brains of the female and male differ as well. A mother's aggression is driven by the limbic system. Females respond to impending danger or harm to their offspring. Why? Because they were designed to protect their children. Mothers are often more aggressive than fathers in intervening on a child's behalf. I have seen this in my own family. If there's a danger, Marilyn would see it and take action. She'd look at me and say, "Didn't you see what was happening?" Often I hadn't seen it, not because I don't care, but because we are wired differently.

Another difference, very offensive in modern culture, relates to how men and women know things. Both intuition and reason, both art and science, are founded in God Himself. Both are needed to fully represent the image of God.

TWO WAYS OF THINKING

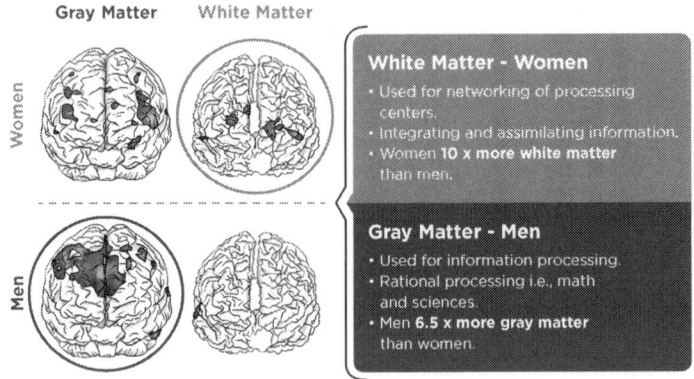

Gray Matter **White Matter**

Women

Men

White Matter - Women
• Used for networking of processing centers.
• Integrating and assimilating information.
• Women **10 x more white matter** than men.

Gray Matter - Men
• Used for information processing.
• Rational processing i.e., math and sciences.
• Men **6.5 x more gray matter** than women.

Human biology reflects this. The brains of males and females exhibit different distributions of gray matter and white matter. White matter is used for networking. It acts as a processing center. Women are able to integrate things and assimilate more information than men. Women have ten times more white matter than men. This is a good thing. Men have more gray matter, used for information processing. Men don't network and assimilate as well as women do. Rational processing in math and science generally comes easier for men. Both gray matter and white matter are good. On average men have 6.5 times more gray matter than women. Peterson says that, in general, men are more interested in things, women in people.

HUMAN ANATOMY

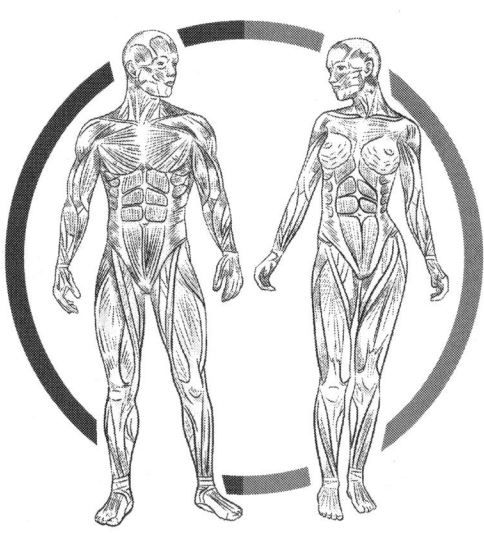

Overall, women and men have physical, emotional, psychological, and biochemical differences that complement one another. The bodies of males and females differ in complementary fashion. This reality is no accident, something to be explained away or corrected through surgery. It is God's design. If we deny it, we deny who we are. We live in contradiction to our own nature.

Knowing this, how can any rational-thinking postmodern person claim that we are identical and interchangeable? Our external sex organs, our body systems, and our structures are different. These differences go to the genetic level.

We are wonderfully different and wonderfully alike! Let us celebrate the significance of our human identity and the wonderful and corresponding differences of male and female.

STUDY GUIDE

1. What does Elisabeth Elliot mean when she says, "Our sexual differences are the terms of our life, and to obscure them in any

way is to weaken the very fabric of life itself"? Do you agree or disagree with Elliot? Why?

2. If creation shows that we are made for a purpose, why might some people choose to live as though there is no purpose? What is the result?

3. List four ways that men and women are similar and four ways they are dissimilar. Two Israeli researchers, Gershom and Pietrokovski, have "identified around 6,500 genes with activity that was biased toward one sex or the other." What are the implications of this discovery as it relates to the nature of human sexuality? What impact does this discovery have on "gender identity"? Can the removal of external sexual organs change one's sex?

4. How might understanding the biological differences in how men and women assimilate knowledge be helpful? Have you observed this? What examples can you think of?

Section 2

PART 3

Imago Dei

CHAPTER 8

Made in God's Likeness: The Structural View

A GOOD FRIEND of mine, Elizabeth Youmans, founder of Chrysalis International, likes to say:

> Every child has name . . .
> . . . a purpose
> . . . a story
> . . . and a place in HIS-story!
>
> Every child is unique![93]

When poor children on the street come into view, what do you see? Rags? Bare feet, sores, bloated bellies? Do they appear to you as stray dogs? Or do you see them as God does? Every child is the very image of the living God.

One of these children may become a scientist who finds a cure for cancer, or the president of a nation to bring peace from war. How can this be? Because a human is not primarily identified by his or her physical characteristics or economic status. We must learn to see every child with the eyes of God, made in the image of God. There are no ordinary children, nor, as C.S. Lewis would say, ordinary people:

> There are no ordinary people. You have never talked to a mere mortal. Nations, cultures, arts, civilizations—these are mortal, and their life is to ours as the life of a gnat. But it is immortals whom we joke with, work with, marry, snub, and exploit— immortal horrors or everlasting splendors.[94]

Women and men are made in the image of God. But what does this mean?

Theologians generally agree that there are three aspects to the image of God built into humans: the structural, the relational, and the functional. These are seen in Genesis 1:26–28.

> Then God said, "Let us make man in our image, after our likeness. And let them have dominion over the fish of the sea and over the birds of the heavens and over the livestock and over all the earth and over every creeping thing that creeps on the earth."

> So God created man in his own image,
>   in the image of God he created him;
>   male and female he created them.

> And God blessed them. And God said to them, "Be fruitful and multiply and fill the earth and subdue it, and have dominion over the fish of the sea and over the birds of the heavens and over every living thing that moves on the earth."

These three verses frame our understanding of what it means to be human, to be made in the image of God. They establish the nature and purpose for which we have been created. The structural view, which is the subject of this chapter, is simply that *human beings are like God*.

Humans are creatures. At the biological level, we are animals. But we're not merely animals, as Darwinism theorizes. We are also made like God. In our spiritual or transcendent dimension, we are like God; in our physical nature we are related to other created things. We are unique in kind. We are the humankind. We occupy that unique space between earth and heaven, between time and eternity.

The Hebrew word אָדָם (*'ā·ḏām*) is used three ways, depending on the context.

First, it is a generic name for human beings (Genesis 1:26–27). "Let us make man (*'ā·ḏām*) in our image, after our likeness. And let them have dominion . . . So God created man (*'ā·ḏām*) in his own image, in the image of God he created him; male and female he created them." This use includes female and male, a collective word encompassing humankind. We are all *imago Dei*. It is not that males are the image of God and females are not. Second, Adam is the name of the first human being (Genesis 3:17, 21; 4:1, 25; 5:1). Third, the word is used for the male of the species (Genesis 2:5, 7, 8, 15, 16 18, 19, 20).

The first Adam was responsible for the Fall. Jesus Christ is referred to as the second Adam and provided our salvation. The Apostle Paul speaks of the two representative Adams in Romans 5:15, 17–19:

> But the free gift is not like the trespass. For if many died through one man's trespass, much more have the grace of God and the free gift by the grace of that one man Jesus Christ abounded for many. . . . For if, because of one man's trespass, death reigned through that one man, much more will those who receive the abundance of grace and the free gift of righteousness reign in life through the one man Jesus Christ.
>
> Therefore, as one trespass led to condemnation for all men, so one act of righteousness leads to justification and life for all men. For as by the one man's disobedience the many were made sinners, so by the one man's obedience the many will be made righteous.

When we speak of being made in the image of God, we need to clarify how we are like God and how we are not. God's nature has two kinds of attributes. His *communicable* attributes are shared with humans, his *incommunicable* attributes are not.

Here are some examples of God's *in*communicable attributes:

- Self-Existence—I AM WHO I AM (Exodus 3:13–14; Isaiah 40:28–29)

- Unchangeable—God never changes (Psalm 102:25–27; James 1:17)
- Eternal—God stands outside of time (Psalm 90:2; Revelation 1:8)
- Omnipresent—God stands outside of the universe (1 Kings 8:27; Psalm 139)

In these ways human beings are unlike God. We are not self-existent. We are not unchangeable, eternal, or omnipresent. So how are we *like* God? What of his nature has God shared with all human beings?

In three critical areas we are like God and unlike the rest of the created order. All human beings are endowed with a mind, heart, and will. The *mind* is the attribute of intellect and includes knowledge, understanding, and wisdom. The *heart* is the attribute of morals and includes holiness, love, grace, goodness, mercy, righteousness, and patience. Last is the *will*, the attribute of purpose. Human beings are free moral agents who can make decisions that shape history.

As found in human beings, these three critical areas may be described as *internal capital*. This internal capital, combined with the human body, allows humankind to fulfill the Cultural Mandate as stewards of creation. The external stewardship of creation requires the internal self-government of the mind, heart, and will. In short, humankind stands apart from the rest of creation in design and function. Human beings are the *imago Dei*. This glorious fact separates us from the rest of creation.

Evolutionism, however, says man is a highly evolved animal. We are like chimpanzees. We are derived from a mindless process. But when God chose to make humans, He did not look at chimpanzees for the pattern. In the Grand Design, God looked at Himself. You are more like God than you are like a dog or a monkey. You are made in God's image. This is a remarkable truth.

Atheists may liken us to mere animals or confuse us with robots or machines. But our nature establishes our inalienable human rights and dignity. Most cultures suppress human nature and fail to create a space where people can dream and fulfill their aspirations. Think of all the tyrannies in the world both on the right and the left, fascist or Marxist.

God made you as an image of himself. He gave you the attribute of intelligence. You have a mind; you can reason. You have an imagination. God imagined the universe and built it. He shared His creativity with humans. Humans have imagined all they have made, working from God's primary creation.

You may have read about the land of Narnia or Middle Earth. Where did Narnia come from? From the imagination of C.S. Lewis. Middle Earth came from the imagination of J.R.R. Tolkien. God is the great imaginer. He imagined the universe and built it, and we are like Him.

God gave you a mind and a heart. These are the seat of your emotions and of moral attribution. We are moral creatures. We can choose between right and wrong. We have a will, the attribute of purpose. We can make decisions, choices that will affect time and eternity! Hindus say humans are like pebbles thrown into a pond that make no ripples. But the Bible affirms that humans affect eternity. God gave us a will; our decisions impact time and eternity.

This awesome reality is true because a human is not an animal but a God-image bearer. We look toward the heavens while we are fully engaged on the earth. Man is God's agent to carry out His heavenly mandate on earth. And what is heaven's mandate? "Be fruitful, multiply, fill the earth, and have dominion over creation" (see Genesis 1:22, 28).

Human beings were made to walk the boundary between heaven and earth. Man is the one creature whose eyes are toward heaven and whose feet and hands are in the soil. Man alone carries out the heavenly mandate on earth. A husband and wife conceive a child who will not only walk on earth but will dwell in eternity.

According to Genesis 1:26 (NIV), God said, "Let us make mankind in our image, in our likeness, so that they may rule . . ." We are co-creators with God, put here to govern, to develop wonders from God's primary creation.

A striking example is Favio Chavez, a scientist who went to a garbage dump in Paraguay to solve the massive environmental problems through principles of land stewardship. When his initial strategy did not work, he launched a radical idea, based not on his vocation as a scientist but on his avocation as a musician. Favio taught people who lived and worked on the dump to make musical instruments from the garbage. And he taught their children to play classical music on those instruments, creating the Landfill Harmonic Orchestra. These children, born into poverty, learned to play beautiful music using instruments made from recycled trash. How could they do this? Because they are not like the stray dogs and cats wandering on the garbage dump. They are *imago Dei*, human beings capable of godlike creativity and beauty.

Animists and Postmoderns see man as a ghost, more of an insubstantial being subject to the spirits than a creature of flesh and blood endowed with godlike qualities.

Atheists see man as an animal. We have a mouth and a stomach, we consume. Our modern society is built around this conception of human beings. We have no inherent dignity; our dignity comes from what we consume. Our value is defined by what we have, not who we are. Radical feminism, born out of this lie, does not acknowledge the significance of women as feminine. Feminists believe women only have significance when they produce and consume things.

Judeo-Christian theism and atheism play out in very different systems with reference to what a woman is. Theism leads to maternal feminism. All human beings are made in the image of God; all human life is sacred, to be protected from conception to natural death. Theism says male and female are equal in dignity and value and have complementary functions. In God's creation, a woman is designed to nurture.

Atheism, on the other hand, produces modern egalitarian feminists. The nurturing of children has no value and interferes with a woman's right to a career. The evolutionism that underlies modern feminism leads to abortion on a large-scale, dictating that her right to choose is more significant than a human's right to live.

Carrie Lynn DeKlyen was a pregnant thirty-seven-year-old mother of six when she was diagnosed with cancer. Her doctors recommended an abortion so they could treat her cancer and save her life. She refused the abortion, and thus the cancer treatment. She gave birth to a little girl, Life Lynn, and Carrie Lynn died three days later. Believing in the sanctity of human life, she sacrificed her life for her baby's right to live.

Another mother, Irene Vilar, proudly calls herself the "abortion addict." Her book, *Motherhood: Testimony of an Abortion Addict*, tells her story. In the course of sixteen years, she conceived and aborted fifteen children. Irene Vilar was a moral relativist who lived a life of license without taking moral responsibility for her choices. Her worldview differed greatly from Carrie Lynn's, leading to a very different understanding of who she was, who her babies were, and what motherhood is. She lived as a narcissist who put her ego above the lives of her fifteen babies.

Ideas have consequences. A biblical worldview leads us to understand that we and our children are made in the image of God. An atheistic worldview makes self the center of the universe: Your life, your career, are more important than your children.

Special Olympics athlete Frank Stephens was called to testify before the United States Congress, where he said,

> About abortion, I don't want to make it illegal, I want to make it unthinkable. Politicians change laws. I want to change people's hearts. I want to change people's hearts by changing people's minds and hearts together.[95]

Here's the irony: Frank has Down syndrome. He was speaking before a Congress that often debates what to do with people like him while still in the womb. Abortion is not the answer, not even for the classic exceptions of babies conceived in rape. To say, "I'm pro-life except in cases of rape," is to say, "A child conceived in rape does not deserve to live." Ryan Bomberger, conceived in rape, said,

> I should have been aborted, at least that's what the pro-abortion side believes. I am always that 1% that is used 100% of the time to justify abortion. My birth mom experienced the horror and the violence of rape but chose to be stronger than her circumstances. Her courage not only enabled me to live but to be adopted and loved.[96]

Rebecca Kiessling is a pro-life lawyer seeking to outlaw abortion in circumstances of rape. She has asked,

> Have you ever considered how really insulting it is to say to someone, "I think your mother should have been able to abort you"? It's like saying, "If I had my way, you'd be dead right now." And that is the reality with which I live every time someone says they are pro-choice or pro-life "except in cases of rape" because I absolutely would have been aborted if it had been legal in Michigan when I was an unborn child, and I can tell you that it hurts.[97]

Valerie Gatto, Miss Pennsylvania 2014, was also a product of rape. She testifies,

> I believe God put me here for a reason, to inspire people, to

encourage them, to give them hope that everything is possible and you can't let your circumstance define your life.[98]

All human life is sacred. A woman's life, a preborn baby's life, a black life, a white life, a Down child's life, an elderly life, a baby girl's life, the life of a child conceived in rape. Her life is sacred. Why? Because we're made in the image of God.

STUDY GUIDE

1. Before having read this chapter, how would you have described what it meant to be made in the image of God?
2. What are the three aspects of being created in the image of God? What does each mean?
3. What is the difference between God's communicable attributes and His incommunicable attributes?
4. In what three critical ways are we like God? What is "internal capital"?
5. How does the concept of man being *imago Dei* differentiate Judeo-Christianity from all other philosophies and religions? What are some of the social, political, and economic policy consequences of this fact?
6. How should this view of human worth and potential affect our perception of even the most destitute, difficult, or degraded people?
7. What does it mean that human beings were made to walk the boundary between heaven and earth and time and eternity? How does this contrast with your culture's view?

Made for Relationship: The Relational View

WALT HEYER WAS born male and raised as a boy. When Walt grew up, he got married, and he and his wife had two children. Then in April 1983 Heyer decided to become a woman and began taking female hormones. Later, Walt underwent radical sexual "reassignment" surgery.

Walt lived for eight years as a female named Laura Jensen, saying, "At first I was giddy for the fresh start."[99] But after a few years he began to regret the transition to a woman. Then, in 1991, he decided to de-transition back to a male.

During Walt's years living as a woman, he realized something basic about human nature. "I learned the truth: Hormones and surgery may alter appearances, but nothing changes the immutable fact of your sex."[100] He recognized that our sexuality is more than skin deep. It is part of the terms of our existence.

Walt has started a ministry to engage with others who are considering reassignment surgery or to help those who, like himself, regret their decision to transition.

We live in an age of confusion, where even our basic sexual nature is undermined. Our culture no longer knows God and the Grand Design of people being made in His image, male and female. We do not know the Bible and no longer recognize reality.

Our forebears, of course, knew the Bible as the grand narrative explaining all of human life, a life built on relationship. The Bible reveals that before the creation of the world, a divine community existed, Father, Son, and Holy Spirit—a *community* of three persons, bound together in love. Before the creation of the world, there was *communication*. In Genesis 1:26–28, the curtains of eternity are pulled back and we overhear a conversation from eternity past, among the divine community, about the creation of men and women.

> Then God said, "Let us make man in our image, after our likeness. And let them have dominion over the fish of the sea and over the birds of the heavens and over the livestock and over all the earth and over every creeping thing that creeps on the earth."

> So God created man in his own image,
>   in the image of God he created him;
>   male and female he created them.

> And God blessed them. And God said to them, "Be fruitful and multiply and fill the earth and subdue it, and have dominion over the fish of the sea and over the birds of the heavens and over every living thing that moves on the earth."

Before the creation of the world there was communion, a face-to-face intimacy within the divine community. John 17:22–24 is very clear about the unity in the relationship between the Father and Son. Jesus prays,

> "The glory that you have given me I have given to them, that they may be one even as we are one, I in them and you in me, that they may become perfectly one, so that the world may know that you sent me and loved them even as you loved me. Father, I desire that they also, whom you have given me, may be with me where I am, to see my glory that you have given me because you loved me before the foundation of the world."

Speaking of the Godhead as three distinct divine persons, the great

American theologian Jonathan Edwards noted, "There is such a wonderful union between them that they are after an ineffable and inconceivable manner one in another; so that one hath another, and they have communion in one another, and are as it were predicable one of another. As Christ said of himself and the Father, 'I am in the Father, and the Father in me.'"[101]

This grand narrative is about the relationship between God and His creation, God and His people, Christ and His bride. And it is about the relationship between man and woman. The idea that the narrative is about relationship, and particularly on the human level between man and woman, will seem strange to a world that worships at the altar of individualism. In the West we often define ourselves as separate, independent human beings. We don't need anyone or anything else. As Simon and Garfunkel sang, "I touch no one and no one touches me / I am a rock I am an island."[102]

But we were not meant to be alone. Canadian neurologist and psychiatrist Karl Stern speaks of the great "and" with intriguing language: "The unspeakable mystery of the *and,* of God *and* His Creation, of God *and* His people, of Christ *and* His church. . . . The sexual '*and*' [as in male *and* female] is a reflection [that] all being is nuptial."[103] Because God is community, we have been made for relationship. The Bible signifies the importance of this by beginning and ending with a wedding. In Genesis our first parents wed; at the end of Scripture, Christ marries His bride, the church.

The Grand Design begins in Genesis 1 and 2 and establishes human identity and function in God's creation. Genesis 1 focuses on our *being* as male and female in the image of God. In Genesis 2, we begin to see a diversity of *function*, the unique design of male and female for a shared purpose.

We have already explored three distinct understandings of the relationship between male and female. *Sexism* begins with inequality, both in being and function, of male and female. *Feminism* begins with interchangeability of male and female in both being and function. *Complementarianism* affirms both the equal value of male and female and the equality of being and diversity of functions.

Humankind is the crown of creation—the *imago Dei*. Human beings are the high-water mark, the crown of God's creative activity.

Let's take a moment to reflect on the significance of these words.

Genesis 1:1–2 says, "In the beginning God created the heavens and the earth. Now the earth was formless and empty, darkness was over the surface of the deep, and the Spirit of God was hovering over the waters" (NIV).

Note that in the beginning God created the raw materials for the universe. They were without form and the universe was empty and dark.

In Genesis 1:3, 6, and 9, God begins to form the unformed. With each creative act, God refines and brings a higher order to what was less refined and less ordered. Think of a potter shaping the clay and bringing more refinement as she works. Or think of a painter who adds more detail to the painting as he works.

At each stage of His creative activity, God stands back to see if what He has made meets His expectations. And it does. Over and over, God proclaims that His work is "good."

After He has shaped the inanimate part of the universe, God moves to create higher order, bringing life into existence—first plant life (Genesis 1:12–13) and then animal life (Genesis 1:20–25). Each creative act requires more refinement and a higher order.

Now God comes to the crown jewel of His creative activity. In Genesis 1:26–28, He makes human beings, imprinting them with the image of God. Their purpose is to form families and govern creation.

At each stage of creation, God establishes more refinement, a higher order, a greater glory. In Genesis 1, we see God crown His creation with humankind. But in Genesis 2, we see the pattern of refinement continue. In Genesis 2, God creates Adam first, of course, but He is not finished. A finer and more radiant human being is still to be created. The woman, following Adam in order of creation, is the crescendo of God's creativity, the crown of the crown of creation.

Human beings walk the boundary between heaven and earth. We are creatures, united with creation and therefore are responsible to care for it. On the other hand, God made us in His image and likeness and in this way distinct from creation, sharing the transcendent dimension with the angels and with God.

Scripture clearly shows that God identified us, male and female, as *adam,* the generic term for the human race. This identity stands in contrast to the particular *ish,* man (as opposed to woman) or husband, and *ishshaw,* woman (as opposed to man) or wife. As Genesis 5:2 affirms, "Male and female he created them, and he blessed them and named them Man (*adam*) when they were created."

Yet this is not the end of the matter when it comes to the relational understanding of the *imago Dei.* God creates humankind in His image reflecting the One and Many. Thus, He creates us not only *adam* (unity) but also *ish* and *ishshaw* (diversity). One man could not fulfill the image of God. It took *ish* and *ishshaw* to fully display the image of God.´

We were made male and female, created equal but not the same, to complement one another. Genesis 1:26 indicates that male and female have a common origin. We share the imprint of God's character and nature. We are not merely animals, as evolutionism insists.

Genesis 1:27 establishes that we are equal in the source of our identity. God named us and defined us as male and female.

We are equal in the Cultural Mandate of Genesis 1. Both male and female are required to fulfill it. Genesis 1:26 says, "*They* will rule" (ERV), not "*he* will rule." The image bearers of God, kings and queens of creation, rule as equals.

Both have moral and rational agency and are able to say yes or no to God. We are not machines, automatons, or puppets. We may say no to God, and choose death, or yes to God, and find life.

Our communion with God has been equally broken. Male and female are sinners. And we are equal in Christ's work of redemption. In Christ there is no male or female (Galatians 3:28). Both come to the same God. And we stand equally in hope of the return of Jesus Christ.

THE THREE FACETS
OF THE IMAGE OF GOD

The **Structural View - Nature of Humanity:** Gen. 1: 26a: Then God said, "Let us make man in our image, after our likeness."

The **Relational View – Community:** Ge. 1:27: So God created man in his own image, in the image of God he created him; male and female he created them.

The **Functional View – The Cultural Commission:** Gen. 1:26b, 28: "And let them have dominion over the fish of the sea and over the birds of the heavens and over the livestock and over all the earth and over every creeping thing that creeps on the earth.... And God blessed them. And God said to them, "Be fruitful and multiply and fill the earth [the social commission] and subdue it, and have dominion [the developmental commission] over the fish of the sea and over the birds of the heavens and over every living thing that moves on the earth."

The Cultural Commission of Genesis 1:26–28 includes three facets of our *imago Dei* nature. This foundational passage tells us what it means to be made in the image of God. It tells us who we are and why we are here.

Genesis 1:26 says, "Then God said, 'Let us make man in our image after our likeness.'" We are made *like* God. This is the *structural* dimension. It's our nature. All human beings, young and old, male and female, are made in the image of God.

In verse 27 we see the *relational* dimension. "So God created man in his own image, in the image of God he created him; male and female he created them." *We are made for community.*

The Cultural Commission has two subordinating clauses, which I call the social mandate and the Developmental Mandate. The social mandate—to form families, have children, create communities, and populate the earth—is the relational dimension of our being made in the image of God, male and female.

The Developmental Mandate, on the other hand, is the *functional* dimension of our purpose. This is the third aspect of our *imago Dei* nature. God created us for a purpose. We can see this in both our design and our function. We read this in verse 26 (and again in 28): "And let them have dominion over the fish of the sea and over the birds of the heavens and over the livestock and over all the earth, and over every creeping thing that creeps on the earth."

We typically find our identity from our culture. Our culture tells us who and what we are. For most of history the culture has told us that men are superior to women. Women are objects to be conquered. And we live out this lie at the individual and cultural levels.

The Bible, however, presents us with the ultimate counterculture—the Grand Design. Before the creation of the universe, God existed as three in one, a model unique among all other gods, philosophies, and religions. It profoundly establishes our unity and diversity in the human family. It allows us to celebrate our distinctives. God says, "Let *us* make man in *our* image," not "Let *me* make man in *my* image." God is unity without uniformity, diversity without superiority. God is community who creates us for community. The Hebrew word *adam* captures the unity of humankind. Our diversity is found in male and female: *ish*, the husband, and *ishshaw*, the wife.

God is unity and diversity. Humans also display unity and diversity: We have unity as humans and diversity as female and male. We are made for a complementary relationship. We are binary.

We see binary reality over and over in the creation account (also shown on page 85). Heaven and earth (Genesis 1:1); light and dark (verse 4); day and night (verse 5); the waters above and the waters beneath (verse

7); the sea and the dry land (verse 10); the greater light and the lesser light (verse 16). And, at the climax, we see man and woman, the crown of creation, male and female (verse 27).

Male and female together manifest the integrated, comprehensive, complementary, and transcendent nature of the triune God. And the family they produce is a united one (*echad*), not a single one (*yachid*).

Often in today's modern culture two individuals live in the same household—maybe married, maybe not—but they don't function in community. They function as individuals. Elisabeth Elliot put it this way in her book, *The Mark of Man*: ". . . it took two different modalities to represent the divine image. It took male and female."[104] This is the unity. This is the place of our equality. Both male and female are of equal worth, of *infinite and eternal value*.

> **Male and female together manifest the integrated, comprehensive, complementary, and transcendent nature of the triune God.**

The first two chapters of Genesis tell the whole story. Chapter 1 reveals how we are *equal in being*. Chapter 2 explains how we are *diverse in function*. First, let's focus on the latter, our diversity.

Procreation requires a man and a woman. Today's postmodern culture celebrates pregnant "men" with beards. But a man cannot be pregnant. A pregnant woman can take male hormones and grow a beard, but she is still a woman. Male and female complement each other to fulfill the social mandate.

In the social mandate, the male *adam* will most fully manifest the paternal heart of God. The female *adam* will most fully manifest the maternal heart of God. God said, "This is my world. I give it to you. Do something with it" (see Genesis 1:26). God's nature is characterized by both a maternal heart and a paternal heart. The latter is manifest largely in protection, the former in nurturing. Both aspects are conveyed in the creation order.

To prioritize the male's brute strength is to lose half the universe. The male alone cannot reflect the image of God or fulfill the Cultural Mandate. Male and female govern as the kings and queens of creation. We are placed together to fulfill the Cultural Mandate as the vice-regents of God.

Does this mean a man has nothing of the nurturing nature, or the woman nothing of the protective nature? No, of course not. But the paternal heart of God is most fully manifested in the man, and God's maternal heart most fully manifested in the woman. In the diagram, you see the image of God. The man is the natural defender, but a mother is a fierce protector of her children. An angry mother bear is not to be challenged.

GOD'S CHARACTER

Protector ⬅ **GOD IS BOTH** ➡ Nurturer

both aspects conveyed
in creation

Men - tend to be
more protecting

Imago
Dei

Women - tend to be
more nurturing

Protecting   **Nurturing**

No doubt, a man is not without ability to nurture, and a woman not without ability to protect. But each has a strong propensity according to his or her hardwiring. Again, see the diagram. Male and female are involved in both spheres, the public and the private, but each has his or her primary responsibilities and secondary responsibilities.

Children require both protection and nurturing. In a family, the female's primary responsibility is the domestic sphere, nurturing her children, governing the home. She also has a secondary obligation to speak in the public sphere for the sake of future generations.

The male, on the other hand, has a primary responsibility in the public sphere for "governance," and secondarily in the domestic sphere in nurturing and raising the children. This calls for a "dance" between the husband and wife. Each supports the other's primary role without usurping it while fulfilling his or her primary role in all its glory. As with a literal dance, it takes time, practice, and perseverance to learn to do it well!

The father-heart of God is the eternal masculine, which is demonstrated in self-sacrificing, agape love. The paternal heart protects, provides, and redeems. He is the kinsman and the loving head of his wife. The wife is to respect her husband. So the father-heart of God is the eternal masculine and is manifested most clearly in male. Masculinity comes from God.

Where does femininity originate? From God. Eve came from Adam's side, but Adam is not her source. God fashioned her from Adam's flesh and bones, but her femininity is sourced in God Himself. The maternal heart of God is the origin of the feminine just as God's paternal heart is the origin of the masculine.

As English minister Michael Ferebee Sadler writes, "God did not begin to love when He began to create angels or men whom He could love . . . from eternity there was Father, Son, and Spirit loving One Another in the Godhead."[105] The eternal feminine is compassion, nurturing, suckling. This is God as the teacher and the *ezer*, that is, the suitable helper.

In Genesis 2:24 we come to a sacred mystery: "Therefore shall a man leave his father and mother and shall cleave unto his wife and they shall be one flesh" (KJV). How can two be one? This sacred mystery bookends the narrative of Scripture. The first wedding is the glorious finale of the creation story. The first couple is a prototype for all humans who will leave their parents' homes and establish their own. And they picture the final wedding at the end of history when Christ returns for His bride.

The Trinitarian God is *echad*, the united, compound one, not *yachid*, the single, absolute one. We are not talking about uniformity—no distinction between the parts—which is egalitarianism. This would make man and woman equal, as in interchangeable or the same. As the postmodern construct would argue, the categories of binary male and female would cease to exist.

Neither are male and female absolute diversity, the sexist model in which male is seen as superior to female.

Rather, the Trinitarian principle is unity without uniformity and diversity without superiority. These principles shape our lives together as men and women, husbands and wives, within the larger community. God is the source of the paternal and maternal hearts. And God's paternal heart and maternal heart are transcendent patterns that become the pattern for male and female.

STUDY GUIDE

1. Before the creation of the world, there was *Community*. How does Scripture teach us this? How does creation reveal this?
2. How does God's creation of humankind reflect the one and the

many? Why does it take both male and female to fully reflect the image of God?

3. What are the three aspects of being created in the image of God? How does each of these three aspects challenge the narrative our culture gives us about where we should find our identity?

4. Examine the graphic of God's character manifesting Himself in masculine and feminine terms. Are men's and women's strengths mutually exclusive, or do they overlap?

5. What does this suggest about men's and women's roles in society?

6. Where does femininity originate? Should the church worship or depict God as female in art, or use female pronouns for God? Why or why not?

CHAPTER 10

Made Kings and Queens to Govern Creation: The Functional View

ONE DAY, THE great American agronomist George Washington Carver read Genesis 1:29 during his devotional time with his Lord: "And God said, 'Behold, I have given you every plant yielding seed that is on the face of all the earth, and every tree with seed in its fruit. You shall have them for food.'" The Hebrew "behold" is meant to call attention to something. "Look at the seed!" Do you see a tiny, meaningless bit of matter? Or do you see the vast potential of the seed? What can that seed produce? Can you see the forest in the seed? Can you see the wonder it holds?

Carver was holding a humble peanut. He realized that God was telling him to BEHOLD—look at—the seed. So he asked a simple question: "God, what did you make this seed for?" At that moment he beheld the wonder of the simple peanut and began a lifetime of studying it. As a result, Carver discovered over two hundred uses of the simple peanut that would bless the human family.

Imitating the God who conceived and brought the universe into existence, we are called to bring into existence what we imagine by our words, actions, and networking. When God finished His work, it was perfect, but not complete. What God made was not static; it was alive with living things, alive with potential. It remains for us, made *imago Dei*, to complete the tasks God has given us as kings and queens of His creation. We are the *imago Dei*. We have been made "like God" (structural aspect) to fulfill the Creation Mandate by filling the earth with families and community (relational aspect) in order to fulfill God's purpose to develop the earth (functional aspect).

When it comes to the functional aspect, the purpose for which we have been made as human beings (the subject of this chapter), think of the *seed principle*. My African friends have a remarkable proverb: "You can count the seeds in a mango, but you cannot count the mangos in a seed." How many seeds does a mango have? One! How many mangos are in that seed? A number you cannot count! This is the hidden potential of a seed.

> Culture in the broadest sense is the purpose for which God created man after His image.
> Herman Bavinck

God "finished" His part of the work and gave it to human beings to see what we will do with it. He was saying, "Take what I have given you and do something with it." This is the Cultural Mandate—to form families and cultivate culture and creation. It is the reason we are on this earth. He not only gave us the mandate, but, as we read in Genesis 1:28, "God blessed them." In other words, He equipped us with what we need to do the task: power for success, prosperity, and fruitfulness.

That blessing includes internal capital and external capital. We need both. The astonishing power of a seed is analogous to the abilities God has given you. With the internal capital God has given you—your intellect, imagination, and emotions—what will you create, discover, and develop?

God has also given us external capital—the material world, such as the land, the sun, the water, forests, and flowers. After we learn to govern our internal capital, we can also learn to govern external capital.

Humans are makers of culture. Herman Bavinck said, "Culture in the broadest sense is the purpose for which God created man after His image."[106] God has put us here to govern His creation and bring it to a point of flourishing. Vishal Mangalwadi says, "God speaks and creates the universe. Man speaks and creates culture which shapes the universe."[107] We have been given dominion to finish His work on this planet. What an awesome calling!

We see the grand purpose of our existence in Psalm 8:3–8:

> When I look at your heavens, the work of your fingers,
> the moon and the stars, which you have set in place,
> what is man that you are mindful of him,
> and the son of man that you care for him?
> Yet you have made him a little lower than the heavenly
> beings
> and crowned him with glory and honor.
> You have given him dominion over the works of your
> hands;
> you have put all things under his feet,
> all sheep and oxen,
> and also the beasts of the field,
> the birds of the heavens, and the fish of the sea,
> whatever passes along the paths of the seas.

In the vast universe, on a tiny planet, in an insignificant solar system, why are we important? What is man that God would even consider him? And yet God *does* consider us. We are not nothing. We are a little lower than the angels, made to rule over the works of God's hands.

Is that how you see your life? Scripture says we are to practice *oikonomia*, governing or stewarding the house. The Bible makes it clear that we are called, positioned, and equipped to do the task, and do it well. So how has God asked us to steward the work of His hands?

God has given us two dimensions to our stewardship. The first is found in Genesis 2:15, "The LORD God took the man and put him in the Garden of Eden to work it and take care of it." God gives the human two assignments in this passage: Work the garden and care for it. We have a body with which to work. We are to conserve and make progress. The Hebrew word for *work* is wonderful and revealing: *avodah*. The root of this word (עָבַד) is used over 1,000 times in the Old Testament. The three main ways it is translated are *work*, *worship*, and *service*.

We Christians tend to separate work from worship. We worship on Sunday and work on Monday. Sunday is more important to us as we divide life into the sacred versus the secular. But the Hebrew recognizes no such division. *Avodah* is both work and worship. We've been placed here to worship the living God. And how do we worship Him? By transforming what

He has given us into something for His glory. In this first dimension of stewardship, we are called to physically care for creation, and in so doing, we are worshiping God.

עָבַד | AVODAH

A Hebrew word used 289 times in the Old Testament translated variously as worship, serve and work.

Work:
Genesis 2:5, 15; Exodus 20:9 "to cultivate" the land.

Worship:
Exodus 8:1, 12:31; 20:5 to worship and serve the Lord.

Reveals the Hebrew mind:
• Integrated mind and life.
• No sacred/secular dichotomy.

Avodah is the integrated action of worship and work:
• The Cultural mandate is to cultivate: to sacredly work.

A second dimension of stewardship is seen in Genesis 2:19, when God gives Adam the privilege of naming the animals:

> Now out of the ground the LORD God had formed every beast of the field and every bird of the heavens and brought them to the man to see what he would call them. And whatever the man called every living creature, that was its name.

What a remarkable text! God could have said, "Look up in that tree. See that creature? I call that a bird. I want you to memorize that name." Instead, God said to Adam, "Look up there in the tree. There's an animal. I have made that animal, but I am giving you the privilege to name it. And whatever name you give that animal, that's what I will call it. That will be its name." Our words have creative power. Adam named the animals. We govern by creating words, by classifying and naming. God spoke the universe into existence and, not incidentally, made us in His image to be word makers.

When our first child was due, Marilyn and I joyfully picked out a girl's name and a boy's name. I said to Marilyn, "We're going to name our child and whatever we name our child that will be the name God calls our baby!"

We named our baby Nathan, and God has been calling him Nathan for fifty years. Even more amazing, God will be calling him Nathan for eternity. We are made to be stewards, and part of that stewardship is naming things. This is part of what it means to be made in the image of God.

We are made to use our imaginations. God *imagined* us in His *image*. Then He willed what He had imagined into existence. He is the God of imagination, and He gave us an imagination. He gave us not only a body to work the *soil* but an imagination to cultivate the *soul*. He has given us a mind and a heart—a mind to reason and discover, a heart to imagine and create.

Before God created the universe, He imagined it. Then He created the raw material through His speaking words; God formed the universe to reflect His imagination. Human imagination is clearly implied in God's mandate to Adam and Eve to develop the creation out of the raw materials He provided. And human imagination has been at work ever since. The power of human imagination is on display in this quote from an anonymous author: "A bar of iron costs $5, made into horseshoes its worth is $12, made into needles its worth is $3,500, made into balance springs for watches, its worth is $300,000."

The value of an item is often not found in the item itself. For something to have value, it must first be discovered by a human. Human imagination must then be applied to envision its potential.

Imagination is linked with discovery. For generations, oil existed underground, brimming with hidden potential. But only after humans discovered oil did that potential begin to unfold. Someone wondered, "What is this black, sticky stuff good for? Why did God put this here? What is its hidden potential?" *Imago Dei* people invented multiple uses for oil: light for lamps, heat for homes, and power for machinery. With oil we have flown around the world and to the moon.

"By faith we understand that the universe was formed at God's command, so that what is seen was not made out of what was visible," (Hebrews 11:3, NIV). This text establishes that the unseen God produced the seen universe. The invisible produces the visible. The minds of individuals transform the "worthless" into the priceless.

Human imagination enables people as secondary creators working with God's primary creation. In other words, it is not the limited physical capital in commodities that contributes value to the world but the vast metaphysical capital in human beings. The capital of human minds leads to discovery. Human imagination transforms rocks and flowers into colors and transforms colors into paints that are applied to canvas to produce a priceless masterpiece.

This is the "capital" that can transform "worthless," insignificant sand into glass, that remarkable invention that admits light while barring weather. Sand is converted into a chip to power a computer or cell phone. It is this capital that fired the imagination of George Washington Carver to take the small peanut and transform it into more than 300 products to bless the human family.

Metaphysical capital is found in the human heart (moral imagination) and mind (worldview). It is the metaphysical capital articulated by Judeo-Christian theism that provides the greatest source for transformation of raw materials, communities, and nations. Human imagination is yours to apply to the world! Behold, the seed!

So the first dimension of stewardship is to use our bodies to cultivate the soil. The second level is with our minds, hearts, and words to cultivate our imaginations. We are creating culture.

As we have seen, the word "culture" comes from "cult," meaning worship. Cult is the worship of a divine being. Culture is the temporal manifestation of a people's faith. It is religion externalized. We make cultures like the gods or God we worship. Cult and culture are related to the word "cultivate," preparing the earth for seeds and physical flourishing. But we not only cultivate the soil, we cultivate the mind, we cultivate virtue. The purpose of education is to cultivate the mind, to produce virtue. Tragically, the concept of virtue has largely disappeared from our vocabulary. We rarely hear about cultivating virtue or cultivating the mind.

> Metaphysical capital is found in the human heart (moral imagination) and mind (worldview). It is the metaphysical capital articulated by Judeo-Christian theism that provides the greatest source for transformation of raw materials, communities, and nations.

The Cultural Mandate of Genesis 1:28 to steward His creation, however, is comprehensive. It happens in time—over all of human history and in space—over all the earth. It is comprehensive over all the spheres of society: family, business, political governance, science, education, the arts, agriculture. We are to bring *everything* under the Lord-ship of Jesus Christ. This is why we're here.

Too many Christians live with the sacred-secular dichotomy and limit their scope of concern to spiritual things. If it's not religious, or spiritual, it's not important. But that's not biblical; it is the product of a dualistic Greek mindset.

Genesis 2:15 helps us better understand the functional aspect of being imago Dei. Here we find the purpose for which God put man in the garden: "The LORD God took the man and put him in the garden of Eden to work it and keep (*šā·măr*) it." Here we find two Hebrew words, one translated "work" and the other "keep."

"Keep" is the Hebrew *šā·măr,* meaning to care for, to protect, to guard. Note the balance here between progressing and conserving. The garden is to be tended, it is to be worked that it might produce abundantly. And it is to be protected and guarded. We mentioned above the Hebrew word *avodah*, a term that means "worship" or "work," a word that captures the wholistic Hebrew mind. Let's focus on *avodah*.

Avodah comes from the root word עָבַד, which is used over 1,000 times in the Old Testament. Sometimes *avodah* means *work*, as in to cultivate the field or do common labor:

- Genesis 2:5—"and there was no man to work (*avodah*) the ground."
- Genesis 2:15—"The LORD God took the man and put him in the garden of Eden to work (*avodah*) it and keep it."

Other times, the same word is translated as *worship*, as in worshiping the Lord.

- Exodus 8:1 (NIV)—"This is what the LORD says: 'Let my people go, so that they may worship (*avodah*) me.'"
- Exodus 12:31 (NIV)—"During the night Pharaoh summoned Moses and Aaron and said, 'Up! Leave my people, you and the Israelites! Go, worship (*avodah*) the LORD . . .'"
- Joshua 24:15 (NET)—"If you have no desire to worship the LORD, choose today whom you will worship, whether it be the gods whom your ancestors worshiped beyond the Euphrates, or

the gods of the Amorites in whose land you are living. But I and my family will worship (*avodah*) the LORD!"

Here is the entry from a noted Hebrew lexicon (with my emphases added):

> עָבַד *('ā·ḇăḏ):* v.; . . . work, labor, do, i.e., expend considerable energy and intensity in a task or function . . . give considerable energy and intensity **to give aid to another** (Lev. 25:46; 2Sa. 16:19); . . . **worship, serve, minister, work in ministry, i.e., give energy and devotion to God** or a god, including ceremonies (Exo. 23:24, 25); **cultivate, plow, i.e., work soil** (with or without an animal) as part of the agricultural process (Gen. 4:2; Isaiah. 30:24); **plowed, be cultivated** (Deu. 21:4; Ecc. 5:8; Eze. 36:9, 34).[108]

Take note of the diverse spectrum of meaning. Note as well the connection of the word *work* and *worship* to the act of cultivating the land. In fact, we see a family of words.

1. **Cult**: the "worship or reverential homage rendered a divine being."
2. **Cult**ure: "the temporal manifestation of a people's faith;" "*religion externalized.*"
3. **Cult**ivate: "tilling and preparing the earth for growth or the culture of the *mind*, the culture of *virtue.*"[109]

Simply put: Culture is the manifestation of worship! We were put here, as the Westminster Shorter Catechism states, "to worship God and glorify Him forever."[110]

Historian Russell Kirk stated this connection as a reminder for people living in the modern era:

> [C]ulture arises from the cult . . . when belief in the cult has been wretchedly enfeebled, the culture will decay swiftly. The material order rests upon the spiritual order. . . . The culture can be renewed only if the cult is renewed; and faith in divine power cannot be summoned up merely when that is found expedient.[111]

As we witness the deterioration of our own cultures and nations today, the solution is not more money, government, or more laws. To reverse the cultural collapse, we need to return to the worship—cult—of the Creator and Living God of the universe. And this is not to be done primarily for pragmatic reasons, but because God exists and He is True, Good, and Beautiful. He is worthy of our worship.

Historian Thomas Carlyle puts it simply:

> *Laborare est Orare*, Work is worship . . . All true Work is sacred; in all true Work, were it but true hand-labour, there is something of divineness . . . No man has worked, or can work, except religiously.[112]

The Avodah Institute further elaborates:

> What a powerful image to think that the word for working in the fields is the same that was used for worshipping the God of Abraham, Isaac and Jacob.
>
> The Israelites understood that work could be a way to honor God and neighbor, to serve God and neighbor, and yes, to worship God and serve neighbor.[113]

[C]ulture arises from the cult . . . when belief in the cult has been wretchedly enfeebled, the culture will decay swiftly. The material order rests upon the spiritual order. . . . The culture can be renewed only if the cult is renewed; and faith in divine power cannot be summoned up merely when that is found expedient.
Russell Kirk

Avodah provides the framework for a theology of work. All legitimate work is sacred to God. The Hebrew mind, unlike the Greek, makes no division between labor and worship. Worship is not only for Sunday, but for Monday as well. Worship is not limited to a religious meeting in a building or a public evangelistic effort. Worship is to take place in the midst of our everyday lives, in our homes, in the office, in the factory. The God of the Bible is not a part-time God. Our worship should not be thought of as part-time praise.

And then we find something incredible. This Cultural Mandate appears at the beginning of history and again at history's end.

The mandate is comprehensive. It encompasses all the earth; it engages all sectors of society: family, business, governance, science, education, the arts, agriculture, etc.; and it includes all of human history.

At the end of history, we will understand the fullness of the purpose of the mandate.

Throughout Scripture we see a message: *The kingdom of God is coming.* Sometimes this is described as the coming of the New Jerusalem, the city of God. Both Isaiah 60 and Revelation 21 capture this vision. In the New Jerusalem,

1. The gates will never be shut (Isaiah 60:11; Revelation 21:25).
2. There will be no night; God is the source of the light (Isaiah 60:19–20; Revelation 21:23).
3. There will be no more death, sorrow, or suffering (Isaiah 60:18; Revelation 21:4).
4. The nations of the earth will be drawn there to worship the King of kings (Isaiah 60:1–3; Revelation 21:24).
5. The kings of the earth will bring the glory of their nations there (Isaiah 60:6–7, 9, 13, 17. Revelation 21:24, 26). These gifts will be the fruit of the Cultural Mandate and will be presented to Christ and His bride.

Christ will return to get married. He will gather all the nations to Mount Zion, to Jerusalem.

This great day is foreshadowed in 1 Kings 10, where the Queen of Sheba (probably today's Yemen) recognizes Solomon's supremacy above all human kings. And she brings gifts—gold, spices, and precious stones—representing the glory of her nation to Solomon.

Matthew's Gospel records magi from the east visiting the Christ child. They are Gentiles coming to the king of the Jews with gifts from their nations, the best their nation produced. And they present these finest gifts to this baby, Jesus.

Revelation 21:23–26 records these incredible words about the end of history.

And the city has no need of sun or moon to shine on it, for

the glory of God gives it light and its lamp is the Lamb. By its light will all nations walk, and the kings of the earth will bring their glory into it, and its gates will never be shut by day—and there will be no night there. They will bring into it the glory and honor of the nations.

In the beginning of the biblical narrative, we find the Cultural Commission to take what God has made and do something with it. At the end of history, when Christ returns and the great wedding of the Lamb is to take place, all the nations are drawn to the New Jerusalem by the glory of God. The Lamb is the lamp. The nations don't come empty handed; they bring their glory, the God-honoring products of their cultures, for Christ and His bride on their wedding day. Genesis 1 and 2 record the Cultural Commission. At the end of the biblical narrative, the "why" of the Cultural Commission is revealed: The glory of the nations will be given to Jesus Christ. This is the end of the story.

Why are we here? Why did God create humans? Why are we made in God's image, female and male? The answer, according to the functional dimension of the *imago Dei*: to take what God has made and do something with it for his glory. This requires the nature and giftings of both men and women as male and female. And at the end of history, what we made in our cultures for His glory will be the wedding gifts of the kings and queens of the earth to Jesus Christ.

In the immensity of the universe, what is man that you are mindful of him? God says, "I've made you kings and queens to rule over what I have made." It's a huge calling, but one that can be clearly discerned even in a humble peanut.

STUDY GUIDE

1. How does the story of George Washington Carver reveal both external capital (the inherent potential of the physical, created world) and internal capital (the vision to see that potential and do something with it)?

2. What are the two dimensions of humanity's stewardship of the earth? How do these dimensions relate to external and internal capital?

3. What are the possible meanings of the single Hebrew word *avodah*? If English had a similar word, how would it challenge our concepts of a "sacred" and "secular" divide? How would it change our understanding of worship and work?

4. What is the relationship between "cult" and "culture"? If someone encountered the culture of the nation in which you live for the first time, what do you think they would learn about your people's deepest-held beliefs?

5. What does Revelation 21 say will ultimately happen to "the glory and honor of the nations"? What does this reveal about the ultimate purpose of the Cultural Mandate?

6. Think personally! What are the implications of this understanding of the image of God and of the concept of *avodah* for your work? For your life calling?

PART 4

The Glorious Eve

CHAPTER 11

Woman, the Crescendo of Creation

IN THE BEGINNING God created the heavens and the earth. Now the earth was *formless* and *empty, darkness* was over the surface of the deep, and the Spirit of God was hovering over the waters.[114]

At the beginning of the biblical narrative, we notice a number of remarkable things.

This is the moment when God creates the raw material from which He will form creation. Before this moment, God had imagined the universe in all its grandeur. But the thought didn't just stay in His mind. God willed what He had imagined into existence.

The title of the first book of the Bible, Genesis, is the Hebrew word רֵאשִׁית, literally the first three words of the Scripture, "in the beginning." The Hebrew lexicon defines it as "what is first, the beginning, i.e., the initiation of an action, process, or state of being."[115] The word signifies the origin or point at which something comes into existence. This is the moment of conception, the beginning of gestation.

First, the Creator, the First Artist, creates the raw material from which He will form what He had imagined. Think of God as the Potter who must first create the ball of clay. Genesis 1:2 records the original status quo, "Now the earth was formless and empty" (NIV). Not deformed, but without form, empty, and void.

Here's another descriptor of the status quo: obscurity. "Darkness was over the surface of the deep" (NIV). Without light, things are indistinguishable. At the beginning, all was formless, void, and dark. Into this reality the Creator shaped the raw material.

What happened next? "The Spirit of God was hovering over the waters." The word "hover" (meaning to tremble, shake, or quiver) brings to mind a mother bird hovering over her nest, settling gently on the eggs at the point of incubation. Here begins the process of gestation, the creation moving from one state (formless, empty, and dark) to another.

What does God do next? He says, "'Let there be light,' and there was light. And God saw that the light was good. And God separated the light from the darkness. God called the light Day, and the darkness he called Night. And there was evening and there was morning, the first day" (Genesis 1:3–5).

This is the first day of creation. The sun and moon would not be created until the fourth day (Genesis 1:14–19). Light is created and separated from darkness so that things may be distinguished, one from another. There is a wonderful symmetry between Genesis 1:3–5 and Revelation 21:23. At the beginning of time, there is light without the sun, moon, and stars. How can this be? At the end of time, we understand this more completely: "And the city has no need of sun or moon to shine on it, for the glory of God gives it light, and its lamp is the Lamb." It is the glory of God that provides light. History, as we know it, begins as it ends.

Light and darkness comprise the first in a string of binary pairs that will climax with man and woman, the complementary couple who appear in Genesis 1:26–27.

The unformed earth brings to mind the potter who begins with a ball of clay, the painter with the blank canvas, the writer with her words, the carpenter with his wood, the chef with her ingredients. We begin with our imagination and the raw materials.

Note, then, the order of God's creation activity: Inanimate objects—Genesis 1:3–10, 14–19; and animate objects:

a. Plants—Genesis 1:12–13
b. Animals—Genesis 1:20–25
c. *Imago Dei*—Genesis 1:26–27

The Creator forms inanimate things (Genesis 1:3–10, 14–19): the sun, moon, and stars. Verse 3 says, "'Let there be light' and there was light"; verse 6, "Let there be an expanse in the midst of the waters"; verse 9, "Let the waters under the heavens be gathered together into one place, and let the dry land appear." God forms what was unformed.

Then He adds magnificent complexity, creating living things, beginning with plants (1:12–13).

Each stage adds more form and a higher, more refined order. "Let the earth sprout vegetation, plants yielding seed, and fruit trees bearing fruit in which is their seed, each according to its kind, on the earth" (1:11). God creates plants with seeds that allow the plants to multiply. A seed multiplies, reproducing in kind. Even plants are given the power of the seed to replicate endless future generations.

In forming living creatures, God gives higher form and greater complexity. Now we see the breadth of life. "'Let the waters swarm with swarms of living creatures, and let birds fly above the earth across the expanse of the heavens.' . . . And God said, 'Let the earth bring forth living creatures according to their kinds—livestock and creeping things and beasts of the earth according to their kinds'" (Genesis 1:20, 24).

At the completion of each day and each point of creation, the Artist stands back to reflect on what He has made. Does it conform to His imagination and expectations? Six times we see His judgment: "It is good" (precious, beautiful) (1:4, 10, 12, 18, 21, 25). We also see another assessment: It is "so" (well, right, correct) (1:7, 9, 11, 15, 24, 30).

But the Creator is not yet finished. He comes finally to the high point of His creation, human beings. Like the rest of creation, these also are able to multiply. But they are distinct from the rest of creation in that they are made in the likeness of the Creator. They are the *imago Dei.*

Most of us were taught in public school about Darwin and evolution as an ideology that asserts that we are descendants of apes. But the Bible provides a radically different narrative. When God made human beings, God looked at Himself. We're not patterned after animals; our pattern is based on the nature of God himself. This is stated in Genesis 1:26–27:

> Then God said, "Let us make man in our image, after our likeness. And let them have dominion over the fish of the sea and over the birds of the heavens and over the livestock and over all the earth and over every creeping thing that creeps on the

earth." So God created men in his own image. In the image of
God he created him; male and female he created them.

We don't live in a *man's* world. This is *God's* world. To fulfill God's image
required male and female. The man alone could not fully reveal the image
of God. Neither could a woman alone, nor two men, or two women. Male
and female are required to reveal the image of God!

At this point in creation, the Creator reflects on what He has made: "It
was very good," that is, utterly or exceedingly good, "pertaining to a high
point on a scale of extent" (Genesis 1:31).[116]

The creation has a Grand Design. While human beings may be small in
the immensity of creation, they stand at the threshold of time and eternity,
on the boundary between earth and heaven. David, perhaps contemplating
his own existence as he tends his sheep on a star-filled night, asks God
about this sublime truth.

> O Lord, our Lord,
>   how majestic is your name in all the earth!
>   You have set your glory above the heavens.
>   Out of the mouth of babies and infants,
>   you have established strength because of your foes,
>   to still the enemy and the avenger.
> When I look at your heavens, the work of your fingers,
>   the moon and the stars, which you have set in place,
>   what is man that you are mindful of him,
>   and the son of man that you care for him?
> Yet you have made him a little lower than the heavenly beings
>   and crowned him with glory and honor.
>   You have given him dominion over the works of your
>   hands;
>   you have put all things under his feet,
>   all sheep and oxen,
>   and also the beasts of the field,
>   the birds of the heavens, and the fish of the sea,
>   whatever passes along the paths of the seas. (Psalm 8:1–8)

Genesis 2 unpacks the creation of the *imago Dei* human. Genesis 1 may
be seen as the headline of the story; Genesis 2 is the more detailed story.

The headline is that "Human Beings Are Made *Imago Dei.*" Now we will examine, with more detail, the unfolding creation of male and female.

Genesis 2:7 tells us, "Then the LORD God formed the man of dust from the ground and breathed into his nostrils the breath of life, and the man became a living creature." Now we have a man—part of the image of God—but God's not finished yet. At each stage He adds more detail, creates a little higher form. The higher more refined form is in God's imagination but has not been manifested. Michelangelo captures this in his beautiful Sistine Chapel fresco of the creation of Adam. Eve is there, under God's arm. The higher, more refined form is coming!

Genesis 2:21–22 records the dramatic moment: "So the LORD God caused a deep sleep to fall upon the man, and while he slept took one of his ribs and closed up its place with flesh. And the rib that the LORD God had taken from the man he made into a woman and brought her to the man." So while Adam is made from the dust of the ground, Eve is made from the very DNA of Adam, taken from his side.

> My sisters, *you are the crescendo of creation.* My brothers, you are near the finale, but you are not the finale. After God made the male, he made the female. The woman is the crescendo of creation, the high-water mark of God's creative activity.

Creation is progressive. Here *at last* is the woman, as Adam put it. The narrative progresses from the unformed in Genesis 1:1–2 to the creation of woman, the highest, most refined work of God's creation.

Note that it took one verse (2:7) to describe the creation of Adam, but it takes six (2:18–23) to describe the creation of the more refined Eve.

My sisters, *you are the crescendo of creation.* My brothers, you are near the finale, but you are not the finale. After God made the male, he made the female. The woman is the crescendo of creation, the high-water mark of God's creative activity.

Our world tends to ignore this fact, but we Christ-followers need to recognize and celebrate it. The culture tends to see women as inferior to men, but in fact, woman was the climax of God's creative activity. The man is the crown of creation, and woman is the diadem in the crown.

Let's briefly explore two extensions of this powerful truth. First, woman is a manifestation of what I call the maternal heart of God, a vital, little-understood concept into which we will delve more deeply later in this book. For now, suffice it to say that Eve is "the mother of all living" (3:20). The name Eve means life-giver. God gives life, and the woman gives life.

Second, the bride of the first Adam is the prequel to the bride of Christ, the Second Adam. At the end of history, Christ will return to get married. The Bible begins and ends with a wedding. It begins with the beautiful bride of Adam and ends with the beautiful bride of Christ, the Church.

Gene Edwards's epic poem, "The Divine Romance," tells the story of the creation of Eve. Enjoy!

Slowly the revelation subsided, giving angels a moment to wonder what ultimate thought had coursed through His being, what masterpiece might now fall from His hand. At last they could pierce the light and see again the face of God. Upon that face was etched exaltation and joy.

Whispered one angel as he staggered to his appointed place, "He has contemplated man's counterpart and seen her in the eye of His mind. But somewhere beyond that sight, methinks, He has glimpsed a higher, far greater, revelation. But what?"

"'Tis mystery, hidden in unapproachable light," rejoined another.

Now it was with trembling hands that the Builder did build, and mold, and fashion, and mold again. And while the being He fashioned took on its final form, awed and dumbfounded angels fell once more to their knees at the wonder of the sight before them.

One angel, most irreverently, cried aloud the thoughts of all: "He is not making another Ish. This one is alike, yet different. As the lioness is to the lion, so is this out-of Man. But never, never," cried the wayward angel, "was lion or lioness so beautiful as this."

Another angelic being broke the confines of restraint, his exclamation foretelling the advent of thunderous peals of praise which would follow his words.

"Nor was ever Man so beautiful as this," he exclaimed.

With that, the vaults of heaven broke open, and in one full-throated shout, all heavenly beings proclaimed:

"Never was
Nor e'er shall be
A being
As beautiful as she.
All host in heaven's court,
All creatures on earthen sod,
It matters not the tribe nor race,
One sight alone can be
More beautiful than she.
It is the face of God."[117]

STUDY GUIDE

1. In what sense is the Spirit of God's "hovering" over the face of the deep a maternal image?
2. What is the order of God's creation activity? What happens at each new stage? What does this suggest about woman's being created last?
3. How does the biblical narrative differ from the theory of evolution? Who are human beings patterned after?
4. What does the name Eve mean? How does this make her like God in a different sense than Adam?
5. How is Eve a prequel to the Bride of Christ? In what sense is the church more beautiful than anything God has yet made?
6. Again, think personally! If you are a man, what does it mean for you that women are the crescendo of creation? If you are a woman, what does the fact that you are the crescendo of creation and the "mother of all living" make you think? Do you see yourself differently?

CHAPTER 12

The Maternal Heart of God

"THE RETURN OF the Prodigal Son," a famous work of the great Dutch painter, Rembrandt, demonstrates a profound understanding of the heart of God.

We all know the story of the prodigal son. A man had two sons. The younger son was impetuous. He went to his father and asked for his inheritance. The father gave him the inheritance, and he went out and squandered it. Within a short time, his money was gone.

He needed food, so he went to work on a pig farm. We all know what Jews thought of pigs. They were filthy, unholy, and for a young Jewish boy, it didn't get any lower than that.

One day this young man realized he should go home to his father. A slave in his father's household lived in better conditions than he had on the pig farm. So he returned home to ask his father if he could just be a servant in the household. While he was still off in the distance, his father saw him coming and ran to embrace him. That's the moment Rembrandt captured in his painting.

If you look carefully at the father's hands, you'll see they are not identical. The left hand is thick and muscular. The right hand is more delicate; it has longer, thinner fingers.

Rembrandt clearly had the ability to paint identical hands. So why didn't he? Because he understood something of God's heart. He painted a female hand and a male hand to show God's nature; the father heart comes from God, and so does the maternal heart.

REMBRANDT'S *THE RETURN OF THE PRODIGAL SON* (1669)

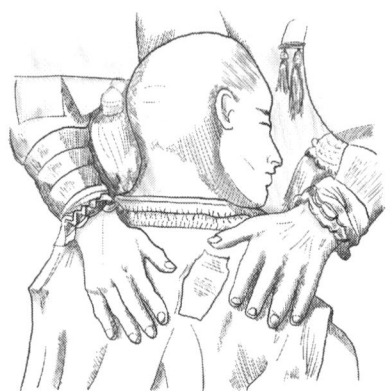

In his book, *The Return of the Prodigal Son*, Dutch priest, pastor, writer, and theologian Henri Nouwen writes:

> As soon as I recognized the difference between the two hands of the father, a new world of meaning opened up for me. The Father is not simply a great patriarch. . . . He touches the son with a masculine hand and a feminine hand. . . . He is, indeed, God, in whom both manhood and womanhood, fatherhood and motherhood, are fully present. That gentle and caressing right hand echoes for me the words of the prophet Isaiah: "Can a woman forget her baby at the breast, feel no pity for the child she has borne? Even if these were to forget, I shall not forget you. Look, I have engraved you on the palms of my hands."[118]

In Matthew 23:37 we can hear the plaintive voice of the "maternal heart" reflected in the words of our Lord Jesus Christ as he sits overlooking the city of Jerusalem : "O Jerusalem, Jerusalem, the city that kills the prophets and stones those who are sent to it! How often would I have gathered your children together as a hen gathers her brood under her wings, and you were not willing!"

Christ identifies with a mother bird calling her flock together to spread her wings of protection over them. We see here the maternal heart of God. God has a paternal heart—and is the source of the maternal heart as well.

But before I go further, I need to make a distinction between a metaphor and a simile, or someone might claim I am saying, "God is a mother." But I am *not* saying that. That would be a heresy. The distinction between a metaphor and a simile might seem minor, but it isn't.

A metaphor compares the *whole* of one thing to the *whole* of another. A simile compares *part* of one thing to *part* of another. To say "God *is* a mother" is to use a metaphor and is to fall into a pagan error.

The Bible, however, uses *simile* to compare God and a mother. God is *like* a mother. A mother is *like* God. When speaking of God's maternal heart, the Bible uses simile: God is *like* a woman giving birth, *like* a nursing mother, *like* a mother hen, *like* a mother eagle. These are similes that Scripture uses to picture God's maternal heart.

With that necessary distinction out of the way, let's dig into what Scripture says about this vital topic. How are we to understand God's maternal heart? One way is to study what he has made. Pastor John Piper says, "All things exist to demonstrate something about God's infinite perfection."[119] God has made the female body and soul to demonstrate to the world something of His infinite perfection. A quote attributed to Thérèse of Lisieux, a member of the Carmelite community near Normandy in France, captures this: "The loveliest masterpiece of the heart of God is the heart of a mother."[120]

This makes perfect biblical sense. In Romans 1:19–20, the Apostle Paul makes a powerful assertion that God reveals Himself not only through His Word, the Bible (special revelation), but God also does this through what He has made.

Paul describes this second source of revelation in Romans 1:19–20 (KJV, emphases added):

> Because that which may be known of God is manifest *in* them; for God hath shewed it unto them.
>
> For the invisible things of him from the creation of the world are clearly seen, being understood *by the things that are made*, even his eternal power and Godhead; so that they are without excuse.

God has revealed Himself to all human beings through His creation.

Paul argues that God has revealed Himself in two ways through creation. First, He manifested Himself *in* them. He made us in His image as creatures who can think and analyze, who have moral emotions, and can make moral decisions. We can look at ourselves and reflect on our own existence and conclude that we are more than rocks or even more than mere animals. We can look inside ourselves.

God has also manifested himself *outside* of us in the external world. People in an earlier generation would recognize this in what Plato and Aristotle represent. Plato is the philosopher, the man of reason, who focused on the ability to think logically and critically. Aristotle is the man of science, who used his senses to look at creation and draw conclusions from reality—the material world. So revelation, reason, and reality are sometimes called the three books in which God has revealed Himself. And in Romans 1, Paul is saying people who look at what God has made and conclude there is no God are without excuse.

So revelation, reason, and reality are sometimes called the three books in which God has revealed Himself.

We spoke above about Rembrandt. Suppose you were with friends in Holland and went to a museum that displayed Rembrandt's paintings. What could you learn about Rembrandt by looking at his paintings?

You could see the subjects he was interested in, the features of the world and culture he inhabited. You could recognize his great skill, his vivid imagination. You would no doubt be struck by his sense of perfection in portraying beauty, his sensitivity to color, his mastery of light. You would note his extraordinary attention to detail.

All that relates to Rembrandt's artistry, but you could also observe his techniques. How did he apply the base? What kinds of brushes did he use? How did he use textures? You could learn all sorts of things about Rembrandt simply by looking at what he made.

Imagine walking out of the museum after a day of admiring Rembrandt and hearing a friend say, "You know, this was an amazing day. The trouble is, there was no Rembrandt." How would you reply to such a statement?

"Are you crazy? Where did these paintings come from? Did they just drop out of the sky and materialize on the wall? What a thing to say!"

But people say such things about God all the time. In the face of what

God has made, modern man and postmodern man say there is no God. Paul's retort: Such people are without excuse. The clarity of God's general revelation allows no justification for unbelief, no legitimate apology for ignorance. Disbelief in God makes men not skeptics and unbelievers, but idolaters.

What can you learn about God by observing flowers? He loves beauty. He loves diversity, colors, and fragrances. A simple bunch of flowers reveals much about God: form and function, beauty, design, ornamentation, excellence, diversity, order, pleasure.

Scientists would ask different questions: How do flowers work? How can this array of beauty and design come from brown earth? They would look at the structure, the system, biology, chemistry, hydrology, etc. All sorts of things would be revealed through the eyes of a scientist.

We can learn a lot about God by looking at what He has made.

God is a romantic. Ladies, do you love to receive flowers? Men, when was the last time you gave your wife or girlfriend flowers? God is romantic; He has given *us* flowers.

Here's another thing God made that teaches us a lot about Him. My sisters, God made *you*. What does the female body teach us about God?

The female body was made for a purpose: to have compassion, to nurture, and to protect. The design of a female body reveals the transcendent nature of God's compassion, nurture, and protection. A woman's body is functional. It has a physical-ness to it; it was designed for a particular purpose. But it's not merely functional; it also reveals something of God's transcendent nature. He designed the female body to say to the world, "I am here. This is what I am like." The female body reveals the maternal heart of God.

Every one of us has, or had, a mother. We were all carried inside her womb. Most of us received our first nourishment from our mother's breast and were held in our mother's arms.

The essence of female is to reveal the maternal heart of God to a watching world. A woman does not have to be a mother to do this, of course. Her love, self-sacrifice, and nurturing manifests God's maternal heart.

Two famous single women were exemplary in the way they manifested the maternal nature. Florence Nightingale, considered the founder of modern nursing, trained other women to serve wounded and dying solders during the Crimean War. Also, Mother Teresa of Calcutta and her Sisters of Charity modeled God's maternal heart in their care for the poor and dying in India and around the world.

Now let us return to God's special revelation in His Word. We find in Scripture three powerful similes. Womb love pictures God's compassion. Nurturing breasts speak of God's sufficiency. Maternal arms, or sheltering wings, reveal God's protection.

Womb Love

God has revealed himself not only through what He has made, but also through His self-descriptions. Exodus 34:6–7 is God's first self-disclosure, in which he says, in essence, "I am the compassionate and gracious God."

The female body reveals the maternal heart of God.

The Hebrew word for compassion is *racham*. It means to love deeply, to have mercy, to have tender affection.[121] Thirty times this word is translated *mercy*. Four times it's translated *compassion*. And four times it's translated *womb*. One of the things God sought to demonstrate in His Grand Design of the woman was His compassion. He sculpted a place of compassion in a woman's body: the womb.

In 1 Kings 3:16–28, each of two prostitutes had a baby, but one of the babies died. In the night, the mother of the deceased child secretly exchanged the dead baby for the other mother's living baby. The text goes on as follows:

> "When I rose in the morning to nurse my child, behold, he was dead. But when I looked at him closely in the morning, behold, he was not the child that I had borne." But the other woman said, "No, the living child is mine, and the dead child is yours." The first said, "No, the dead child is yours, and the living child is mine." Thus they spoke before the king. (1 Kings 3:21–22)

They had an audience with King Solomon, wisest of kings, and each told her side of the story. Solomon listened and called for a sword. "Divide the living child in two, and give half to the one and half to the other" (3:24). Then the woman whose son was alive was filled with compassion for her baby and said to the king, "Oh, my lord, give her the living child, and by no means put him to death" (3:26).

Immediately Solomon knew who the mother was. How? Not by magic. He recognized the womb love and knew the identity of the mother.

Nurturing Breasts

One of God's names is *El Shaddai*, the all-sufficient one, the satisfier, the Almighty. This name is found forty-eight times in the Old Testament. *Shaddai* comes from the root word *shad*, which means breast; *El* means God. So El Shaddai is the God who fully nourishes, supplies, and satisfies His people, the way a mother would provide for her child. God is the God of nurturing.

God's maternal heart is manifest in the feminine nature and the female body, and profoundly in a woman's breasts. A woman's body, including her breasts, are reduced to "sex objects" in many societies. Too often the wonder, beauty, and function of the woman's breasts are lost.

My wife, Marilyn, is mother of four children. For much of her life, she worked as a nurse in labor, delivery, and post-partum wards. At one period in her life, she coached women in breastfeeding, which was becoming a lost art in North America. In modern culture, the world of second-wave feminism, the bottle replaced the breast so a woman could more easily return to the workplace, leaving someone else to feed her baby.

Marilyn spent six months studying to be a lactation therapist. She'd come home from class excited about something she had learned. "Darrow!" she once said. "I can't believe that people study a woman's breast and don't conclude there's a God!" What follows came from these conversations.

A baby's bonding with the mother actually begins in the womb. Early on, the baby hears the mother's heartbeat, and learns the rhythm of her mother's heart. As the baby's ears develop, she learns to distinguish the mother's voice from other voices. The baby in the womb can hear the mother's music and learn the pace of the mother's reading when she reads aloud. The baby can learn the mother's culinary tastes through the spices in the amniotic fluid. After birth, these same tastes come to the baby through the mother's milk.

Mothers and infants bond even before the baby leaves the womb. *Being There* is a remarkable book by Erica Komisar about the importance of a mother's time spent bonding with and nurturing her baby in the first three years. Komisar notes:

> Mothers are unique in their connection to their babies from an intrinsic biological and emotional perspective. From the moment they enter the world, babies know the difference between their mothers and everyone else, and they know the

difference from the moment they enter the world because they have been in the mother's womb and have been learning while they have been in the womb.[122]

What a remarkable understanding! Doesn't this blow your mind? God's Grand Design for mothers and babies is a wonderful manifestation of God's existence and character.

What a wonderful opportunity for the mother and baby to develop intimate knowledge and bonding through "being there." The subtitle of Komisar's book's is *The First Thousand Days* and points to the importance of the mother being there for the baby for her first three years of life.

In the modern world, however, a mother often has little to no time to be there. It's considered normal for a woman's value to be found in the marketplace. After she's had a baby, she doesn't hang out with the baby; she goes back to work. But mother-infant bonding in the first thousand days is critically important.

Komisar writes:

> There have been a number of studies that document just how accurately babies recognize the uniqueness of their mothers. In research . . . babies who were presented with a breast pad soaked with their mother's milk on one side, and one with a stranger's milk on the other side, turn their heads towards their mother's very specific smell. Babies will also turn towards their mother's voice, which they've heard since they were in utero, and away from the voice of another caregiver.[123]

You may have experienced a time when you cried out to God and seemed to get no response, a time when your prayers seemed to bounce off the ceiling. Be assured that our nurturing God did not forget you, and He never will.

In Isaiah 49:13–15 we read,

> Shout for joy, you heavens; rejoice, you earth; burst into song, you mountains!
>
> For the LORD comforts his people and will have compassion on his afflicted ones.
>
> But Zion said, "The LORD has forsaken me, the Lord has forgotten me."

"Can a mother forget the baby at her breast and have no compassion on the child she has borne? Though she may forget, I will not forget you!" (NIV)

One of the most difficult times in my life was when our grandson died at six months old. He was alive in the morning, and by the evening he had died. I remember the pain, kneeling in front of his tiny casket, looking at his little lifeless body. I cried. I asked God, "Where are you? I'm an old man, you could've taken my life and spared this baby. Where are you?" Everyone in the family was crying out the same way. The pain of the loss of this child was immeasurable.

We all have moments like this. Zion is experiencing this moment in Isaiah 49. "How can we rejoice? How can we celebrate? God is not listening to us. He has forsaken us." And what does God say? "Can a mother forget the baby at her breast?"

Few things are more profound than the bond between a mother and her baby. What is the source of this intimacy? The maternal heart of God. Even if a woman should forget the baby at her breast, God will not forget you.

As we have said earlier, God is Trinity, one God in three persons, a divine community bound by love and noted for intimacy. The Hebrew word for this kind of intimacy is *yada,* meaning face-to-face, intimate knowledge. God sees us face to face. We can know God, not simply know *about* God. It is the face-to-face intimacy of a husband and wife, of a mother and child. As J.I. Packer noted, "Knowing God is a relationship calculated to thrill a man's heart."[124]

When Marilyn was taking the breastfeeding class, she taught me the concept of latching on, skin-to-skin contact, and eye-to-eye contact. If a newborn is placed on the mother's tummy, within a half-hour, the baby will make his or her way to the mother's breast without any prompting or touching. Why? The first sound a child in the womb hears is his or her mother's heartbeat. After delivery, the baby will go to that sound. What does the baby find? Nourishment.

When a mother breastfeeds her baby, she looks into the child's eyes. This maternal-infant bonding isn't just flesh-to-flesh. It is soul-to-soul.

Marilyn came home one night very excited. "Guess what I learned tonight?" she asked. "When a baby's eyes begin to focus, the first focal length is eight inches. The first thing the baby sees in clear focus is the face of the mother." This didn't just happen; this is by intention from the Master Designer who made us.

Another night Marilyn came home and said, "They're doing experiments on women who are lactating, putting foreign substances into the mother's body to see what her body will do. And the mother's breasts produce the antibody for the baby before her body produces the antibody for itself!"

God has built nurturing into a woman's nature, an automatic setting to think of the other first. A woman may tend to think of herself before she thinks of her child, but at the chemical level, her body is built to protect the child before her own interest.

Another thing Marilyn learned is that human milk is perfectly designed for human babies. An elephant's milk is designed for elephant babies. A cow's milk will not take care of an elephant's needs. Likewise, a baby daughter needs her mother's milk. Komisar writes, "Not only is breast milk the ideal food for infants, but the act of breastfeeding is the most intimate connection you will ever have with another human being."[125] Is this intimacy explained by happenstance or Darwin's theories? No. It is part of the Grand Design.

The Mother's Arms

The mother's arms reflect God's protection. We see this protection referenced in the spreading of the wings of the mother bird, as illustrated in Psalm 91:1–4 (KJV):

> He that dwelleth in the secret place of the most High shall abide under the shadow of the Almighty. I will say of the LORD, He is my refuge and my fortress: my God; in him will I trust. Surely he shall deliver thee from the snare of the fowler, and from the noisome pestilence. He shall cover thee with his feathers, and under his wings shalt thou trust: his truth shall be thy shield and buckler.

The believer lives under the shadow of the Almighty, under the wings of God's protection.

The Hebrew word *rachaph* means to brood, to flutter, or to move. Picture a mother bird settling over the nest or flapping her wings over her chicks to circulate the air. The same word is used in Genesis 1:2, depicting the Spirit of God hovering over the earth at creation. We find this concept throughout Psalms, Ruth, Isaiah, and Matthew.

A modern parable in the United States captures this concept: A ranger was examining a forest that had been burned by a massive fire. At the base of a tree, he found the body of a dead mother bird, covered with dust and ash, her wings spread apart. As the ranger flicked the bird's body away, baby birds scampered from under the protective wings. This mother bird could have flown away and saved her life, but instead she had gathered her brood and covered them with her wings. By saving them, she died in the process.

I shared these things in Guatemala some years ago to a group of 150 mostly young people. When I finished, a young man asked to speak. He came forward, weeping. By the time he got to the front, he could hardly control his emotions. I put my arm around him for comfort, and when he had calmed down, he said,

> My father was "machista," a macho man. He'd go out drinking at night and come home drunk. He would beat my mother, and me, and my sister. One night he came home drunker than normal. He found his gun, backed me into the corner, pointed the gun directly at me, and pulled the trigger. Just as he pulled the trigger, my mother jumped between the gun and me.

He began sobbing again but managed to finish. "She took the bullet that was meant for me. I have never known where this love came from, and today I know. This is the heart of God." He continued sobbing for a long time.

God spreads His wings over us, sheltering us under His wings.

Rebekah Holsapple effectively expresses the maternal heart of protection in her poem, "Scars of Love":

> If a man came to me and said, "I am your Christ," I would ask him to show me his hands. I know my Christ by the love which defines His character—the love that gave Him the strength and desire to give His life in exchange for mine.

> "There is no greater love than this, that a man lay down his life for his friend."

I have never seen Jesus, but He knew me and loved me even before I was born. He gave me life, and when my own sin threatened that life, He died on the cross to save it, and no mark was left on me. When I see Him, I will know Him by the scars that bear witness to the unfathomable magnitude of His love for me.

I know my mother by the love which defines her character—the love that gave her the strength and desire to offer her life in exchange for mine.

"There is no greater love than this, that a man lay down his life for his friend."

My mother knew me and loved me even before I was born; she gave me life. When I was a baby, twelve stone steps threatened that life, but she held me so tight and close that every cut and bruise fell on her own body, and no mark was left on me.

So mother, if when I get to heaven I don't recognize you, show me the scars on your arms that bear witness to the unfathomable magnitude of your love for me.[126]

—————————— STUDY GUIDE ——————————

1. Why did Rembrandt paint the hands of the Father different and distinct? How does Henri Nouwen relate that to what the Bible reveals about the heart of God?
2. What does the design of the female body reveal to us about God's nature?
3. What are the possible meanings of the Hebrew word *racham*? How does this relate to the story of King Solomon and the two women?
4. What is the connection between God's Hebrew name "El Shaddai" and a mother's nurturing act of breastfeeding?
5. What is maternal-infant bonding? Have you thought deeply

about what this means, or have you accepted what society teaches—that what a woman carries in her womb is not human, it is "a product of conception," or merely "tissue"? What is the significance of the title of Erica Komisar's book *Being There: The First Thousand Days* for the mother and baby, for the family, and the future of a nation?

6. What image does Psalm 91 use for God's protective love? What experiences have you had of a mother's protective love?

CHAPTER 13

Eve, the Life Giver

ONE OF MY heroes as a young man was Elisabeth Elliot, a missionary to the unreached Huaorani tribe in the jungles of Ecuador. Elisabeth became a well-known author and speaker. She said two things that relate to the design of men and women. "Men and women are two creatures, amazingly alike and wondrously different," and, "In order to learn what it means to be a woman, we must start with the one who made her."[127] To understand male and female, we need to apprehend the mind of the Designer.

One of my favorite passages in Scripture is Hebrews 11:10. The writer is reflecting on the call of Abraham in Genesis 12. Abraham had left his home in Ur of the Chaldees and was following the voice of God to the Promised Land. In Hebrews 11 we find out, in more detail, what Abraham was looking for: the City of God, the New Jerusalem: "For he was looking forward to the city that has foundations, whose designer and builder is God" (11:10). Here we find two developmental terms: designer (Greek: *technitēs*) that is, architect or craftsman, and builder (Greek: *dēmiourgos*), that is, maker, builder, or creator.

Men and women are binary creatures by design. They are equal and different at the same time, designed to complement each other. To understand the design of women is to automatically understand something of the design of the male counterpart and vice-versa.

Several years ago, I received a letter from a Chilean friend, Eduardo Krauss. Shortly after hearing me speak about the maternal heart of God, he wrote a long letter of reflection. His wife was pregnant with their first child. He realized motherhood was going to change his wife. Paulina was going to learn more about God because she was going to be a mother. She would understand that her maternal heart came from God. Eduardo's reflections inspired me to think further about the creation of the woman. I will do so using some key points from the Genesis creation account.

Creation and gestation

Genesis 1:1–3 records what we might call the gestation of creation.

> In the beginning, God created the heavens and the earth. Now the earth was formless and empty. Darkness was over the surface of the deep and the spirit of God was hovering over the waters. And God said, "Let there be light," and there was light.

As we noted in a previous chapter, "hovering" translates the Hebrew word for a mother bird brooding over her chicks or incubating the eggs to keep them warm between the moment of conception, as it were, and the birth of the chicks.

Gestation is God's idea. He conceived of the universe, gestated, and gave birth to creation. Amazingly, but perhaps not surprisingly, this pattern is built into our design for creating new human beings.

To understand male and female, we need to apprehend the mind of the Designer.

Gestation is the human capacity for conception to give and sustain life. The male provides the seed. Genesis 1:29 says, "I have given you every plant yielding seed." We think of seeds in relationship to plants, but the man provides the seed, while the woman provides the egg and the womb where the new human life is incubated.

Something that has not existed before comes into existence. What a wonder is this! The *imago Dei* male and female coming together have the ability, designed by God, to create life that will live for eternity. Birth marks the end of gestation. Like God, the woman has the ability to conceive, gestate and give birth to new life. Sisters, this is who you are!

In his letter Eduardo mused, "Has God ever been pregnant?"[128] Figuratively, yes, at creation and at the birth of the nation of Israel. In the plan of salvation, God gives life to what was dead. At this moment in history, we await the coming of the Kingdom of God in its fullness. This is the period of gestation of the Kingdom of God. It is coming.

Eduardo concluded, "So God can understand the process of gestation."[129] God knows what birth pains are. Pregnant mothers can feel privileged to approach God in a unique way. They can know what a man cannot, the ability to incubate a life. They can achieve a unique bond no man can understand.

Light in the darkness

At this point in the creation, it was dark: "Darkness was over the surface of the deep" (1:2). And what did God say? "'Let there be light,' and there was light" (1:2). And the waters became full of living things. God is giving birth to creation.

Eduardo pointed to a Spanish phrase—*dar a luz*—which means "giving birth." *Dar* means "to give" and *luz* means "light." Spanish recognizes a relationship between giving birth and light. Genesis 1:2 says that during the gestation of creation, darkness was over the face of the waters. At the beginning of the creation, as the unformed is given shape, light penetrates the darkness. In Spanish, "give birth" and "generate light" share a common root.

THE WONDER AND GLORY
OF THE MOMENT OF CONCEPTION

DESIGNED FOR MALE AND FEMALE

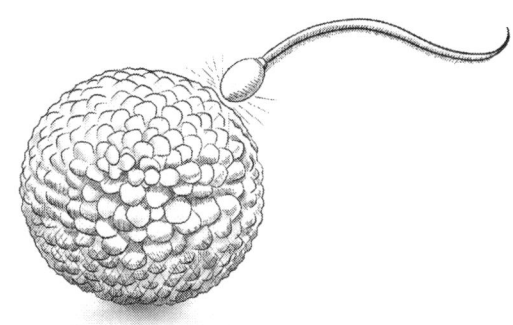

Astonished scientists have photographed the moment the sperm enters the egg and have seen a flash of light occurring at that instant. In like manner, Genesis 1:1–3 reports that, at the point where God began to form the unformed, light appeared in the darkness.

One plus one equals one

Here's another mystery from the creation account. Genesis 2:24 says,

"Therefore a man shall leave his father and his mother and hold fast to his wife, and they shall become one flesh." We all know that one plus one equals two. So why does the Scripture indicate that one plus one equals *one*? How do we understand this?

As we discussed earlier, English has only one word for "one," and it means a "single one," an "absolute one." This is true for most languages. But the ancient Hebrew of the Bible has two words for "one." The first, as in English, means a single one or an absolute one. But another word, *echad*, is found in Genesis 2:24: "The two will be *echad*." *Echad* means a "united one," a "combined one." One plus one equals a combined one flesh.

> When a man and a woman conceive a child, something comes into existence that did not exist before. A new life is created, a person who did not exist before and will live into eternity.

When a man and a woman conceive a child, something comes into existence that did not exist before. A new life is created, a person who did not exist before and will live into eternity. Just thinking about what it is to conceive a baby gives me chills. It's not merely just about a physical act; it's something sacred. Today we have reduced the wonder and beauty of human sexuality to entertainment or recreation. Conception is often seen as an unfortunate consequence of unprotected sex. This is utter folly. What comes from that intimacy is something that never existed before, someone who will live for eternity, a unique human being.

It takes a binary relationship to produce life. It takes a complementary relationship, a man and a woman who are marvelously equal and very similar but not the same. It is the whole, the man and the woman coming together in *echad*, that creates something that did not exist before—a new life.

This binary human couple is sourced in the Three-in-One God; all that is human, both male and female, comes from Him. In Deuteronomy 32:18 we see the paternal and maternal love of God. It was God who conceived of the nation of Israel, bringing her out of captivity in Egypt and carrying her in the desert until she made it to the Promised Land.

But Israel was not thankful: "You deserted the Rock who fathered you. You forgot the God who gave you birth" (NIV). God led Israel out of Egypt into the Promised Land as "the Rock who fathered you" . . . "the God who gave you birth." In this verse we see God's paternal and maternal heart.

The Keil and Delitzsch commentary on the Old Testament says this about Deuteronomy 32:18:

> To bring out still more prominently the base ingratitude of the people, he [Moses] represents the creation of Israel by Jehovah, the rock of its salvation, under the figure of generation and birth, in which the paternal and maternal love of the Lord to His people had manifested itself.[130]

Because both the paternal and maternal natures come from God, women possess inherent dignity. This sublime truth refutes all those repugnant arguments about the alleged superiority of men. A woman is designed to do what a man can never do. Feminism says that sacred truth is worthless. Sexism says it's worthless. Both feminism and sexism claim worth is found in being like a man. No, my brothers and sisters, a woman's *glory is in doing what she alone can do.*

Adam and Eve as complementary

In Genesis 2, God forms Eve from the body of Adam and gives him the privilege of naming her. "The man said, 'This at last is bone of my bones and flesh of my flesh; she shall be called Woman, because she was taken out of Man'" (Genesis 2:23).

These are among the very first recorded human words: "She shall be called Woman, because she was taken out of Man." Adam uses a play on words. She shall be called *ishshah* (woman), because she was taken out of *ish* (man). This poetic expression signifies the complementary design of woman and man. We are equal in dignity and worth, but we are not the same. We were designed by the Creator of the universe for a binary relationship to bring forth something that never existed before—a human life.

Dennis Prager captures another important truth when he observes that "'Eve' means 'life' in the same way 'Adam' means 'earth.' These names, 'earth' and 'life,' suggest Adam and Eve are prototypes for all of humanity."[131] The symmetry and complementary nature of their work is reflected in Genesis 3 where the woman will labor to bring forth life from her womb, and the man will labor to bring forth food from the ground.

Not only are they prototypes for all humanity, but they are also the prologue for the wedding of the ages at the culmination of the narrative, that of Christ and His Church. Between the beginning and culmination of the narrative, they each bring forth life: The man brings forth food from the ground and the woman brings forth human life from her womb. The male and female are binary, and their work is complementary.

Eve, the life giver

Adam *identifies* his counterpart with the word for woman. But he *names* her "Eve." The Hebrew word means "life" or "living." The root is simply and profoundly *Life-Giver*.

Who gives life? God! But what name did Adam give his wife? Life-giver. Why? Because she was the mother of all the living. The first giver of life is Jehovah God, but He envisioned a universe filled with life and thus created woman. He designed and created the woman to replicate what He had done to give life, to be a life-giver.

> A woman is designed to do what a man can never do.

Can we stand in awe of the God who conceived all this? Can we stand in awe of you, sisters, for who you are, for what God has made you to be? We need to repent for how poorly we have treated women, for how we have objectified women, reducing them to objects.

My sisters, you are life-givers, and we honor you. Modernism says that a woman carries a product of conception in her womb—a foreign invasion of her body, something to be discarded. This mentality reduces a woman to a producer and consumer of things.

But the biblical worldview asserts that what is in a woman's womb is a human life, someone who will receive a name, who will live into eternity. While not every woman can carry a child to term, every woman is designed by God to be a life-giver and a nurturer of nations. Elisabeth Elliot knew this, and so should we.

STUDY GUIDE

1. How does the experience of pregnancy relate to the "gestation" of creation and redemption? Does this shed new light on Jesus' description of the tribulations of the church age as "the beginning of the birth pains" (Matthew 24:6–8)?
2. Does it surprise you that Deuteronomy 32:18 refers to God as "the God who gave you birth"? How might recognizing God's

maternal qualities add to a Christian's understanding of the value of women?

3. What does the fact that women in feminist societies feel pressured to do everything men do to be "equal" say about the value society places upon things men cannot do? How might Christians model a better way forward for women and girls?

4. Who is the Giver of Life? What is the significance that Adam named his wife Eve meaning life-giver because she was "the mother of all living" (Genesis 3:20)?

5. What does Adam's name for his wife say about the wonder with which he viewed her? How can we cultivate the same wonder today?

6. Why do modern feminists want to be like men and do everything men can do when they were designed to do everything a man cannot do?

CHAPTER 14

Nurturer of the Nations

WENDELL BERRY COMES from a long line of Kentucky farmers. He understands the relationship between the family and the land. His life is uniquely balanced as an American poet and novelist, a cultural critic and a conservationist, in the classic sense of conserving what is important. For Berry, what is important is the land and the connection between the family and the farm. Berry writes:

> The word "husbandry" is the name of a connection. In its original sense, it is the name of the work of a domestic man, a man who has accepted a bondage to the household. To husband is to use with care, to keep, to save, to make last, to conserve. Old usage tells us that there is a husbandry also of the land, of the soil, of the domestic plants and animals—obviously because of the importance of these things to the household. And there have been times, one of which is now, when some people have tried to practice a proper human husbandry of the nondomestic creatures, in recognition of the dependence of our households and domestic life upon the wild world. Husbandry is the name of all the practices that sustain life by connecting us conservingly to our places and our world; it is the art of keeping tied all the strands in the living network that sustains us.[132]

Genesis 2:7 records the creation of the first human male from the dust of the ground: "Then the LORD God formed the man of dust from the ground and breathed into his nostrils the breath of life, and the man became a living creature."

Berry no doubt would agree that God placed the male of the species in the garden "to work it and keep it" (Genesis 2:15). Genesis 3:23 picks up this theme: "Therefore the LORD God sent him out from the garden of Eden to work the ground from which he was taken." The Hebrew uses a wonderful play on words, *adam* for the man and *adama* for the ground.

The *Theological Wordbook of the Old Testament* points out this play on words:

> Initially, God made *adam* out of the *adama* to till the *adama* (Gen 3:23), to bring forth life. The *adama* was God's possession and under his care (Gen. 2:6). Thus, the first *adam (the man,* Adam) and his family were to act as God's servants by obeying him in maintaining the divinely created and intended relationships vertically and horizontally.[133]

Adam, the first human being, was born out of the earth (*adama*) to bring forth life from the abundance of the garden. The first Adam and his family were to act as God's servants by maintaining the divinely created relationships, both vertical (with God) and horizontal (with creation). We stand at the intersection of earth and heaven and of time and eternity.

Yes, God placed Adam in the garden to work it and take care of it. But in Genesis 2:20 we read this startling claim: "But for Adam, there was not found a helper fit for him." Adam was alone. However, this was not the first time something in the unfolding creation was unfinished.

> These are the generations of the heavens and the earth when they were created, in the day that the LORD God made the earth and the heavens.
>
> When no bush of the field was yet in the land and no small plant of the field had yet sprung up—for the LORD God had not caused it to rain on the land, and there was no man to work the ground, and a mist was going up from the land and was watering the whole face of the ground—then the LORD God formed the man of dust from the ground and breathed

into his nostrils the breath of life, and the man became a living creature. And the LORD God planted a garden in Eden, in the east, and there he put the man whom he had formed. (Genesis 2:4–8)

It's not hard to guess why there was no vegetation. First, there was no rain, and second, there was no man to work the ground. So God filled both needs. He provided the water and the steward. Yet, even so, there is still something "missing." It is not good for the man to be alone (Genesis 2:18)!

But why would God say Adam was alone?

In Christendom we talk about the need for human beings to have their relationship with God restored. Christ's death and resurrection provide for that restoration. In the Garden of Eden, there's an unbroken relationship between God and man. This most primary of all relationships is unbroken. Yet God says it's not good for Adam to be alone.

In addition to his "vertical" relationship with God, Adam also had bountiful "horizontal" relationships with the rest of creation—the land and the animals. He is not alone. And yet God says that Adam *is* alone. Yes, he has a relationship with God. Yes, he has a relationship with creation, but there is no one like him. His counterpart is missing.

> **We stand at the intersection of earth and heaven and of time and eternity.**

Remember that by design, God's nature is reflected through male and female. A single male cannot reflect all it means to be made in the image of God. It takes male and female.

Adam was alone *in kind*. His complement, his equal-yet-different counterpart, by design, was missing. So at this point God stoops, once again, to complete humankind, to present the man with a gift of profound wonder and completion and delight.

So the LORD God caused the man to fall into a deep sleep; and while he was sleeping, he took one of the man's ribs and closed up the place with flesh. Then the LORD God made a woman from the rib he had taken out of the man, and he brought her to the man. The man said, "This is now bone of my bones and flesh of my flesh; she shall be called 'woman,' for she was taken out of man." (Genesis 2:21–23, NIV)

Michelangelo, in his wonderful painting on the ceiling of the Sistine Chapel, captures the moment. During the creation of Adam, the right hand of God reaches out to release the man while the left hand of Adam reaches toward God. Adam has been created, the first human being.

And where is Eve? Eve is not there. But she has not been overlooked. The figure of a woman appears under God's left arm. This is Eve. She has not been brought forth into life, but she has been conceived. And how will she be born into life? Not from the dust of the ground, but from the DNA of the man.

It takes the male and female counterparts to fulfill the Cultural Commission. Both female and male are required to procreate, to beget life, which is the societal part of the Cultural Mandate, "Be fruitful and multiply and fill the earth" (Genesis 1:28). The second part of the mandate is to steward the creation, to govern what God has made. The tasks of procreation and stewardship require not a single one, but a complementary one!

> **The second part of the mandate is to steward the creation, to govern what God has made. The tasks of procreation and stewardship require not a single one, but a complementary one!**

Male and female have complementary roles in this process. Each is to bring forth life, the man from the garden, the woman from her womb. Both are to nurture. The man's primary, but not exclusive, responsibility is to husband the soil; the woman's primary, but not sole commission is to nurture their children. This work of nurturing, while different, is of equal and fundamental importance to the flourishing of the human family and the Cultural Commission.

The first couple was placed in a garden to have children, form families, and tend and keep the garden, a task known, variously, as the Cultural Mandate, the Creation Mandate, or the Development Mandate. Man is placed in the midst of creation to be a steward, to husband the land (Genesis 2:15).

At the level of language, the relationship between "husbandry" and "husband" is obvious. The relationship transcends the merely superficial. In Genesis 2:15, Adam is placed in the Garden of Eden to husband the land. But God says the stewarding family is not complete (Genesis 2:18, 20b). From the man's side, God creates a complementary partner, *Ishshah*. Adam will now husband—"care, keep, save, conserve"—his counterpart, Eve, as well as their family, and the land they will share.

Genesis 3 builds on this sharing theme; they will share in the sorrow and consequences of disobedience. After the Fall, both forms of nurturing will require greater labor (see Genesis 3:16–19). The man and the woman shared responsibility for the Fall and therefore would share the consequences for their rebellion in each one's nurturing responsibility.

> To the woman, God said,
>> I will surely multiply your pain in childbearing;
>> in pain you shall bring forth children . . .
> And to Adam God said,
>> . . . cursed is the ground because of you;
>> in pain you shall eat of it all the days of your life;
>> thorns and thistles it shall bring forth for you;
>> and you shall eat the plants of the field.
>> By the sweat of your face you shall eat bread,
>> till you return to the ground,
>> for out of it you were taken;
>> for you are dust,
>> and to dust you shall return.

The woman will have increased toil in childbearing, the man in weeding. Note that their responsibilities have not changed. Both have primary roles—he brings food from the ground; she brings children from her body.

As we saw earlier, the first Adam came from the ground (*adama*); the second, complementary *adam*, the female, was formed from the first adam. The man's source was the ground, and the woman's was the man. English nonconformist Pastor John Angell James (1785–1859) said this about the counterpart:

> She was not taken from the head to show she was not to rule over him; nor from his foot, to teach that she was not to be a slave; nor from his hand, to show that she was not to be his tool: but from his side, to show that she was to be his companion.[134]

They complemented each other. She didn't just complement him. The very nature of a complementary relationship is they each complement the other. The woman is no slave to be ill-treated. She is not property to be bought and sold nor an object for a man's pleasure. Here is one not to be despised and crushed by sexism nor to be discarded by feminism. Neither sexism nor radical feminism understand the nature of feminine and female or of masculine and male.

In the creation account, the man is the crown, and the woman is the crown of the crown. Here in human form, from the hand of the Creator himself, is the manifestation of the maternal heart of God. Here is the wife of the first man, the mother of all the living.

Here is the counterpart of the man, providing what he cannot. Please note this. The woman foreshadows the bride of the Son of God, the one who, by the self-sacrificial love of her Husband, will be made worthy of God Himself.

Women are *free* to do whatever they want, but they have been *designed* for one particular purpose: to nurture. A woman in the very fiber of her being was made to nurture the nations.

A woman is free to do a million things. She may be a lawyer, pilot, corporate executive, politician, soldier, or kickboxer. While this is all true and good, she has been designed to do one thing above all else: to nurture the next generation. Women are *free* to do whatever they want, but they have been *designed* for one particular purpose: to nurture. A woman in the very fiber of her being was made to nurture the nations.

The word *nurture* is the Hebrew word *kuwl.* What, exactly, does this word mean? To feed, to sustain, to nourish, to hold, and to cherish. Notice this is not simply to physically feed, as in feeding or nursing the baby. There is transcendence here, the maternal-infant bonding as the woman holds, cherishes, and nourishes her child.

Two New Testament Greek words are translated "nurture." The first is *trepho,* to feed or nourish, to bring up, and to raise up. This word is derived from another Greek word, *entrepho,* which means to nourish a person or thing, and metaphorically, to educate, to form the mind. It is not simply physical nurture but shaping the soul.

The second New Testament word translated "nurture" is *paideia,* a term normally used in the context of education. *Paideia* means to nurture, to instruct. It also means chastisement, to give shape to, as a mother says to her child, "This is right, and this is wrong." *Paideia* relates to the cultivation of the mind and the character, the development of virtue, the whole training and education of children.

Despite all the "character counts" programs rushed into our public schools in recent years, modern educators, tragically, know very little about cultivating virtue or cultivating the mind. *Paideia*, by contrast, aims to increase wisdom and character, to develop virtuous lives.

Nurture relates to the transcendent nature of female. To nurse is a physical manifestation of that nurture. A mother nursing her baby gives a picture of something transcendent. This explains the soul-to-soul contact of a nursing woman and her baby.

The English word "nurse" means to tend an infant or nurture at the breast. It means to manage with care and economy, with a view to increase. The mother manages with care and economy the healthy development of the child. Note the intimate relationship captured here between the mother and child. It includes physical comfort, growth, and the reaching of potential.

We need to encourage women to regain their unique place in God's order, to understand who the Creator designed them to be, not only to conceive and gestate a baby, but to nurture that child and, in doing so, to *nurture nations*.

While the female is called to be the nurturer of the future, the man's responsibility, as Berry saw, is to *husband*. He nurtures the land so it will thrive and provide for his family. He serves his wife so she will flourish in her calling of nurturing the children.

In *Letters to Young Ladies*, Lydia Sigourney writes of the dual points of responsibility between the woman and the man to create the whole:

> While her partner toils for his stormy portion of that power or glory from which it is her privilege to be sheltered, let her feel that in the recesses of domestic privacy, she still renders a noble service to the government that protects her, by sowing seeds of purity and peace in the hearts of those, who shall hereafter claim its honours or control its destinies.[135]

While her husband toils against the weeds in the garden (Genesis 3) to provide for his family, the woman is sheltered. He is her servant, not her tyrant. She is protected, not for a life of ease, but for the critical task of nurturing. While the government affords protection for her, she performs a noble service of educating the future leaders of the community and nation. Her husband and the government create a protected space for her to fulfill her glorious calling. She is developing the character of future citizen leaders, those who will claim its honors or control its destinies. The woman and the man fulfill a Grand Design, a complementary partnership designed by God for the fulfillment of His purposes on this planet.

It is time to repudiate both sexism and radical feminism. Men are not superior to women. Women do not find their identity in becoming like men. The two become one in complementary partnership, fulfilling the Grand Design.

Ann Crittenden has been a journalist in economics and was nominated for a Pulitzer Prize. She was well-known in social circles; at parties, everybody wanted to talk with the famous Ann Crittenden.

Then she got married, had a baby, and left her journalism career to be a mother. In her circles, the reaction was very negative. At a party someone said to her, "Didn't you used to be Ann Crittenden?" Because she had left a very successful career to be a mother, she had supposedly lost her identity. This is modern feminism.

Crittenden wrote a profound book, *The Price of Motherhood: Why the Most Important Job in the World Is Still the Least Valued*. Here's one of its gems: "Mothers themselves often refer to the essence of child-rearing as simply 'being there,' putting one's time at the disposal of another and signaling that the other's needs come ahead of one's own."[136]

Today's world puts the individual at the center: You exist for yourself. You may have a child, but you don't have to be there for the child. You're there for *you*. In many countries daycare facilities are prolific and mothers are encouraged to go back to work in the marketplace as quickly as possible. Many people today are having a single child so they can say, "I had a kid." But they're not functioning as fathers and mothers. The child is just a new toy. When Ann Crittenden turned her back on her career to fully be there for her child, she ceased to exist in the modern world.

As we saw in an earlier chapter, Erica Komisar discovered that too often the root of personal brokenness is an absent mother in the child's early years. Children and mothers are designed for an attachment, a connection vital for the health of the child, as an infant, a teenager, and an adult. Will today's mothers embrace this essential role? Or will they be drawn away from their nurturing by the culture's lies?

An unattributed quote on social media states this wisely:

> The lioness does not try to be the lion. She embraces her role
> as the lioness. She's powerful, strong, and nurturing. She does

not mistake her meekness for weakness. The world needs more kind, humble, faithful, persevering, confident, fierce, bold, pure, and tender-hearted women. The lioness does not look at the lion and say, "I want to be a lion." She celebrates her being a lioness.

Eve is the life-giver. Women and mothers are the nurturers of nations. You may never have a child, but you have been designed to nurture a generation.

—————— STUDY GUIDE ——————

1. Does Wendell Berry's definition of the word "husband" expand the concept beyond simply "a man who has a wife"? What else can this word mean?

2. What is the Cultural Mandate? What are the two subordinating mandates? How do both men and women work to fulfill this mandate?

3. Why does God say that "it is not good for man to be alone"? Doesn't man have everything he needs in God alone?

4. After the Fall, what are the consequences for the man and woman? How does this reflect their original responsibilities before the Fall?

5. How are you impacted by the following quote? "Women are *free* to do whatever they want, but they have been *designed* for one particular purpose."

6. What do the two Greek words the New Testament uses for the idea of "nurturing" mean?

7. Even though modern and postmodern culture do not value the concept of nurturing, why is the work of nurturing incredibly important to the family and the health of a nation?

Section 3

PART 5

Nurturing the Nations

CHAPTER 15

The Hand That Rocks the Cradle

NINETEENTH CENTURY LAWYER and poet William Ross Wallace had the heart of a maternal feminist. His famous 1865 poem, "The Hand That Rocks the Cradle," acknowledged the influence of mothers in shaping, not just children, but the cultures and nations those children will lead. One of the stanzas affirms:

> Woman, how divine your mission
> Here upon our natal sod!
> Keep, oh, keep the young heart open
> Always to the breath of God!
> All true trophies of the ages
> Are from mother-love impearled;
> For the hand that rocks the cradle
> Is the hand that rules the world.[137]

It's a very provocative idea, especially in a generation that does not revere the maternal, that dismisses a mother's role in shaping the lives of children and the future of society.

Only the Judeo-Christian ethic elevates women and motherhood in this way. Sadly, our regard for the maternal has crumbled before the battering ram of pagan sexuality. Pagan sexuality has been normalized around much of the globe. It allows sex between men, sex with multiple partners, sex with children, sex with animals, sex with things. In the postmodern world it has sought to obliterate biology and the concept of binary sexuality. In such a world, the Judeo-Christian concept of human sexuality deviates radically from the norm.

Dennis Prager published an article called "Judaism's Sexual Revolution: Why Judaism (and then Christianity) Rejected Homosexuality" in which he noted the monumental changes in our understanding of sex wrought by biblical faith.

> When Judaism demanded that all sexual activity be channeled into marriage, it changed the world. The Torah's prohibition of non-marital sex quite simply made the creation of Western civilization possible. Societies that did not place boundaries around sexuality were stymied in their development. The subsequent dominance of the Western world can largely be attributed to the sexual revolution initiated by Judaism and later carried forward by Christianity.[138]

Prager's ideas, rooted in his Jewish faith, are foreign to modern and postmodern cultures. He went on:

> This revolution consisted of forcing the sexual genie into the marital bottle. It ensured that sex no longer dominated society, heightened male-female love and sexuality (and thereby almost alone created the possibility of love and eroticism within marriage), and began the arduous task of elevating the status of women.[139]

The Jewish and Christian concept of sexuality marks a dramatic departure from the pagan sexuality so common around the world. Thus the link between a sexual ethic and the regard (or contempt) for the maternal. As author George Gilder says, "The crucial process of civilization is the subordination of male sexual impulses and biology to the long-term horizons of female sexuality."[140]

Generally speaking, the man wants sex without constraints; his biology is wired to a short-term timeframe. A woman's biology and physiology are geared to the long term. A man has sex and walks away; a woman has sex and conceives a baby. Thus begins a nine-month journey and then years of mothering. Only the Judeo-Christian concept of marriage provides stability by harnessing a man's sexual energies into caring for his wife and children.

The pagan culture, by contrast, enables men to sire children without fathering them. A man, focused on immediate pleasure, simply abandons the mother and his child.

All over the world we see the tragedy of unchained male sexuality. In America, many young children are fatherless, the offspring of men whose sexual appetites were unconstrained. A moment of selfish pleasure creates a new human being who will live forever.

But in creating civilization, women transformed male lust into love, channeled wanderlust into jobs, homes, and families, linked men to specific children, reared children into citizens, and changed hunters into fathers. The prime fact of life is the sexual superiority of women.

> When Judaism demanded that all sexual activity be channeled into marriage, it changed the world.
> Dennis Prager

Another force in the West that diminishes the maternal is feminism, which pushes women out of the home and into the marketplace. While many will cheer this development, it is not without significant downsides. Is anyone considering the consequences? Nothing is more important than mothers and children. Suzanne Venker, a maternal feminist, wrote *The Flipside of Feminism*. She calls "working mothers" an absurd and misleading term. Mothers at home work harder than anyone. But according to feminist culture, mothers at home are not working. They are idle.

Erica Komisar notes,

> We have a values dilemma in the United States. We focus on giving our children (and ourselves) things rather than our time, attention, and engagement. We don't want to recognize that raising healthy children requires putting their needs ahead of our own for a time.[141]

In Western feminized culture, the woman's needs are deemed more important than the children's needs. It's supposed to be more important for a mother to be in the workforce than with her children.

Because of the spread of feminist culture and modernism, we assume material things are more important than functioning fathers, mothers, husbands, and wives. Having is better than being. The woman who does not get married, or the couple who doesn't have children, are often captive to today's culture, which regards children as unimportant.

Sadly, the church has conformed to the world. Mary Pride, in her book *The Way Home,* said,

> At every turn, Christian women found that their biological, economic, and social roles were considered worthless. It was men's ministry, men's money, men's buildings and programs. These were the areas that mattered. It wasn't just out there in society, it's that this mentality has come into the life of the church.[142]

Maternal feminists of the second half of the nineteenth century were homemakers and nurturers. This was normal. Feminists understood that their children would someday inherit the world and needed to be prepared. Who would prepare them? The nurturer. They also understood that the home was the foundation for a healthy society. Maternal feminists functioned, consciously or unconsciously, from a biblical worldview.

But this changed. The Judeo-Christian worldview was steadily replaced by the materialistic worldview of atheism. Pride continues:

> The sad truth is that the "traditional" role which feminists attacked in the fifties had already lost its scriptural fullness. Christian women were staying home out of habit, not out of conviction. Women had been robbed of their role, even though they were "in their place." And they were robbed by the church.[143]

The churches in this country had actually paved the way for feminism to succeed, even as preachers orated about the sanctity of motherhood! Denominations endorsed family planning and "therapeutic abortion." Church meetings were scheduled for every night of the week, giving a clear message that family life was unimportant. Ministry was considered more worthwhile than motherhood, and missionaries working abroad were expected to leave their children in boarding schools. Church life centered on the church building, not the home.

Here's one way to contrast maternal feminism and modern, egalitarian feminism: The former builds on a mother's world, the latter on a money world. The mother's world was about care, connectedness, interdependence, and other values necessary for nurturing human beings and building human relationships. The ideal was more mothers at home and fewer in the factories and sweatshops.

MOTHER WORLD VS. MONEY WORLD

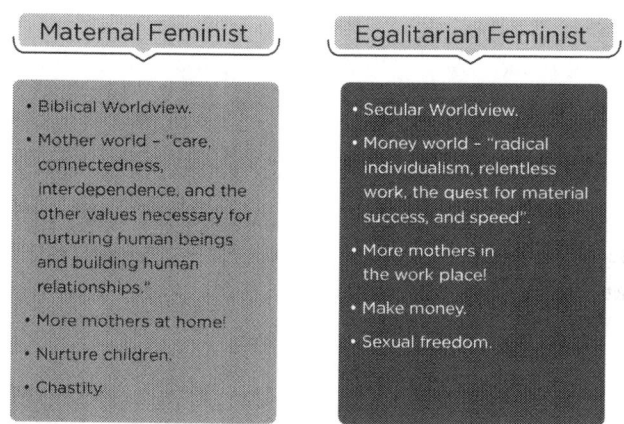

Maternal Feminist

- Biblical Worldview.
- Mother world – "care, connectedness, interdependence, and the other values necessary for nurturing human beings and building human relationships."
- More mothers at home!
- Nurture children.
- Chastity

Egalitarian Feminist

- Secular Worldview.
- Money world – "radical individualism, relentless work, the quest for material success, and speed".
- More mothers in the work place!
- Make money.
- Sexual freedom.

For egalitarian feminists, by contrast, only material things are real, only consumption is important. This is the money world. It's marked by radical individualism, relentless work, and the quest for material success. Egalitarian feminists celebrate more mothers in the workplace, even when children are harmed in the process.

Maternal feminists of the past were interested in being; modern feminists are focused on having. Maternal feminists were interested in ideas, modern feminists in things. Maternal feminists were interested in the future of their children and of society; modern feminists are interested in the present. Maternal feminists were interested in the good of the family, modern feminists in self-fulfillment. Maternal feminists cared about the entire human family; modern feminists cry, "Be true to yourself."

With the shift from a biblical to a secular worldview, the focus shifted from nurture to money, from chastity to sexual freedom. It has moved from women being women, making homes and nurturing children, to women being "men," abandoning hearth and children for an elusive equality in becoming a promiscuous corporate man. This fight for a new world order was led by the egalitarian feminists.

These are two different worldviews. Different ideas produce different outcomes. Daniel Webster, one of the greatest orators of the United States, is quoted in his 1852 speech, saying:

> The mothers of a civilized nation work not on frail and perishable matter, but on the immortal mind, molding and fashioning beings who are to exist forever. They work not on the canvas that shall perish, or the marble that shall crumble into dust, but upon mind, upon spirit, which is to last forever, in which is to bear, for good or evil throughout its duration, the impress of a mother's hand.[144]

The maternal feminists sought to extend their maternal reign in the home into the larger world to create a healthy society for their children. Nellie McClung (1873–1951), another earlier feminist, said, "A woman's place is in the home, and out of it whenever she is called on to guard those she loves and to improve conditions for them."[145] How different in tone and goal from today's feminists!

Maternal feminists sought to help create a society that supported the health of the family and the child. They sought to fight the forces that would undermine the family and destroy the nation. They opposed sweatshops (where women were paid low wages and kept from mothering), child labor (where children were kept from learning), and supported a family wage (so the husband could work, and the wife fulfill her maternal call). They fought for temperance (against the abuses of alcohol, so destructive to the family) and for woman's suffrage (to exercise a maternal voice and vote in the public square).

The maternal feminists were cut from a very different cloth than modern career feminists. They fought not to get women into the workplace, but to get women *out* of the workplace and *into* the home. They wanted a woman to be free to do what she was made to do—nurture a nation.

> The mothers of a civilized nation work not on frail and perishable matter, but on the immortal mind, molding and fashioning beings who are to exist forever. They work not on the canvas that shall perish, or the marble that shall crumble into dust, but upon mind, upon spirit, which is to last forever . . .
> Daniel Webster

A woman's voice, her place, is in the home. But not only in the home. Her voice and leadership are also needed in the marketplace and in the public square. Her voice differs from that of a man's. She speaks into the marketplace as a nurturer for the good of children and the future of coming generations. She reminds the culture of the long term for the things that matter the most.

Lydia Sigourney is the epitome of a maternal feminist. In her 1837 book, *Letters to Young Ladies,* she addresses young women who have a maternal heart, who want to be married and have children to nurture. She tells her readers they need to plan to be a mother. She reminds women of their maternal calling to nurture and educate the future citizens and leaders of the nation.

How different this mindset is! Today, young women give more thought to preparing for a career. Forming a family and being a mother may come later, but only after a successful career is established. By then, the pull of materialist culture may be too strong to overcome.

Sigourney's book, written 200 years ago, is stunning. Consider the opening line:

> "The mind of the present age acting on the mind of the next," as it has been happily defined by a living writer, is an object of concern to every being endowed with intellect, or interested either through love or hope, in another generation.[146]

It's easy to pay lip service about the poor, to express concern about what's happening in the world. But who is *shaping* that world? People who were children thirty, forty, and fifty years ago. And who shaped those children? The hand that rocks the cradle rules the world.

How vital it is to make the connection between two things: motherhood and the future of nations. Sigourney wrote that a mother should be equipped with the best education she is able to receive to enhance her ability to shape the mind and soul of a child. "[T]hey who are to nurture the future rulers of prosperous people," Sigourney continued, "should be able to demonstrate from the broad annals of history the values of just law and the duty of subordination."[147]

We all want a free society. But has a mother been educated to understand how to *build* a free society? She needs to study and think about these things in her youth if she is to be the mother of the next generation.

The health of a nation is rooted in just laws and citizens who subordinate themselves to those laws. Women must value education for themselves and be lifelong learners. They need to learn to think and act from biblical convictions. Women are called to nurture children for the development of a nation.

Tragically, much of the materially impoverished world retains little hope of a future for which to prepare a child in order to build a healthy community and nation. Also, our modern, selfish generation thinks mostly of personal fulfillment. How might I have a child, as conveniently as possible, then put the child in daycare and get back to my career as soon as possible?

In contrast, how might a young woman prepare herself for the high calling of the Cultural Mandate of Genesis 1:26–28? Sigourney's exalted language rings true; women are commissioned to "light the lamp of the soul":

> Is it not requisite, that they on whose bosom the infant heart must be cherished, should be vigilant to watch its earliest pulsations of good and evil?—that they who are commissioned to light the lamp of the soul, should know how to feed it with pure oil?[148]

The mother doesn't just *bear* the child. She is the spark that lights the lamp of the soul. Note the intimacy of the maternal heart and the heart of the child. The mother is to concern herself with the moral development of her young charge. Just as God created the first man and breathed life into him (Genesis 2:7), so the mother who brought her child into the world is to light the lamp of her child's soul. God as creator, nurturer, nourisher, and provider is manifest in the maternal.

Darwinism is wrong. We're not merely animals; we are human beings made in the image of God. A child is conceived to live for eternity. This child will have a name by which God will call him or her. "He calls his own sheep by name and leads them out" (John 10:3, NIV).

The mother lights the lamp of the soul. The natural vocation of females is to teach. Sigourney writes:

> [T]he vocation of females is to teach. . . . It is in the domestic sphere, in her own native province, that woman is inevitably a teacher. . . . Is not the infant in the cradle her pupil? Does

not her smile give the earliest lesson to the soul? Does she not enshrine her own image in the sanctuary of the young child's mind so firmly that no revulsion can displace, no idolatry supplant it?[149]

As we have seen, God has given mother and child a unique intimacy. Sigourney observes again, "Does she not enshrine her own image in the sanctuary of the young child's mind so firmly that no revulsion can displace, no idolatry supplant it?"[150]

These are not accidental aspects of motherhood. They are intentional. That baby is a human being made in the image of God. Which does the baby need: a new toy or a mother's (and father's) presence and nurturing? A mother needs to be intentional about her mothering. This is not a secondary calling, something to do when not pursuing a career. It is what she has been designed and made for. It is her purpose. A mother has the ability to intentionally be present to her child. Sigourney continues,

"Does she not enshrine her own image in the sanctuary of the young child's mind so firmly that no revulsion can displace, no idolatry supplant it?"
Sigourney

> Admitting, then, that whether she wills it or not, whether she even knows it or not, she is still a teacher, and perceiving that the mind in its most plastic state is yielded to her tutelage, it becomes a most momentous inquiry what she shall be qualified to teach. . . . Has she not power to impress her own lineaments on the next generation?[151]

A mother, whether conscious of it or not, will pass on her values, virtues, and vices to the next generation. This is the nature of things. It is her nature to nurture and teach. It is her child's nature to "suck" and learn. But what ethic and knowledge will she pass on? Will she do so intentionally or as an afterthought? What will be her priority, family and children, or the marketplace and consumerism?

Whether mother realizes it or not, she is a teacher. She will teach her children *something*. But does she think about it? Does she plan to be a mother, a nurturer of her child, of nations? Does she prepare her soul and mind to build the leaders of the community, of the next generation, and the nation?

Has she not power to impress her own lineaments on the next generation? Yes, she does. Sigourney writes: "If wisdom and utility have been the objects of her choice, society will surely reap the benefit. If folly and self-indulgence are her prevailing characteristics, posterity are in danger of inheriting the likeness."[152]

Is the mother consciously and intentionally being a mother, preparing herself for motherhood, exercising her nurturing for the good of the family and the nation, or is she slothful in mind and body, just going through life?

For good or ill, the hand that rocks the cradle rules the world.

STUDY GUIDE

1. What did William Ross Wallace indicate by his poem *The Hand That Rocks the Cradle*?
2. According to Dennis Prager, how did Jewish sexual activity change the world? Would you agree or disagree and why?
3. In what ways do feminism and the modern world diminish the maternal instinct in women?
4. How did maternal feminism differ from modern, egalitarian feminism?
5. How is motherhood connected to the future of nations? Consider the graphic "Mothers World vs. Money World." In your own words, what would each world lead to?
6. What is a mother's "natural vocation"? What must a mother know or do to be able to "light the lamp" of her children's souls properly?

CHAPTER 16

The Maternal Nature: Essential for Free Societies and Flourishing Economies

AN ISLAND NATION in Asia, home to 5 million people, is a mere 40 kilometers long by 20 kilometers wide. It was so poor that the government had to buy drinking water from another country. To increase its footprint, the island bought soil from other nations and dumped it on the coastline. Today, that country, Singapore, is the tenth wealthiest country in the world in terms of per capita GDP.[153] With virtually no natural resources and very high population density, Singapore has flourished economically.

How did this happen? In a world of materialistic assumptions, a nation with few natural resources and high population density usually means people are hungry and poor. What can change this reality? Understanding that the primary resource is not in the ground; it is in the hearts and minds of the people.

Who nurtures humans to prepare them for enterprise, to foster an entrepreneurial mind, to take what is in front of them and to do something with it? Mothers! Moms are the engine of a nation's economic development. Ann Crittenden, mentioned earlier in this book, speaks of the price of motherhood:

> The idea that time spent with one's child is time wasted is embedded in traditional economic thinking. The extraordinary talents required to do the long-term work of building human character and capital—human character and instilling in young children the ability and desire to learn have no place in the economist's calculation. Modern economic theory sees no value in a mother. Economic theory has nothing to say about the acquisition of skills by those who work with children. Presumably there are none.[154]

This is the ignorance of modern, materialistic culture. This is the flat-earth view of economics, the manipulation of limited resources. Metaphysical and moral capital are not recognized. A mother's life supposedly has no value; she has nothing to contribute to the economic well-being of the nation unless she puts her children in daycare and enters the workplace.

Modern economic theory sees no value in a mother.
Ann Crittenden

Such economic theory is incredibly blind. In 2021, in purely economic terms, salary.com estimated that stay-at-home moms work more than 90 hours a week and, in the U.S., if paid justly, would earn a "median salary of $184,820."[155] And that does not include what the children she nurtures will contribute! But the culture places zero value on a stay-at-home mom. What skills are required to nurture and raise virtuous and free citizens? What is the value of the mother who uses those skills? In the modern world, presumably there are none. In the biblical framework, they are "beyond rubies."

Maternal nurturing shapes a flourishing economy and political freedom. In the modern world, the nurturer's influence on the marketplace and the public square is unrecognized and unrewarded.

Mothers are often unsung contributors to a nation's economic health.

The Greek word for stewardship of the house is *oikonomia*: governance, stewardship, management of the house. As we have seen, the Cultural

Mandate is to create culture and build godly nations. Men and women have been made stewards to create enterprise, to bring economic flourishing. And women, especially mothers, have a unique and powerful role in that creative process.

In 1 Timothy 5:14, Paul advises young widows to marry, bear children, and manage (*oikodespoteo*) their households. The Greek word *oikodespoteo* means to rule a household, to manage family affairs. This is the role of the woman in the home, to guide the house. We see her virtues and comprehensive skill set pictured in the godly woman of Proverbs 31.

Societies often face two contrasting economic visions. The Greek word *oikonomia* describes the first, which is the management of a household so as to increase its long-term value to all its members. In a financial institution, it means investment, not merely trading. It focuses on benefiting the entire community over the long haul.

CONTRASTING ECONOMIC VISIONS

Oikonomia	Chrematistics
• **Management** of a household so as to **increase its value** to all of its members over the long run.	• **Manipulation** of property and wealth so as to maximize **short-term** exchange values.
• "Investing".	• "Trading".
• Focus on benefiting the community.	• Focus on individual consumption.
• Planted olive trees and built olive press.	• Leased all the olive groves.

Chrematistics, another Greek word, is the opposite of *oikonomia*. *Chrematistics* is the manipulation of property and wealth to maximize short-term value for personal gain. In a more sober time this would be called corruption. Today it is simply the way many people do business. An example is the trader who jumps in and out of the stock market for maximum short-term gain. He's not thinking of the future, not thinking long term, not considering the larger community. He's focused on individual consumption to make as much as he can, as quickly as he can. Too often *chrematistics* is what drives the consumer-oriented economy.

These are two contrasting visions. One of them comes from a biblical paradigm in which we are the stewards of God's house, managing it for the long-term benefit of the community. The other represents a materialistic vision of wealth manipulation for quick selfish returns.

So we have two visions at work. Did you know that three types of capital have also been recognized? They are as follows:

1. Natural capital, such as the raw resources in the ground. This includes minerals and oil, as well as fertile soil and abundant rainfall. These are resources external to the human being. Perhaps 25 percent of a nation's wealth comes from natural capital.[156]
2. Infrastructure, which includes simple assets such as roads, bridges, electrical grids, power generation, and communication systems; and more complex assets such as the legal system, academic institutions, and government.
3. Human capital is the most valuable source of a nation's wealth. Human beings are not, as the evolutionist would say, mouths to be fed. They are the very image of God. Human social relationships, moral capital (virtue), and metaphysical capital of the mind, heart, and worldview comprise untold wealth. Human capital is the source of vision, creative imagination, and critical thinking. This amounts to about 60 percent of the nation's wealth.[157]

Considering that institutional capital is the product of human thought and ingenuity and that human labor builds roads, bridges, and power lines, the World Bank has concluded that "in the wealthiest countries, human capital accounts for three-quarters of the producible forms of wealth."[158] Wealth does not come from the ground. It is the product of human imagination and creativity.

The fact is, African nations, plus some places in Latin America and South America, are vastly wealthier in natural resources and human potential. But too many people in their societies think that development must come from the outside. Somebody *else's* resources have to come here, or we will always be poor. This lie is grounded in materialism. I've seen this firsthand through forty years of international development work: "The poor will always be poor, so we must bring resources from the outside." But the source of the nation's wealth is not primarily external and not in the ground. It's the people themselves who are the greatest resource.

And what is most needed to develop a society's human capital? It's parents, with a significant focus on conscientious mothers!

It is absurd to suggest that stay-at-home moms bring no value to a society.

At a recent State of the Union address, the dual chambers of the U.S. House and the Senate, of a horribly divided Congress, gave the president a standing ovation. What brought them together? His statement that the country now had more women in the workforce than at any time in history!

Is this worth a standing ovation? What's the other side of that coin? More children are without a mother present. In the past the problem has been "fatherless children," children whose fathers have abandoned them or who were seldom home. Now, it is often "motherless children" because their mother has joined the father in the marketplace. Parentless children are raised in daycare, by public schools, or in "the hood," resulting in the child being robbed of much of her or his God-given potential. It means fewer families being formed and fewer children being born. *Chrematistics* at a national level leads to short-term outlooks and narcissistic individuals. Too often this can lead to a nation's suicide.

> **Wealth does not come from the ground. It is the product of human imagination and creativity.**

Crittenden speaks prophetically to culture: "Without conscientious mothers, there would be no economic man. . . . Conscientious mothers motivated by feelings of compassion and love, nurture, protect and train children for adulthood."[159]

Unless women nurture children, economic man will disappear. Yet we place no value on motherhood in the West. Conscientious mothers are the contemporary practitioners of *oikonomia*, the building and preserving of long-term communal value that used to be the essence of economics.

So much of life in the West is about consumption. Without a future orientation, everything is consumed, and nations shrivel and die. Gratification is immediate rather than delayed. We make selfish, short-term economic decisions that fail to account for the future of a community and a generation. This is Carl Trueman's expressive individualism.

Crittenden says, "If most of our national prosperity reflects the productivity of our human capital, then the people who provide primary care to children are the single most important source of our most valuable economic asset. . . . Put another way, conscientious mothers are key players in the drama of economic growth, the stars who never receive top billing."[160]

Such irony.

Every mother needs to be conscientiously mothering. Not just having babies, but taking the maternal heart of God seriously, engaging fully as a nurturer of her children. These are the people who will create the conditions for the long-term economic flourishing of nations. Few people today appreciate the maternal influence on the economy.

Which leads us to the second matter, the influence of the maternal in governance.

Mothers also influence the public square, by encouraging virtue and self-governance in their children. We're either governed internally by virtue or externally by government. Who prepares the heart and soul of a free people to govern themselves internally based on God's laws and ordinances? Mothers have a primary role.

American statesman Robert Winthrop made the distinction between freedom and tyranny very clear:

> All societies of men must be governed in some way or other. The less they may have of stringent State Government, the more they must have of *individual self-government.* The less they rely on public law or physical force, the more they must rely on private moral restraint. Men, in a word, must necessarily be controlled, *either by a power within them, or by a power without them; either by the word of God, or by the strong arm of man; either by the Bible, or by the bayonet.*[161] [emphasis added]

If we do not practice individual self-government, only a heavy-handed government will maintain order, whether in the United States, or any other nation. In the United States and other nations, we are witnessing a rise of incivility and lawlessness that is paving the way for more and more laws. That's because moral and spiritual decay leads to the need for more and more laws, more police to enforce those laws, and more courts and prisons to address the violation of those laws.

Order is the first need of any nation. The kingdom ethos lays a foundation for building free, just, prosperous, and compassionate societies, which glorify God in their obedience and allow the glory of the nation to be revealed.

A mother shapes children into adults. If she is wise and good, she will likely shape responsible adults. If she is blessed to live in a free republic, she can shape responsible citizens. She cultivates the minds and hearts of her children. In doing so, she helps to build the next generation of leaders. A free society is established by the character and the teaching of the conscientious mother.

With only a third-grade education, at age thirteen Sonya Carson married a twenty-eight-year-old man, birthing two boys in Detroit. Even though she could not read, Sonya insisted her sons become readers and apply themselves in school. Her older son, Curtis, became a mechanical engineer living in Georgia. Her younger son, Ben, became a world-renowned pediatric neurosurgeon, the first doctor to successfully separate twins conjoined at the head. In 2016, he was a candidate for president of the United States. Ben says, "I not only saw and felt the difference my mother made in my life, I am still living out that difference as a man."[162]

> **Men, in a word, must necessarily be controlled, either by a power within them, or by a power without them; either by the word of God, or by the strong arm of man; either by the Bible, or by the bayonet.**
> **Robert Winthrop**

I first heard about self-government from Elizabeth Youmans. At the time I was in my late fifties. I had always thought self-government was simply the concept of democracy, people governing themselves through democratic elections. Dr. Youmans used familiar words in her lecture, but she was talking about concepts I had never encountered. Here's how she puts it.

The Christian principle of self-government is God ruling internally from the heart of the believer. In order to have true liberty, man must willingly or voluntarily be governed internally by the Spirit and the Word of God rather than by external forces.[163]

Government must begin on the inside. Only then can it extend outwardly into all of life. One cannot change a nation without changing oneself. One cannot govern a nation without first governing oneself.

A quote sometimes attributed to Dutch lawyer and theologian Hugo Grotius described the concept of internal self-government convincingly:

> He knows not how to rule a kingdom, that cannot manage a province; nor can he wield a province, that cannot order a city; nor he order a city, that knows not how to regulate a village. Nor he a village, that cannot guide a family; nor can that man govern well a family that knows not how to govern himself; neither can any govern himself unless reason be lord, will and appetite her vassal; nor can reason rule unless herself be ruled by God, and (wholly) obedient to him.[164]

The more internal self-government a person and nation possess, the more freedom they have (less external government). Freedom flows from the internal to the external. Government is, or may be, employed at the following levels:

- Global
- National
- State
- City
- Family
- Individual

If power flows from the top down, tyranny is the result. Think of North Korea today. On the other hand, self-governing citizens have freedom, and their national government, which derives its authority from the people, is limited.

James Madison, father of the U.S. Constitution, wrote that the Founders of the American system of government had decided "to rest all our political experiments on the capacity of mankind for self-government."[165] The reason the United States is devolving into chaos is that we no longer understand the concept of self-government. We are becoming a lawless people. This is not a new phenomenon. British Statesman and Philosopher Edmund Burke wrote,

> Men are qualified for civil liberty in exact proportion to their disposition to put moral chains upon their own appetites. . . . Society cannot exist, unless a controlling power be placed

somewhere. . . . It is ordained in the eternal constitution of things that men of intemperate minds cannot be free. Their passions forge their fetters.[166]

We either discipline ourselves and live as free men and women, or we allow our passions to dominate us. Which outcome we find is largely determined by parents. If the children of a society are nurtured, they can learn self-governance, and become free and virtuous citizens. Daniel Webster wrote, "It is generally admitted that public liberty, and the perpetuity of a free constitution, rest on the virtue and intelligence of the community which enjoys it."[167]

How is virtue to be inspired? How is intelligence to be communicated? Mothers are the affectionate and effective teachers of the human race. The hand that rocks the cradle is the hand that rules the world. The mother who teaches and nurtures her children shapes the future of the nation toward economic prosperity and political freedom.

Alexis de Tocqueville spent the year of 1831 traveling and observing American life. In 1835, he wrote the classic *Democracy in America.* Toward the end of the book, he said that American women are superior to women anywhere else. But what Tocqueville observed in American women is not exclusive to America. Wherever feminine distinctives are upheld, wherever motherhood is championed, we see strong families and enduring freedom.

> Men are qualified for civil liberty in exact proportion to their disposition to put moral chains upon their own appetites. . . . Society cannot exist, unless a controlling power be placed somewhere. . . . It is ordained in the eternal constitution of things that men of intemperate minds cannot be free. Their passions forge their fetters.
> Edmund Burke

From 2015–2018, Big Ocean Women, a group of "maternal feminists" gave six presentations to the United Nations Commission on the Status of Women defending motherhood, of all things. Their organization advocates for the necessity of women being women and not trying to be men.

As women, we are distinct and different from men. Our contributions, however, are equally valuable and essential. It is with confidence that we claim and embrace our unique feminine nature and biology. We believe that every woman who has the best interest of the rising generation at heart, and willingly gives of herself to nourish and protect the rising generation, is a mother.[168]

> **Mothers are, indeed, the affectionate and effective teachers of the human race.**
> **Daniel Webster**

What contributed to the United States becoming a nation of unparalleled political freedom and economic prosperity? Many factors, no doubt. But one very powerful factor was the influence of nurturing mothers who understood their God-given role as shapers of a nation. As American statesman Daniel Webster put it:

It is generally admitted that public liberty, and the perpetuity of a free constitution, rest on the virtue and intelligence of the community which enjoys it. How is that virtue to be inspired, and how is that intelligence to be communicated? . . . Mothers are, indeed, the affectionate and effective teachers of the human race.[169]

STUDY GUIDE

1. There are two very different economic visions that will produce two very different nations. Look at the characteristics of each. How would you describe the social and economic outcomes of each vision for a nation?
2. Which vision is better at developing human capital?
3. What is a nation's greatest source of wealth? Why does intentional or vocational motherhood lead to the flourishing of a nation? What tends to happen when the mother enters the "workforce" and leaves her children to be raised by others? In what ways do mothers have a primary influence in the public square?
4. What does the concept of "self-government" refer to? What did Edmund Burke say intemperate people are chained by?

5. What remark did Alexis Tocqueville make about American women in the nineteenth century? If what was true then has ceased to be true today, what could be the result?

CHAPTER 17

Making a House
a Home

MY FRIEND BOB Moffitt and I were leading a conference of mission leaders, composed of about fifty men and women from five states. As we began, we asked those in attendance to share who they were, where they were from, and what they were doing. The last person to speak was a young woman in the back who gave her name and said, "I am only a mother."

I was stunned. "Only a mother! Did you hear that?" I asked the group.

This event was hosted by a mission organization that believes in the family, but believes in ministry more. This woman was caring for her children but wasn't in "ministry." So she obviously felt less valued than someone who was in "full-time ministry."

No one is *only* a mother. Nothing in life is more important than being a mother.

Another time I spent a week in Peru with about two hundred men and women and taught on "The Dignity of Women." During the week, a woman came to me and asked why I was talking so much about doing dishes, sweeping floors, and changing diapers. I hadn't talked about those things all week, but she heard me saying "a woman does housework." The strong impact of sexist culture had shaped her understanding of what a woman was to do, and she had assumed that I was advocating the same.

Sexists promote and feminists decry the picture of a barefoot, pregnant woman, enslaved to her mate and imprisoned in her house. The modern feminist movement defines Western culture today. Tragically, the art of transforming a house into a home is too radical an idea for either the sexist or the feminist to understand or appreciate. So, to be clear about the dignity and worth of a woman who intentionally stays home to create a flourishing environment for her family, we would do well to think in terms not of housekeeping but of the "art" of homemaking.

To get there, we must think differently about the nature of a home and the making of a home. A *house* is not a home. A house is a physical place of brick and mortar or wood and sheetrock or adobe and plaster. A *home* is a space, a transcendent place where life occurs, and human beings may flourish. *Housekeeping* is a "flat earth" view of life. It is the concept of a home stripped of its heart, its transcendent nature removed.

At the heart of modern feminism is the goal of removing the homemaker from the home and reducing the transcendent to the material and mundane. It is replacing the maternal glory with a job and a paycheck. As maternal feminist Suzanne Venker says in her book, *The Flip Side of Feminism*,

> Women on the left were motivated by ideological, not eco-nomic, reasons. First, they wanted to achieve independence from men. Second, they wanted to eliminate the full-time homemaker from society. Their purpose was not equality or opportunity for women in the marketplace. Feminists simply wanted to make marriage and motherhood unchic.[170]

It's not cool to be married, to be a mother, to make a home. Political science Professor Nancy Hirschman, a modern feminist, wrote, "[Women who change their children's diapers] have voluntarily become untouchables."[171]

Modern feminism is blind to the art of making a home. Both sexists and modern feminists reduce homemaking to mere housekeeping. According to Betty Friedan, author of *The Feminine Mystique*, "A baked potato is not as big as the world, and vacuuming the living-room floor—with or without makeup—is not work that takes enough thought or energy to challenge any woman's full capacity."[172]

Lydia Sigourney, the maternal feminist from 200 years ago, said a moth-er's calling encompasses far deeper things than baking potatoes and sweep-ing the floor. It involves the study of history, law, and other subjects, and "the structure and development of mind" as mothers "nurture the future rulers of a prosperous nation."[173]

These are two different visions stemming from two very different worldviews.

We're talking about homemaking, not housekeeping. Of *course* mothers (and fathers) change diapers. But the maternal vision provides a larger context for the changing of diapers. It is just part of the larger picture of the care and nurture of a living soul, a one-of-a-kind human being entrusted to a mother's care. Changing diapers is certainly *part* of what a mother does (and in our house a father did, too!). But let's not forget that providing a baby with a clean diaper can be done to the glory of God as an act of worship!

Edith Schaeffer wrote a book called *The Hidden Art of Homemaking*. Edith and her husband, Francis, were a remarkable couple who founded L'Abri Fellowship. Truth seekers (including Marilyn and me) from all over the world came to this place of intellectual hospitality. There they found not only a place to find answers to their questions, but a home to make them feel welcome and cared for.

Edith had transformed a house into a beautiful, welcoming home. Breakfast would last forty-five minutes, lunches an hour and a half, dinners two and a half. The meal wasn't simply fuel for the body but a time of conversation, of feeding the soul. When you arrived in a home at L'Abri, you were welcomed into a space not just into a building. There were always candles on the table. In the spring and summer, fresh flowers graced the table. Classical music played in the background. L'Abri was a place of warm conversation, where anyone could bring questions.

Not everyone knows how to create a home. While living in Switzerland, my wife and I traveled from L'Abri to Vienna to visit an organization smuggling Bibles and Christian literature behind the Iron Curtain. This was at the height of the Cold War. We experienced a stark difference in the level of hospitality. In Vienna, pots were put on the table straight from the stove, and we ate off plastic plates. The food was neither attractive nor healthy, but it was quick, something like Spam or K-rations in the army. The ministry motto was "We are at war." There was neither time nor money to create a welcoming space and good meals.

It wasn't simply a matter of stewardship, however. Neither L'Abri nor this group had much money. But they possessed two very different mentalities. On the one hand, one just threw everything on the table and ate off plastic. On the other, L'Abri was a haven to celebrate beauty and life, even at the table.

God is beautiful. He is love. He exercises hospitality. How do we manifest God's character and his nature in the spaces where we live? Or do we simply keep a house (or maybe not even do that)? Those are two very different things.

Many young people are eagerly listening to Jordan Peterson, a Canadian psychologist and best-selling author, because he is pursuing the truth for which they are hungry. He writes,

> If you want to change the world you start with yourself and work outward because you build your competence that way . . . if you can't even clean up your own room, who the hell are you to give advice to the world?[174]

Peterson makes a powerful point, but a limited one. We are not only to bring order to a home, as he suggests, but beauty. A home should be a welcoming place of grace. A home is much more than a place to sleep and eat and sit in front of the television and play with our electronic devices.

God is beautiful. He is love. He exercises hospitality. How do we manifest God's character and his nature in the spaces where we live?

Unfortunately, the glory of the mother and homemaker in Proverbs 31 is largely forgotten in today's cultural battle—which manifests itself even in the church. The clear instruction in two New Testament passages for nurturing and homemaking is too often ignored, or even belittled, by God's people.

The first is 1 Timothy 5:9–10; 14 (NIV):

> No widow may be put on the list of widows unless she is over sixty, has been faithful to her husband, and is well known for her good deeds, such as bringing up children, showing hospitality, washing the feet of the Lord's people, helping those in trouble and devoting herself to all kinds of good deeds.
>
> So I counsel younger widows to marry, to have children, to manage their homes and to give the enemy no opportunity for slander.

It describes the characteristics of a godly older widow:

- faithful to her husband
- well known for good deeds
- bringing up children
- showing hospitality
- washing the feet of the saints
- helping those in trouble
- devoted to doing good deeds

These verses also describe the conduct of the younger widow. She is called to:

- marry
- have children
- manage her home

Younger widows are to marry, have children, and "manage their homes." Note the two subsidiary elements of the Cultural Commission in Genesis 1. The young widow is to marry and have children ("be fruitful and multiply," the social commission) and manage her home ("rule," the developmental commission).

The Greek word for "manage their homes," *oikodespoteo*, means to guide the house, to manage family affairs. This word is related to *oikonomia*, "to steward the house." The word "economics" is derived from this Greek word. Genesis 1:26–28 comprises the Cultural Commission for the stewardship of God's house and establishes human beings as *homo economicus*, Latin for economic man.

The woman is not a slave; she is queen of the house with incredible opportunities and corresponding responsibilities. She's the maker of the home, an environment conducive to the health of the family, especially the children, and the guests in the home. Younger women are to turn the home into a welcoming and flourishing space. The woman is the queen of the manor, the person in authority, the governor of the house.

This truth is expanded in Proverbs 31:10, "A wife of noble character who can find?

She is worth far more than rubies" (NIV). Proverbs 31 pictures the virtues and skills of the woman who manages her household. She's a vital part of the community. She's the maker of a home, queen of the manor, a vice-regent of creation.

Proverbs 31 does not portray every woman but rather shows a model for godly traits, some of which an individual woman may possess. So these do not represent the ideal standard that every woman should strive to reach, but the kinds of traits that a woman may possess.

Proverbs 31 lists both virtues and skills.

The virtues include:

- Her reputation (31:12, 31)
- Discernment (31:13, 16)
- Work ethic (31:15, 17, 18b, 27b)
- Entrepreneurial nature (31:16, 24)
- Profitability (31:18)
- Compassion (31:20)

Her virtues include her reputation, discernment, work ethic, entrepreneurial nature, profitability, and compassion. She is prepared for the future. She has personal strength, dignity, and wisdom. She fears the Lord.

She also has skills. This woman invests in agriculture. She is skilled in interior design, weaving, sewing, sales, communication, education and instruction, and management and parenting. By these virtues and skills, she transforms four walls and a roof into a thriving place to live.

When Betty Friedan says that "vacuuming the living-room floor—with or without makeup—is not work that takes enough thought or energy to challenge any woman's full capacity," she reveals her ignorance of the high calling and capacity of a woman to make a home and nurture the next generation.[175] Modern, radical feminists have discounted the creators of homes and the conceivers and nurturers of children to be simply "housekeepers."

A second "dismissed" passage is Titus 2:3–5:

> Older women likewise are to be reverent in behavior, not slan-
> derers or slaves to much wine. They are to teach what is good,
> and so train the young women to love their husbands and
> children, to be self-controlled, pure, working at home, kind,
> and submissive to their own husbands, that the word of God
> may not be reviled.

Implied in "caring for the house" or "working at home" is artfully and mindfully working to make a well-ordered home that will serve the family and become the founding order for a healthy society.

Note that these passages are addressed to church leaders about women. Women are to minister to other women, to teach them about motherhood and homemaking. As women tend to be more relational than men, older woman mentoring younger women is a very natural function. This responsibility was not given to husbands or pastors to do for women but for women to do for women.

Older women are to mentor younger women because the latter will become nurturers of nations. This is more than sweeping and doing dishes. Keeping the house is part of being a homemaker, but homemaking is an art that requires *all* the virtue and skill a human can possess. A homemaker transforms four walls into a place where children can be nourished, a husband can rest, and friends can gather.

> Admitting, then, that whether she wills it or not, whether she even knows it or not, she is still a teacher, and perceiving that the mind in its most plastic state is yielded to her tutelage, it becomes a most momentous inquiry what she shall be qualified to teach. . . . Has she not power to impress her own lineaments on the next generation?
> Sigourney

What happens to this God-ordained function when women are busy trying to be men?

As noted earlier, Lydia Sigourney says:

> That the vocation of females is to teach, has been laid down as a position, which it is impossible to controvert. . . . It is in the domestic sphere, in her own native province, that woman is inevitably a teacher. . . . Is not the infant in its cradle, her pupil? Does not her smile give the earliest lesson to its soul? . . . Does she not enshrine her own image in the sanctuary of the young child's mind so firmly that no revulsion can displace, no idolatry supplant it?[176]

A woman is an educator. A mother's teaching begins with her "being there" to smile at her child in the cradle. The child's mind is unfolding and unformed. The mother forms her own image in the sanctuary of her child's unfolding and unformed mind.

It is not only the physical actions of homemaking and being present in the home that informs her child; it also includes her conscious effort to edify herself to be the educator of her child. It is worth repeating what Sigourney wrote:

> Admitting, then, that whether she wills it or not, whether she even knows it or not, she is still a teacher, and perceiving that the mind in its most plastic state is yielded to her tutelage, it becomes a most momentous inquiry what she shall be qualified to teach. . . . Has she not power to impress her own lineaments on the next generation?[177]

So let us encourage women to transform a house into a home. Homemaking is an art. It will take all the creativity a person can muster to turn four walls into a living space where children are nurtured and strangers are welcomed, where a family can grow. This is a lost art in the modern and postmodern world. How badly we need to recover it.

How would a woman rearrange her priorities if she truly believed she had the opportunity to prepare her children for life and flourishing and leadership in their generation? I'm sure of one thing: She would never feel that "I'm only a mother."

———— STUDY GUIDE ————

1. What is the difference between housekeeping and homemaking? What one thing could you do today to make your house more of a home?
2. What is at the heart of making a house a home?
3. What stands out to you about Paul's description of older and younger widows in 1 Timothy 5?
4. Who does Titus 2 say is responsible for mentoring young women? How does this happen in your local community or church?
5. How would a father and mother rearrange their priorities if

they understood that they were in a position to make their home a place where their children are instilled with virtue, educated, and nurtured in order to become leaders in their generation?

CHAPTER 18

The Home: Where Nations Are Nurtured

TOO OFTEN IN the modern/postmodern world, we make the state responsible for our children's education. But the state is not responsible for children's education. Parents are. Parents may delegate to others, but a profound responsibility rests with mothers and fathers to educate their children if they want those children to live as free women and men. The legacy of a free society is at stake. The home is the nursery of the nations.

Wise parents take responsibility for the education of their children. They work to lay a solid foundation for their lives and for the leadership they will provide in the community and nation as mature adults. The Bible clearly lays this responsibility on parents' shoulders. This principle of the parents' role is seen in Proverbs 4:1; 6:20; 23:22.

Proverbs 22:6 reiterates this responsibility for the parents: "Train up a child in the way he should go; even when he is old he will not depart from it." This is further exemplified in Deuteronomy 4:9; 6:4–7; 11:19; and Ephesians 6:1–4.

> The home is the nursery of the nations.

While each parent has a distinct role in this process, the woman by nature is the nurturer of her children. Women, despised by sexists and

213

feminists, are the nurturers of nations. Sexists see them merely as pleasure objects, feminists as producers and consumers of things. But they are
nurturers made in God's image, and this is their glory. Sadly, that glory
is lost to sexist and feminist culture. We need to reclaim the dignity of
women and understand their place not only in shaping their families, but
the future leaders of a society.

During the era of the maternal feminist, President Theodore Roosevelt
wisely said:

> The service of the good mother to society is the most valuable
> economic asset that the entire commonwealth can show, and
> is of infinitely more worth to society than any possible service
> the woman could render by any other, and necessarily inferior,
> form of industry.[178]

The Greek word *pedia* is translated as both "nurture" and "education."
The cornerstones of *pedia*, as education, are the sciences, the arts, and ethics.
These mimic God's kingdom culture of truth, beauty, and goodness. The
same words capture a profound truth about the maternal: The mother is
a nurturer and a teacher. She is the first to light the lamp of the soul and the first to teach her children. Let's consider some of the implications of the mother's role as teacher.

"Every child has a name. Every child has a purpose. Every child has a story, his or her own story, and every child has a place in His story."
Elizabeth Youmans

My dear friend Elizabeth Youmans has taught preschool, has taught at the university level, has started schools, and has also written an incredible curriculum about the principle approach to education. Elizabeth says, "Every child has a name. Every child has a purpose. Every child has a story, his or her own story, and every child has a place in His story."

God intends that every human's personal story becomes connected with
His story. Each child is unique. The modern educational system, however,
functions as one-size-fits-all. It glosses over the diversity of children, mostly
failing to teach them how to think and reason. Instead, we're teaching them
by rote to memorize and regurgitate facts and to uncritically absorb what-

ever worldview the education establishment wishes to present. State-sponsored schooling is more about indoctrination than education.

Another educator friend who teaches worldview has asked Christian parents, "Would you send your child to a Hindu school? A Buddhist school? An animistic school?" Their answer is always a clear "No!" When he asks, "Would you send your children to an atheist school?" The parents often get a puzzled look on their faces. Most send their children to atheistic schools—public schools. Public schools are founded on an atheistic premise and framework. They teach your children that there is no God, no Creator, that we are not made with a purpose but are merely the products of an accidental process. They indoctrinate our children in evolutionism and increasingly in comprehensive sex education—CSE, transgenderism, equity math, critical race theory. No Christian parent wants that, but what will they do instead?[179]

They must teach them to think and act as informed Christians who will function from a biblical worldview and live virtuously. For this to happen, parents, and especially mothers, must educate themselves. As Madame Steinberg stated in her 1855 "Lecture on Female Education":

> How highly cultivated then should the mind of that individual be, on whom devolves the sacred office of "training the child in the way in which it should walk!" What unlimited importance must be the formation of her character, the development of her energies, the right direction of her principles, and opinions?[180]

If a mother is to be the educator of free people, how important is *her* education? She must know more than how to vacuum floors and wash dishes, as noble as this kind of activity may be. She is called to be engaged in home *making*, creating an atmosphere where children can thrive. As Sigourney points out:

> Of what unspeakable importance, then, is *her* education, who gives lessons before any other instructor; who pre-occupies the unwritten page of being; who produces impressions which only death can obliterate; and mingles with the cradle-dream what shall be read in eternity. Well may statesmen

and philosophers debate how *she* may be best educated, who
is to educate all mankind.[181]

Here is a critical and expansive question: "How may she be best educated, who is to educate all mankind?" Many societies assume that a girl
does not need an education. After all, she simply stays home to clean, cook,
have babies, and change diapers. At most, she needs to learn to read and
write. Such a view, however, is fundamentally mistaken. This young mother
will shape the next generation. What an incredible vision of motherhood!
How important is the female of our species! The mother's education is
of prime significance because she will be teaching her child long before
anyone else does. She shapes the first impression and sets the dreams that
will be read in eternity.

My good friend and co-laborer Bob Moffitt likes to say that each child
has been born to "write his or her signature on the universe." It is the
mother who sets the child free to write on the universe. But what will the
child write?

The mother teaches her child by her whole demeanor, from the very
time of breastfeeding. As her milk gives nutrients for physical growth, so
her life and character give moral, spiritual, and intellectual instruction so
the child may reach his or her God-given call. What a contrast to a culture
that puts children in daycare so the mother may focus on her career! In
such an arrangement, who shapes the dreams of that child? Today, mothers
find their fulfillment, not in shaping the destiny of nations, but in the mere
marketplace. How sad. Instead of receiving the mother's time and nurture,
the child receives *things*, products that money can buy, mind-numbing toys,
video games, and videos.

Here is a call for women to attain the highest educational preparation.
This is not a call for women to be experts in a limited field of knowledge, to
know a lot about less and less. Quite the contrary. She must know something about everything. John Amos Comenius (1592–1670) was a Czech
leader who thought deeply about the role of education in transforming
society. During the Reformation, most of the world was poor and unedu-
cated. The Reformers understood that all people, young and old, male and
female, rich and poor, needed to be educated for a nation to be lifted out of
ignorance and poverty. Comenius led the movement to educate the masses.
He was known as the "father of modern education."

Comenius articulated a thought that would change the world: the "pan-sophic principle" that everything must be taught to everyone.[182]

This Reformation movement led to two educational principles that have helped to build free, just, and flourishing societies. "Everything must be taught" is the concept of a *unified field of knowledge*. People should study broadly. And what they study needs to be integrated. Each subject is to be related to every other subject. You do not study music without understanding its roots in math. You don't study history without studying geography, etc. In the West, this approach is often called the Liberal Arts.

The second principle is that everything must be taught to *everyone*. This is the concept of *universal education*. Most countries today would affirm this principle, but not all countries practice it. The principle implies that all children, no matter their economic or social background or sex, need to be taught, especially if they are going to be citizens of a free and prosperous society.

> **Everything must be taught to everyone.**
> **John Amos Comenius**

Women are born to be nurturers. What kind of an education ought a woman to have to be able to fulfill her calling to be the first, and perhaps foremost, educator of her children?

Here's a call for women to think broadly, outside the box, to be creative. Women have the incredible opportunity to shape the life of a child, and not just the life of the child. They will shape the life of the future, of the community, and of the nation. Paula Giddings, an African-American historian, says, ". . . it was my mother who gave me voice. She did this, I know now, by clearing a space where my words could fall, grow, then find their way to others."[183] Yes, *all* women (whether mothers or not) are nurturers and have the ability to create a space for people, for children, to gain their voices.

A mother can teach, for example, the importance of diligence. As Sigourney said, "Sloth and luxury must have no place in her vocabulary."[184] Earlier in our marriage, my wife was consulting with young, poor mothers about breastfeeding. One day she entered a house and found it dark inside. The drapes were pulled and the great grandmother, the grandmother, the mother, and a newborn girl—four generations—were sitting on a couch watching television. The vision of the maternal in this house was watching television.

"Sloth and luxury must have no place in her vocabulary. Her youth should be surrounded by every motive to application, and her maturity dignified by the hallowed office of rearing the immortal mind."[185]

Young women must be pointed to the rigor of their high calling. The mind and character of the present generation will determine the mind and character of the next. Thus the natural human tendency to idleness or opulence must be fought.

A young woman should receive the best education and its practical application. Such training is not merely about cramming facts into one's head to pass tests. True education must work toward wisdom, the godly application of the knowledge learned.

Why all this care and preparation to be a mother? Because the task is not merely feeding children or supplying them with toys and entertainment. Every child has an immortal soul that will shape eternity. That child's ideas can shape the destiny of nations. Motherhood is an awesome and holy calling!

The mother has a sacred office; she is rearing an immortal human being. This truth should shape our lives. Let us turn a deaf ear to the words of sexist culture and feminist culture. Let us hear the words of the Trinitarian culture that speak of the dignity of women and the hallowed place of their lives as the nurturers of children.

Suzanne Venker, in *The Flip Side of Feminism*, says this:

> Today when we talk about power, we're referring to money and status. That makes sense, for this kind of power reflects modern values. In the past, when marriage and family took center stage, women were exalted on the home front. Husbands deferred to wives on virtually all household matters, including child rearing. Women were revered for their unique sensibilities.[186]

At one time women were revered *as women*, revered for nurturing and teaching the next generation. Today's culture, however, virtually spits on women who want to be home and nurture their children. There is no place for them in modern, materialistic society. Some opinion-shapers advance the argument that a woman should be forced into the marketplace, that it is slothful to stay home and be a mother because she isn't contributing to society. That's preposterous!

Against this kind of anti-woman feminism, Sigourney writes that the home is a place of privilege for wives and mothers, saying, "While her partner toils for his stormy portion of that power or glory, from which it is her privilege to be sheltered . . ."[187] While the husband must toil in this stormy world, she is sheltered.

Note, the husband is not her tyrant. He is her servant. She is protected, not for a life of ease, but for the critical task of nurturing the future citizens of the nation. The mother has queenly powers to shape the destiny of a child in the name of the God who caused this child to be born.

As she concludes her essay on education, Sigourney speaks of a commission for women to fulfill their calling:

> And now, Guardians of Education, whether parents, preceptors, or legislators—you who have so generously lavished on woman the means of knowledge—complete your bounty by urging her to gather its treasures with a tireless hand. Demand of her as a debt the highest excellence which she is capable of attaining. Summon her to abandon selfish motives and inglorious ease. Incite her to those virtues which promote the permanence and health of nations. Make her accountable for the character of the next generation. Give her solemn charge in the presence of men and angels. Gird her with the whole armour of education and piety, and see if she be not faithful to her children, to her country, and to her God.[188]

For a nation to survive and flourish requires the virtue of motherhood. Without this, its citizens will not have the requisite character, knowledge, and wisdom to govern a just and prosperous society. The role of the mother is to form character in her children. From the wellspring of character will come, as we have seen, internal self-government. A well-ordered home will contribute to a well-ordered society.

A well-ordered home will contribute to a well-ordered society.

We must create the space for women to be all God intended them to be: nurturers of nations, shapers of those who will shape the nations. This is so because the parents, not the state, bear responsibility for bringing up children. As Sigourney notes, "[T]he strength of a nation, especially of a republican nation [a republic] is in the intelligent and well-ordered homes of the people."[189]

STUDY GUIDE

1. How would you respond to the statement: "The home is the nursery of the nations"?

2. Why does Madame Steinberg say a woman's education is important even if she never holds a job in the marketplace?

3. Is education merely a matter of gaining knowledge and marketable skills, or is something deeper required?

4. John Amos Comenius, the Czech Reformer was the "Father of Modern Education." He famously said, "Everything must be taught to everyone!" What are the implications of this for education at home or for the larger community?

5. Suzanne Venker writes, "Today, when we talk about power, we're referring to money and status." How would Jesus define power instead?

6. Why has the state taken over more and more of the family's responsibility for educating our children? What are the consequences of this?

CHAPTER 19

Women as Leaders: Bringing Wholeness to Society

IN MY YEARS of lecturing about the dignity of women, I've been asked a lot of questions. About 90 percent of the time, the first question is, "What do you think about women in leadership?" As we begin to answer that question, I urge you to keep in mind all that you have read so far, along with a popular saying: "In essentials, unity. In non-essentials, liberty. And in all things, charity."

Rejecting modern feminism, which recognizes no limits to women in leadership, and sexist culture, which allows no place for women in leadership, I will promote a countercultural alternative that reflects the Trinity.

Christians grappling with this question cannot help but notice that Jesus Christ brought a profound change to the Jewish and Roman cultures of His day. He was the first feminist. He who created women recognized in His life and teaching that men and women are equal in dignity. Their distinct functions are also equally valued. Matthew, Mark, and Luke mention women in 112 distinct passages. This was unheard of in ancient literature.

Paul's letters also achieve this balance of attention to men and women. In Romans, Paul sends personal greetings to 15 women and 18 men. In chapter 16, he mentions seven women by name, not a common feature in letters of that day. He even names Priscilla before Aquila in Romans 16:3, something totally unheard of in the culture. Paul likely offended many Jews by regarding women as fellow saints and free-thinking coworkers.

Jesus certainly offended many Jews by openly treating women with dignity. In fact, Jesus took it much further. Consider this question: Why did Jesus die on the cross? To redeem us? To reconcile us to God? To open heaven to us? Yes, to all of those. But Jesus also died as a troublemaker, in part because of the open respect He gave women, the way He addressed them, how they related to Him and He to them. Women were part of Christ's kingdom mission team (Matthew 27:55–56; Mark 15:40–41; Luke 8:1–3). He also made them heroes in His stories (Matthew 12:42; 15:28; Luke 4:26). All this certainly caused great ire among the Jewish authorities.

The equality of the sexes is seen throughout Scripture, beginning with our being male and female as the *imago Dei*. In the Old Testament, the sign of the covenant was circumcision. But in the New Testament, baptism is the sign of the new covenant, administered to both men and women. On the day of Pentecost, 120 believers, both men and women, were gathered. In Acts 2, the Spirit of God comes upon the assembly of men and women.

The New Covenant priesthood is for all believers, men and women. Men and women serve in ministry. The *diakonos* (deacons and deaconesses) were male and female ministers and servants, co-workers of the Apostle Paul and others.

In Romans 16:1–2 we read, "I commend unto you, Phebe our sister, which is a servant of the church which is at Cenchrea . . . for she hath been a *succourer* of many and of myself also" (KJV emphasis added). The *succourer* had an important ministry in the community, which was to help others in suffering or difficulty. This word is rare in the Scriptures but is applied to Phebe and carries authority. A *succourer* even to Paul . . . "and of myself also."

In this context, at least, a woman's gift to nurture and care for others represents a position of authority. As we have seen, this is unity without uniformity, diversity without superiority. Men and women are equal in their being. Their gifts are equally important, though not the same. No gift is higher than or better than another. Women prophesied, women led worship, women danced, women taught.

There was just one limitation on women's ministry opportunities. Jesus had many followers who traveled with Him as He taught, some of whom were His disciples—His pupils. The Bible speaks of seventy-two people who were disciples, men and women.

From these disciples Jesus chose twelve—the apostles—whom He gave special authority to represent Him. Again, masses followed Him, seventy-two disciples learned from Him, and twelve apostles received special authority. How did the Lord choose these twelve from the larger group? He spent the night in prayer (see Luke 6:12ff.) seeking the Father's will. In the morning, Jesus called the disciples (men and women) to Him and chose twelve men to become apostles.

Note here that Jesus rejected the sexist order of diversity as superiority. He also rejected the feminist notion that men and women are interchangeable. He restored the Trinitarian order: men and women equal in their being with different functions—equally valuable, necessary, and glorious. Do women teach? Yes. Do women minister? Yes. Do women lead in worship? Do they prophesy? Yes. To the question, "Are women in leadership?" the answer is *yes*. But He chose twelve men to be apostles.

Earlier, we have seen the importance of a mother's presence in the life of her young children. Can a woman run a corporation? Yes! Can a woman have children? Yes! We have exposed as a fallacy the notion that a woman can "have it all," that is, she can bear children and run a corporation at the same time. Children need a mother's presence. The woman was created to nurture, and to do all those things a man cannot do.

> **The *succourer* had an important ministry in the community, which was to help others in suffering or difficulty. This word is rare in the Scriptures but is applied to Phebe and carries authority. A woman's gift to nurture and care for others represents a position of authority.**

But it is also true that, once the nurturing work is finished, she can also be the president of the country, of a corporation. She can lead in all spheres of society. The one limitation is the *episcope*, or office of bishop. This is the only restriction in Scripture on a woman ministering, teaching and leading. And this is a limitation of governance *in the church*. Furthermore, most men are also not part of that governing authority.

Amazingly, Revelation 21:1–4 pictures the Trinitarian order in its description of the city of God.

> Then I saw a new heaven and a new earth, for the first heaven and the first earth had passed away, and the sea was no more. And I saw the Holy city, new Jerusalem, coming down out of heaven from God, prepared as a bride adorned for her husband. And I heard a loud voice from the throne saying, "Behold, the dwelling place of God is with man. He will dwell with them, and they will be his people, and God himself will be with them as their God. He will wipe away every tear from their eyes, and death shall be no more, neither shall there be mourning, nor crying, nor pain anymore, for the former things have passed away."

Then in verses 12–14 we read these words about the structure of the city.

> It had a great, high wall, with twelve gates, and at the gates twelve angels, and on the gates the names of the twelve tribes of the sons of Israel were inscribed—on the east three gates, on the north three gates, on the south three gates, and on the west three gates. And the wall of the city had twelve foundations, and on them were the twelve names of the twelve apostles of the Lamb.

Gates protect a city. The foundations are its strength. Note that the gates and the foundations are identified as masculine. The great high wall of protection had twelve gates named with the twelve sons of Jacob, representing the twelve tribes of Israel. And the walls of the city were on twelve foundations inscribed with the names of the twelve apostles. The gates had male names; the foundation had male names. Why? Because they represented the Bridegroom!

What about the bride? What is the feminine manifestation?

> Then came one of the seven angels who had the seven bowls full of the seven last plagues and spoke to me, saying, "Come, I will show you the Bride, the wife of the Lamb." And he carried me away in the Spirit to a great, high mountain, and showed me the holy city Jerusalem coming down out of heaven from God, having the glory of God, its radiance like a most rare jewel, like a jasper, clear as crystal. (Revelation 21:9–11)

The gates of the city and foundations of the walls are masculine in representation, but the city itself, the New Jerusalem, is *feminine*!

We begin the biblical narrative in Genesis with the creation of man; first the male was created and then the female, the crown of the crown. At the end of history, the city of God comes from heaven to earth with both masculine and feminine representations. This is a model of the Trinitarian nature of unity and diversity. God made us in His image, male and female, and the New Jerusalem is a reflection of the masculine and the feminine. As a bride beautifully dressed for her husband, it shines with the glory of God, its brilliance like a sapphire, the wife of the Lamb, the feminine. The bride of the Lamb is the city of God.

> **The gates of the city and foundations of the walls are masculine in representation, but the city itself, the New Jerusalem, is feminine!**

How we need this complementary/Trinitarian model in leadership to bring wholeness and full value, imagined as great high walls and strong foundations coupled with the radiance like rare jewels, glorious, brilliant, and clear as crystal. We do not replace a sexist culture with a feminist culture. The culture of the Trinitarian order is the beginning of the story, and it is the end of this story. It helps us answer the question about women in leadership in the world God is redeeming with a resounding *Yes*!

——— STUDY GUIDE ———

1. How were Jesus and the early church countercultural in their treatment of women?
2. For what reasons did Jesus die on the cross?
3. How does the new covenant differ from the old with regard to women?
4. What is the only restriction Scripture places on women and most men, in the church?
5. Reflect deeply on the revelation on the nature of the New Jerusalem in Revelation 21. How does this vision undermine both the sexist and feminist order and affirm the Trinitarian, complementarian order?

PART 6

Recovering a Biblical Feminism

CHAPTER 20

The First Wave: Maternal Feminism

AS MENTIONED IN chapter 16, French political thinker, social observer, and historian Alexis de Tocqueville (1805–1859) spent the year of 1831 traveling and observing American life. Later, he gathered his thoughts about what he saw in the 1835 classic, *Democracy in America*. Toward the end of the book, Tocqueville asserted that American women are superior to women anywhere else in the world.

Tocqueville identified what raised American women above all others: the understanding of female and male as complementary, equal and different. Working from its biblical foundation, American society affirmed that these two modalities, while different, are intrinsically equal, both in their being and in the value of their distinct natures. In Tocqueville's words:

> Thus the Americans do not think that man and woman have either the duty or the right to perform the same offices, but they show an equal regard for both their respective parts; and though their lot is different, they consider both of them as beings of equal value. They do not give to the courage of woman the same form or the same direction as to that of man; but they never doubt her courage: and if they hold that man and his partner ought not always to exercise their intellect and understanding in the same manner, they at least believe the understanding of the one to be as sound as that of the other,

and her intellect to be as clear. Thus, then . . . they have done all they could to raise her morally and intellectually to the level of man; and in this respect they appear to me to have excellently understood the true principle of democratic improvement. As for myself, I do not hesitate to avow that, although the women of the United States are confined within the narrow circle of domestic life, and their situation is in some respects one of extreme dependence, I have nowhere seen woman occupying a loftier position; and if I were asked, now that I am drawing to the close of this work, in which I have spoken of so many important things done by the Americans, to what the singular prosperity and growing strength of that people ought mainly to be attributed, I should reply—to the superiority of their women.[190]

Such perceptive (and from my perspective, thrilling) comments would likely draw the ire of many today who claim the mantle of feminism. But that is because Tocqueville and others of his day two centuries ago possessed insights that are far truer to the nature and dignity of women than they will ever know.

> **To what the singular prosperity and growing strength of that people ought mainly to be attributed, I should reply—to the superiority of their women.**
> **Alexis de Tocqueville**

Tocqueville found that American women did not have to become like men to be equal to men. They were equal in their being, but their gifts, roles, and functions were different from men's . . . and equally important.

Most of the time when we hear the word "feminism," we think of modern feminism. But feminism existed before its modern iteration. In this chapter, we will look at the first feminists. In the next two chapters, we will address their modern and postmodern successors and where they went wrong.

The first wave of feminism existed in the late nineteenth century into the twentieth century. It was known as maternal feminism or first-wave feminism. There are still many people who are maternal feminists today. This was not just a movement of women. First-wave feminists, both women and men, had the worldview of the Bible, or at least the memory of a biblical worldview.

They understood the concept of male and female and what feminism meant from this biblical framework. Many were committed Christians.

Maternal feminists were primarily interested in others. They were focused not on themselves but on their children, their families, and society. They understood that individuals are part of a larger community. The women were homemakers, mothers, and nurturers. The family was the center of human life. They grasped the truth that their children would inherit the world and needed to be prepared. They recognized the home as foundational for the health of the society.

Women were valued both for their being and their function. They knew all human beings are made in the image of God and thus have intrinsic dignity, dignity not bestowed by the state. Every human being, man and woman, not only has intrinsic dignity, but infinite value. They further knew that men and women are moral equals. What is more, maternal feminists knew that men's and women's distinct functions were equally valuable and necessary to fulfill the Cultural Commission—that is, the command to fill and care for the creation. Maternal feminists recognized that women have a nurturing nature. They were designed and built to nurture children and nations. Maternal feminists understood that a woman's biology had significance, that her role in procreation assured the future. Nurturing was to take place in the domestic sphere, but it also had a place in the public sphere.

Nellie McClung, a Canadian first-wave feminist and supporter of woman's suffrage, spoke of the need for maternal instincts in both the domestic and public spheres: "A woman's place is in the home; and out of it whenever she is called on to guard those she loves and to improve conditions for them."[191] First-wave feminists worked to extend their domestic, maternal influence into the larger world to create a healthy society for their children. A maternal feminist prepared her children for citizenship and prepared society for her children.

Maternal feminists sought to help create a society that supported the health of the family and the child. They wanted to defeat the forces that undermined the family and destroyed the nation. They fought against sweatshops (where women were paid low wages and prevented from mothering) and child labor (where children were precluded from education).

They fought for a family wage (so the father could provide and the mother could nurture), for temperance (against alcohol's harm toward the family), and for women's suffrage (to give maternal concerns a voice in society).

This was the first wave of feminists. In their era, society honored and respected motherhood. As a consequence, men learned something of their own identity as they engaged with their female counterparts. Maternal feminists affirmed female nature and the wonder and glory of a nurturing spirit. They opposed a male-dominated value system and power structure.

They knew that society needs the leavening of thoughtful women. A woman's understanding and intellect are as needed as those of a man. But the two are different in nature. The woman's judgment is based more on intuition, while the man's is based on reason. Both intuition and reason come from the Creator Himself. Both are required to reflect the fullness of the image of God.

"For centuries, women considered marriage and motherhood to be their highest calling and they planned their lives accordingly. And as a young girl, you ordered your life to fulfill that calling."
Suzanne Venker

Men and women have the ability to reason abstractly and intuitively. However, the woman's propensity is the intuitive; the man's tendency is the abstract. Both are equally honorable and vitally needed.

First-wave feminists, not surprisingly, were pro-life. They understood abortion not only destroyed the life of a baby, but negatively impacted the life and well-being of mothers and family. Alice Paul, a maternal feminist who authored the original Equal Rights Amendment in 1923, called abortion "the ultimate exploitation of women." Victoria Woodhull, a first-wave feminist and the first woman to run for president of the United States in 1872, stated unequivocally that "pregnancy is not a disease, but a beautiful office of nature."

Author and columnist Suzanne Venker agrees. "For centuries, women considered marriage and motherhood to be their highest calling and they planned their lives accordingly," she writes. "And as a young girl, you ordered your life to fulfill that calling."[192]

First-wave feminists were strong women, often working side-by-side with their husbands on farms or ranches. They knew what they wanted and fought for it. Today's world needs maternal feminists who embrace motherhood as the foundation for a healthy society, and, like mother grizzly bears, defend their cubs at home and in the public arena, nurturing us back to marriage and the family as the root of a healthy social order.

The expression of first-wave feminists clearly communicates that the female voice, born out of a maternal nature, is badly needed in building healthy families and sustainable futures. Women have a vital role in building healthy nations, a role born out of their God-given design and dignity. Both the intuitive and the rational voices are necessary for healthy families and societies.

STUDY GUIDE

1. Why did Alexis de Tocqueville believe nineteenth-century American women were superior to all others?
2. List five or six things that maternal feminists understood about women, men, and families.
3. What kind of society were maternal feminists hoping to create?
4. How did maternal feminists view abortion? Why?
5. Maternal feminist Suzanne Venker states: "For centuries, women considered marriage and motherhood to be their highest calling and they planned their lives accordingly." How would women today respond to Venker? What would today's women tend to plan their lives for?
6. What kind of women were first-wave feminists? How do the words and examples of the women quoted in this chapter compare to the picture modern society often paints of oppressed pre-1960s women?

CHAPTER 21

The Second Wave: Modern Feminism

ITALIAN POET, ART theorist, and author Tommaso Marinetti was an early proponent of discarding the great institutions of the West. His 1909 book, *The Futurist*, marked a turning point. Marinetti wrote, "We want to demolish the museums, the libraries, combat moralism, feminism and all the opportunist and utilitarian cowardice."[193]

Of course, Marinetti was referring to *maternal* feminism. While second-wave feminism began to enter the mainstream of culture with the free-speech movement and the sexual revolution of the early to mid-1960s, the roots of these movements began in Europe early in the twentieth century.

The rise of Darwinism and the "death of God" movement brought a seismic shift in Western society, in which the cultural recognition of a moral universe was lost. The concept of human sexuality and the nature of the family began to change also.

As the culture slid faster and faster into the moral abyss, maternal feminism gave way to second-wave, or modern, feminism. Second-wave feminists rose to public prominence in 1966, and not without cause. They were challenging the global sexist lie that men are superior to women, a task the church, to its shame, had dropped. Such a perverse and cruel sexism is born of pagan culture. It demeans women and destroys the natural family.

Modern feminism therefore blessed the world by challenging sexist culture. Tragically, however, modern feminism was not operating from the biblical worldview. Rather, it was born from the worldview of modernism, which denies any transcendent feminine and masculine. The only differences between the sexes, in this view, are biological. Aided and abetted by Darwin's secular humanistic metanarrative, the "self" became the focus of the modern feminist movement.

Second-wave feminists rightly affirm women's intrinsic worth with men. As we have shown in this book over and over, women and men are equal in dignity, value, and honor, because they are made in the image of God. But second-wave feminists do not value the nurturing function of a woman, neither in the family nor in the society.

The 1970s saw an effort to correct some of the errors of modern feminism. A concept emerged called Difference Feminism (AKA Essential Feminism), which acknowledged biological and physiological differences between men and women, including the idea that women are essentially more nurturing than men. While acknowledging these differences, proponents argued that no value judgment could be placed on the differences and that, in fact, both sexes have equal moral status as persons, and their differing functions are of equal importance in the culture.

This concept of feminism is a natural bridge to biblical complementarianism: men and women are similar in many ways, essentially different in other ways, and yet equal in dignity, infinite value, and moral status. Concurrently, as radical feminism roared in the 1980s, in the providence of God, Christians began to examine the sexist culture rooted in the church. As the church engaged in the debate, division arose between those who sided with the Equality Feminists and those who joined, late, with the Difference Feminists.

In 1984, a group of Christians in England formed the organization Men, Women and God to advocate for the egalitarian position in the church. Three years later, in the United States, a sister organization was founded, Christians for Biblical Equality. In the same year, in the United States, the Council on Biblical Manhood and Womanhood was formed. The CBMW is in basic agreement with the Essential/Different Feminists movement. These complementarians argued that men and women have essential, complementary, and important differences and yet are equal in dignity and honor.

If more Christians who were concerned about the dignity of women had engaged in this battle, they would have found natural allies in the Difference Feminism movement and might have turned back the tide of modern feminism. But they didn't. Equality feminism took hold even in large swaths of the church. Mary Pride writes, "At every turn Christian women found that their biological, economic, and social roles were considered worthless. Men's ministry, men's money, men's building and programs—these were the areas that mattered."[194]

The church was leading the way when maternal feminism emerged. More recently the church has been reactive, following the modern culture. We did not confront pagan sexist culture by explaining the beauty and wonder of the Trinitarian God and the archetype His existence made for creation. This is something this book has set out to do. We did not actively proclaim the beauty of binary relationship in male and female covenant marriage. Christians finally joined the party as the debate between Essential Feminists and Equality Feminists was ending. We have, in effect, closed the barn doors after the horses got out.

> "At every turn Christian women found that their biological, economic, and social roles were considered worthless. Men's ministry, men's money, men's building and programs—these were the areas that mattered."
> Mary Pride

Equality Feminism is a subset of Second-Wave Feminism. It focuses on the basic similarities between men and women. Its ultimate goal is the interchangeability of women and men in all domains of life, including the political and economic arenas. Advocates want equal opportunity in the workplace and freedom from oppressive gender stereotyping. They say, the more women out of the home and into the workplace, the better.

Their motto is "make careers, not babies." Their bottom line is to be recognized as indistinguishable from men. And in fact, the goal of the modern feminist movement, whether recognized or not, is for women to *be* like men. While opposing a sexist culture that denigrated women, they stood against a system that valued the feminine. While opposing a patriarchy that sought to confine women to the kitchen, they opposed the nurturing nature, regarding it as the enemy of a woman's life and career opportunities.

Arts professor and social critic Camille Paglia has indicted modern feminism for its failure to recognize the essential place of mothers: "Feminist ideology has never dealt honestly with the role of the mother in human life."[195] She spoke of the practical consequences of modern feminist ideology promoting career over motherhood:

> The overflow of gender theory into real life can conceal developing problems. For example, what are the long-term consequences of the disruption of biologic patterns in our imposing on young women a male-centered career path that occupies women's optimal years of fertility with a prolonged sequence of undergraduate and postgraduate education? By the time our most accomplished young women are ready to marry, they may be in their 30s, when pregnancy carries more risks and when their male peers suddenly have an abundant marital choice of fresher, more nubile girls in their 20s.[196]

The goal of modern feminists was to get women out of the home and into the marketplace, where an individual's worth is supposedly found. In an atheistic, materialistic framework, our worth lies in money and power—things that enable us to manipulate and control the things of this world for our benefit. The family and the home, intangible things that take the spotlight off the self and which must be attained by virtue, are enemies of money and power. Children are barriers to a woman becoming, in terms of a materialistic standard, "all she can be."

Abortion allows a woman to be most like a man. She can have sex at will without taking responsibility for her actions. To be equal to a man is to be un-pregnant.

If this materialistic approach to life is correct, how can a society practically support career over the maternal? Via abortion!

Abortion allows a woman to be most like a man. She can have sex at will without taking responsibility for her actions. To be equal to a man is to be un-pregnant—thus the "necessity" of abortion on demand. Further, having the government pay for the abortion affirms women's "equality." Second-wave feminists inexorably linked their movement to abortion. They had to in order to pursue their agenda. Radical feminism is radical precisely because abortion is its sacrament.

In second-wave feminism, children are an imposition, an interruption to a woman's career. Public schools and universities teach girls they are made for careers. Young women are torn away from their natural purpose to bear and nurture children. Second-wave feminists deny a woman's basic design and function; they reject their actual biology. Eventually, they reject the natural outcome of their biology—children.

Wanting to be like men, to have sex without responsibility, modern feminists supported the sexual revolution. This isn't anything close to "women's liberation." In fact, it's just another iteration of sexist culture, of having sex without taking responsibility for your actions. All over the world we see children without fathers. Why? In these societies, the man's role is to get a woman pregnant. This shows he's a man; he can walk away without taking responsibility for his actions. Women of the second wave wanted the same freedom: to have sex without responsibility. They therefore turn to two technologies for this "freedom": the birth control pill and abortion.

Second-wave feminists speak of "a woman's right to choose." But they don't mean that. They actually insist that women must *not* be free to choose. A choice includes at least two alternatives, but radical feminists demand only one option for women to be fulfilled and reach their potential: abortion. "Pro-choice" is a euphemism. Truth to tell, they are pro-*abortion*.

Paglia identifies abortion as modern feminists' holy sacrament: "[Gloria] Steinem herself can be credited or blamed for having turned abortion into a sacrament, promoted with the same religiosity that she and her colleagues condemn in their devoutly Christian opponents."[197]

Abortion lies at the heart of the culture wars in the United States. Two major paradigms, Judeo-Christian theism and atheism, promote two very different principles: "the right to life" and "the right to choose" to take a life. These principles give birth to very different public policies. One side promotes policies to protect even the most fragile human life, from conception to natural death. The other would destroy that life to guarantee a woman's unconstrained freedom to pursue material ends. Even if her baby survives an abortion attempt, her baby must be allowed to die if the mother wants a dead child.

Such materialism reduces human beings to instruments of production—instruments of consuming things, having money, buying and producing things, which are of ultimate worth in a materialistic society. Linda Hirshman of Brandeis University stated, "Money is the marker of success in a market economy. It usually accompanies power and it enables the bearer to wield power, including within the family."[198]

As we have pointed out in an earlier chapter, the lives and choices of two different women are a good illustration of this divide between the Judeo-Christian worldview and the culture of life and the atheistic-materialistic worldview and the culture of death. The first woman is Irene Vilar—AKA the "Abortion Addict." Vilar was a "mother" of fifteen and the author of the book *Motherhood: Testimony of an Abortion Addict*. In it, she celebrates that she had fifteen abortions in sixteen years. Vilar is a narcissist who put her ego above the lives of her fifteen babies, manifesting a cavalier attitude toward the most vulnerable human life.

The second is Carrie Lynn De Klyen, thirty-seven-year-old mother of six children. After conceiving another baby, Carrie Lynn was diagnosed with cancer. Doctors recommended an abortion so they could treat her cancer. De Klyen refused the abortion and thus the cancer treatment in order to save her baby's life. Carrie Lynn gave birth to a daughter she named Life Lynn. She was able to hold her baby for three days before dying. She sacrificed her own life that her baby might live.

Two women with two belief systems concerning the nature and value of human life. They modeled them for the world to see. Ideas do have consequences! Fifteen babies died so that one mother might fulfill her selfish ambition. Another mother valued the life of one baby so much that she sacrificed her life for her child. Each reveals the character and beliefs of the one making the decision.

So for those who choose death for their babies, the woman's ideal station is the workplace, not the home. Tragically, she's considered to be worth more as a producer and consumer of products than as a mother of children.

Paglia writes,

> But the real-life consequences of this wholesale exclusion of biology from contemporary social thought continue to multiply. For example, second-wave feminism had been habitually

guilty of a callous and to me counterproductive denigration of motherhood. . . . Second-wave feminism glorified the career woman and dismissed the stay-at-home mom as a traitor to the cause.[199]

Pulitzer Prize-winning columnist Kathleen Parker notes,

As it happens, the brand of feminism that insisted equality could be achieved only by women evacuating the home and outsourcing child care found common cause with Communist ideology. Breaking up the family was not incidental but central to that ideology.[200]

Not only did second-wave feminists separate women from their biology. They even managed to assign second-class status to mothers, motherhood, and even marriage. Second-wave feminist Irina Dunn articulated a slogan to define the modern feminist: "A woman needs a man like a fish needs a bicycle." Does a fish need a bicycle? No. Does a woman need a man? No! This is the position of second-wave feminism.

Suzanne Venker says that this is a "tired notion of female independence."[201]

Erica Komisar is a New York-based psychiatric social worker whose research indicates a correlation between absent mothers and children and teens with behavior problems. Komisar, a modern feminist, writes:

If being a feminist means you can do whatever you want without considering the consequences to your children of your absence, that you can act without empathy for your child regarding the pain of their separation from you, then I guess I'm not a feminist [by that definition].[202]

At one time, men used their status to degrade women; now modern feminists use men's status to degrade women. This mentality is leading to a new movement to be free from having children, as seen in NoKidding.net, in the Voluntary Human Extinction Movement, and with International Planned Parenthood. The goal of these movements and organizations is to "free" women from the maternal, from the responsibility of children, so they can achieve perceived success in our modern materialistic culture.

According to the logic of second-wave feminism, equality is achieved by not having children, or having them but shunting them off to professional day care. While they rarely admit this openly, second-wave feminists believe being unpregnant enables a woman to be like a man. And when sexism and feminism define personhood as being male and not pregnant, knives and chemicals can make women like men. How horrible!

Says Lilian Calles Barger, in her book *Eve's Revenge,*

> The widely practiced violence of abortion is not a sign of progress, but a sign that women's reproductive ability needs to be exterminated in order for society to go "forward." In an environment hostile to women's bodies and through abortion, women participate in a war against their own bodies, objectifying them. The feminist slogan "our bodies, ourselves" becomes "our bodies, not ourselves."[203]

This anti-woman philosophy has consequences not just for women and their families, but for nations. Contrary to the common assumption that the world is overpopulated, global fertility rates have been in decline. Some countries, in fact, are slowly dying due to a low fertility rate. A replacement fertility rate of 2.13 children per woman is required demographically to sustain a population. While one hundred of the world's nations have stable or growing populations, about fifty countries register at 2.13 or somewhat less and are in slow population decline. Worse, sixty-six countries have fertility replacement rates of 1.8 or lower and are in a national death spiral. The lowest rates, 1.3 or less, include Singapore, Portugal, Poland, Moldova, Greece, and Taiwan. It is virtually impossible for a nation to recover from such rates. It is national suicide in slow motion, and perhaps not so slow at that.

"The widely practiced violence of abortion is not a sign of progress, but a sign that women's reproductive ability needs to be exterminated in order for society to go 'forward.'"
Lilian Calles Barger

I was in Japan twenty years ago when a medical doctor came to me after a lecture. "Darrow," he said, "we're turning out the lights in Japan." He explained, "We're not having children, so we're closing schools; we're closing maternity wards and hospitals. We're no longer training doctors and nurses in labor and delivery and postpartum because we're not having babies anymore." That was twenty years ago. In 2020, Japan's projected fertility rate was a shocking 1.37.

In South Korea thirty or forty years ago, the average woman gave birth to four children. Today the nation has the world's lowest rate at 0.88. In one generation, the Korean population will be cut in half. Korea is committing national and cultural suicide and is only now waking up to ask, "What are we to do?"

This is the fruit of a radical individualism: me, not us; having, not being. You're defined not by who you are, but by what you have. It's not about self-sacrifice but self-absorption. It's me-centric rather than child-centric, self-serving rather than serving others. It's personal freedom without personal responsibility. This is modern, second-wave feminism. Sadly, this is what most people mean when they talk about feminism today.

RADICAL INDIVIDUALISM

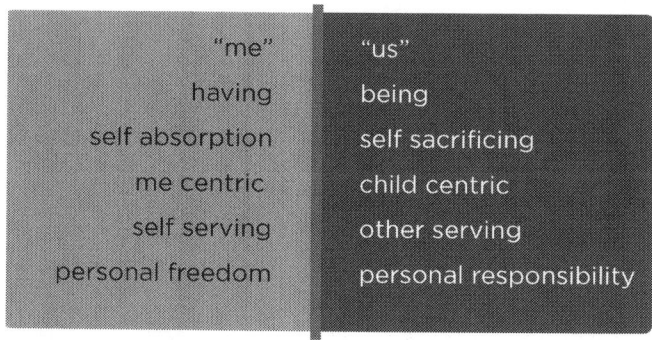

"me"	"us"
having	being
self absorption	self sacrificing
me centric	child centric
self serving	other serving
personal freedom	personal responsibility

And yet all hope is not lost. Maureen Ferguson, a leader of today's maternal feminist movement, writes:

> The vision of women's equality promoted by *Roe v. Wade* . . . assumes women need to be more like men. But women bear children, and that gift is not a deficiency; humanity's very existence depends on our life-giving capacity. Women ought to be valued as they are, and Mom Power embraced. In a culture of true equality and authentic female flourishing, women

would not be told to choose between their children and their success.[204]

Let's do all we can to bring back that kind of culture.

————————— **STUDY GUIDE** —————————

1. How did second-wave feminists differ from maternal feminists? What worldview undergirds second-wave feminism?
2. What two Christian organizations formed in the wake of second-wave feminism? What viewpoints do they represent?
3. Why is the right to an abortion so important to second-wave feminists? What would you say to someone who held this view?
4. What view does second-wave feminism take of motherhood? In what way is this (ironically) a sexist position?
5. What effect has the modern worldview had on the birth rate of developed nations? How can we affirm the value of motherhood in an era of childlessness?

CHAPTER 22

The Third Wave: Postmodern Feminism and the Death of Binary Sexuality

IN THE FATEFUL years before the Second World War, a group of social theorists fled Germany to escape the Nazi regime. The movement began at Goethe University in Frankfurt, rejecting both capitalism in the West and traditional Marxism in the Soviet Union. The goal would be a soft, cultural Marxism.

Threatened by the rise of the Third Reich, they ended up in the United States, where they quickly took up leadership roles in American universities. The influence of these adherents, of what came to be known as the Frankfurt School, goes a long way in explaining why the United States, which won the Cold War against Soviet Marxism, has become, ironically, one of the strongest centers of Marxist thought in the world.

Traditional Marxism is based on a kind of economic determinism that believes capitalist societies will ultimately collapse as oppressed workers rise up against oppressive capitalists to usher in "justice" in the form of communism. When that didn't happen in real life, Frankfurt School theorists redirected their aim at the *culture* that gave rise to capitalism. If that culture could be crushed, the desired revolution could still happen.

Marxist Antonio Gramsci (1891–1937) of Italy understood that Western Civilization came from the God of the Bible and the worldview of Judeo-Christian theism. If the West were to be transformed, it had to be decoupled from its Judeo-Christian roots. Before society could be transformed, culture needed to be transformed. Gramsci argued that this cultural transformation would lead to a wholesale redefinition of traditional institutions such as the family, the church, and civil society.

Adherents attacked education (particularly the history of Western civilization, etc.) through the promotion of a broad approach known as Critical Theory. Simply put, this school of thought is the critique of anything with roots in historically Protestant, Western culture. So Black Critical Theory studies how white Protestant European culture produced systemic and institutional oppression of blacks. Feminist Critical Theory focuses on how white Protestant European culture produces a dangerous patriarchal society that oppresses women. Over time, various Critical Theory courses have replaced the study of American history and Western Civilization, which are now almost completely absent from university curricula.

Outside academia, in the public square, this approach has led to a kind of tribalism of identity politics. Multitudes of non-white, non-Christian, or non-male identity groups claim the status of an oppressed minority, as victims of white, male, Protestant systemic oppression.

But the Critical Theorists were not done. Finally, they attacked the family by fomenting the sexual revolution in hopes of ushering in the desired cultural revolution. Herbert Marcuse (an original Frankfurt School member) borrowed heavily from Sigmund Freud and assaulted the family by encouraging the sexual revolution in the 1960s.

Now, driven by postmodernism, the second-wave feminism that we examined in the previous chapter has morphed into third-wave feminism, which is characterized by social justice language and action. How does this new wave differ from the previous one?

While second-wave feminism denies any transcendent masculine and feminine, third-wave feminism has abandoned biology and physiology altogether. Science was discarded in favor of an irrational and illusionary world that rejected male and female binary categories for androgynous gender identity.

Third-wave or postmodern feminism began to engage culture in the late twentieth century. It seeks to overthrow male-female distinctions. In this view, the two sexes are interchangeable. Male and female are not only equal, they are the same. While maternal feminism was rooted in the metanarrative of biblical theism, and second-wave feminism in the narrative of Darwinism, third-wave feminism is founded within postmodernism and claims to have no metanarrative. There is no essentialism, no reason or reality, just feelings and illusions.

First-wave feminism says men and women are different and equal, second-wave that men and women are different and male is better, and third-wave that there is no difference. The rallying cry is gender identity. It's about the end of binary sexuality. As we will see next, it is about death of family and the death of Western civilization. This form of feminism, like other applications of postmodernist thought, denies any metanarrative. (Of course, that very statement itself is a metanarrative.) Nothing is essential, everything is a social construction, that is, a construction of language. Postmodern, third-wave feminism is rooted in "religious" monism, the idea that "all is one." One religious manifes-

> While second-wave feminism denies any transcendent masculine and feminine, third-wave feminism has abandoned biology and physiology altogether. Science was discarded in favor of an irrational and illusionary world that rejected male and female binary categories for androgynous gender identity.

tation of monism is Hinduism. All apparent distinctions are illusions. The metaphysics and biology of sexuality are practical applications of monism. This is indeed a "toxic new religion."

Again, there is no masculine and feminine, no metaphysical or transcendent sexuality, and no biology, male or female. These feminists oppose a male value system. They deny the existence of reason and reality and consider both to be the social construct of white European males. Postmodern feminists reject sexual distinctions and promote androgyny—male and female as one, undifferentiated.

Describing this approach, Suzanne Venker has said, "All those physical, cognitive and emotional differences you think exist are merely social constructs, the result of centuries of restraints and stereotypes imposed by a male-dominated society."[205] This is androgyny, male and female as one.

A sociological maxim states that before you change a society, you must first change its language. We are seeing this happen before our eyes. We speak no longer of the sacredness of life, but the quality of life. We used to speak of babies, now they are "potential life" or "fetuses." We are abandoning the term *sex* for male and female; now it's *gender*. "Sex" has an essential element, male and female. Gender has no essential element; it's whatever you invent. The word "mother" is being replaced with "birthing person." The word "woman" is undefinable and being removed from postmodern vocabulary.

Whoever controls the language, controls the culture and the future.

We've seen this play out in the changing definition of marriage. In the premodern world, marriage was a covenant between a man and a woman before God. This covenantal relationship existed "until death do us part."

In the modern world, marriage devolved into a social contract, and eventually into a mere "personal commitment." You were married if you wanted to be. When you don't want to be married any longer, you're no longer married. The specific, marital standard of husband and wife has given way rapidly to the androgynous, non-marital concept of "partners."

John Money (1921–2006) was a psychologist and sexologist whose research concerning the Bruce and Brian Reimer twins led to the concept of gender identity, and the idea that our "sexuality" is not fixed but is a social construct. He introduced and promoted the vocabulary of "gender identity," "gender role," and "sexual orientation."[206] By the time Money's research and theory were rejected by the scientific community, the vocabulary of gender identity had been seeded in Western thought and became the fount of the transgender movement today. The tragic story that we told of Chloe Cole, in the introduction of this book, is a direct result of the discredited ideas of John Money. Ideas have consequences! False ideas have tragic consequences.

In postmodernism, the goal is to eliminate marriage, so the word itself disappears from the vocabulary. In fact, we are seeing the deconstructing of sex. Sex is a biological term; gender is sociological. Sex implies distinction, male and female. Gender is defined by societal usage. These are two different concepts. Sex is not elastic; you're born male or female. Gender, as it's used today, is elastic. In fact, you don't even have to identify whether a child is male or female on the birth certificate. Gender is a social construction; you assign to it whatever meaning you want.

The United States reached a legal turning point in 1992 when Justice Anthony Kennedy stated in *Planned Parenthood v. Casey* that the fundamental principle of our liberty is "the right to define one's own concept of existence, of meaning, of the universe, and of the mystery of human life." This was the U.S. Supreme Court recognizing postmodernism.

Is Michael Jackson male or female? What about David Bowie? What's the big deal about Madonna and Britney Spears doing a French kiss? Celebrities are making political statements from a postmodern platform. Jackson, Bowie, and Madonna can be whatever they want. Just make it up as you go because there is no ultimate meaning to our sexuality or our bodies, no role distinctions between men and women.

BINARY SEXUALITY IS PASSÉ IN POSTMODERN WORLD

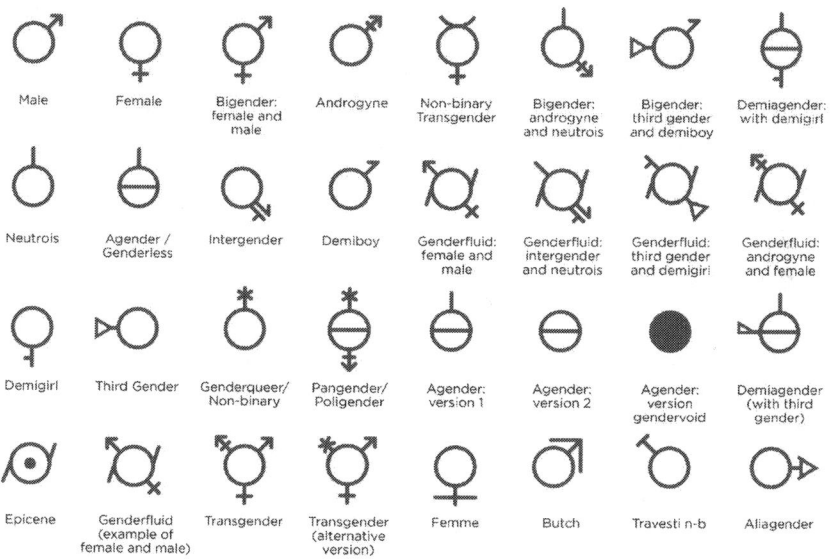

In the 1980s the term LGB was invented as a substitute for "gay" (which, of course, was the new term for "homosexual"). Then T was added to accommodate transgender. Now it's LGBTQIA+. Binary sexuality is passé; we now have a full menu of options. The upper left corner of the graphic shows the sign for male and the sign for female. Note today the other signs that have grown out of this postmodern ideology. Facebook now identifies fifty-eight gender options; Facebook UK identifies seventy-one. What will another few years bring?

These are human-to-human sexual choices. What human-and-animal options, human-and-robot options lie beyond the horizon? Now we have something called "autogynephilia," a man's attraction to the image of himself as a woman. The poster "person" for autogynephilia is Bruce Jenner, recognized as the greatest male athlete in the world in the 1970s. He identifies today as a woman, and it's "deadnaming" and considered hateful to call him Bruce instead of Caitlyn. In some jurisdictions you can be arrested for deadnaming. The force of law is reinforcing postmodernism.

> While we must stand unapologetically for the truth; we must realize that those who repeat those lies are lost and need the grace of Christ every bit as much as we do. So let us speak the truth in love, knowing that ultimately the gates of hell will not prevail.

In postmodernism, reason and reality do not exist. Everything is a social construction. Whatever you think, you are. Western cultures are codifying standards and even laws to require recognizing gender identity. Refuse at your own peril.

The goal of the transgender movement is the destruction of the family and of the transcendent moral order. Admits Riki Wilchins, founder of the Gender Public Advocacy Coalition, "Gay and transgender rights advocates have been quietly dodging the issue of binary heteronormativity, but the sound you are hearing is the other shoe finally dropping hard. . . . Ending our cultural obsession with what's male and female will be our salvation."[207]

Indeed, transgender activists are not merely asking for a place at the table. They're demanding control of the language and the culture. Male and female must disappear. Everyone must affirm non-binary standards.

Russian-American journalist and trans activist Masha Gessen speaks bluntly:

> It's a no-brainer that we should have the right to marry. But I also think equally that it is a no-brainer that the institution of marriage should not exist. That causes my brain some trouble, and part of why it causes me trouble is because fighting for

gay marriage generally involves lying about what we're going to do with marriage when we get there, because we lie that the institution of marriage is not going to change. That is a lie.[208]

The lies in today's modern and postmodern feminist movements represent a sobering challenge to maternal feminists and Christ-followers. We are in a war at the level of culture, but the weapons of our warfare are not carnal. Let us therefore tear down these strongholds by the power of the Spirit.

While we must stand unapologetically for the truth; we must realize that those who repeat those lies are lost and need the grace of Christ every bit as much as we do. So let us speak the truth in love, knowing that ultimately the gates of hell will not prevail.

STUDY GUIDE

1. How does cultural Marxism differ from traditional Marxism? Why does cultural Marxism attack Western culture's Judeo-Christian roots?

2. How does third-wave (or postmodern) feminism differ from both first- and second-wave feminism? What is its metanarrative?

3. Why is it so important to postmodernists to change and redefine words? What are they seeking to accomplish through the redefinition of marriage or biological sex?

4. How does Justice Anthony Kennedy's statement in Planned Parenthood v. Casey differ from the biblical worldview? What would you say to someone who holds this view?

5. Take a moment and reflect on the graphic on the postmodernist response to binary sexuality. What are your thoughts, concerns, feelings? How might you respond to this? What might the church or family groups do to restore the wonder and beauty of binary sexuality and family formation?

CHAPTER 23

Christ, the First Feminist

SEXUAL IMMORALITY WAS normal in the world Jesus entered. Historian Alvin Schmidt observed, "In the Roman and Greek temples sex was a common religious activity. The pagan gods of the Romans or Greeks set no precepts with regard to moral behavior."[209] All that the Scripture deems as vice—infidelity, homosexuality, bisexuality, prostitution (including male homosexual prostitution), infanticide—was considered virtue in Greco-Roman culture. Sexual abstinence was abnormal.

In the Roman world, the law of Manus gave the husband ownership, including absolute control, of his wife. She was his property; he could kill her just as he might destroy a faulty shovel, for any reason with impunity. Women were held in low esteem, the female child even lower. We get a sense of this in a letter from a Roman soldier stationed in Alexandria to his wife in Rome.

> Know that I am still in Alexandria. And do not worry if they all come back and I remain in Alexandria. I ask and beg you to take good care of our baby son, and as soon as I receive payment I shall send it to you. If you are delivered of a child [before I come home], if it is a boy keep it, if a girl discard it. You have sent me word, 'Don't forget me.' How can I forget you. I beg you not to worry.[210]

Note the irony of a very touching letter to a wife, yet so callous about a baby girl. Infanticide of little girls was commonplace. In fact, Rome had 131 males to every 100 females. In the Roman Empire it was 140 males to every 100 females. What happened to the females? They were set outside to die. Put on top of a wall, laid in the bow of a tree, and left to die.

The Greek world was similar. Revered philosopher Plato wrote, ". . . [a]ll those creatures generated as men who proved themselves cowardly and spent their lives in wrong-doing were transformed, at their second incarnation, into women. . . . In this fashion, then, women and the whole female sex have come into existence."[211]

His student Aristotle saw the female as a type of "monstrosity," a deviation from the natural type (albeit one "required by Nature" for reproduction).[212] Thus, a woman is, in a sense, a "deformed male."[213] In a different work, Aristotle asserts, ". . . [the] male is by nature superior and the female inferior, the male ruler and the female subject."[214] Such thinking is akin to Hinduism. Both Hinduism in the East and Plato in the West regard the female as the reincarnation of a male who sinned greatly in his previous life.

THE GREEK DICHOTOMY

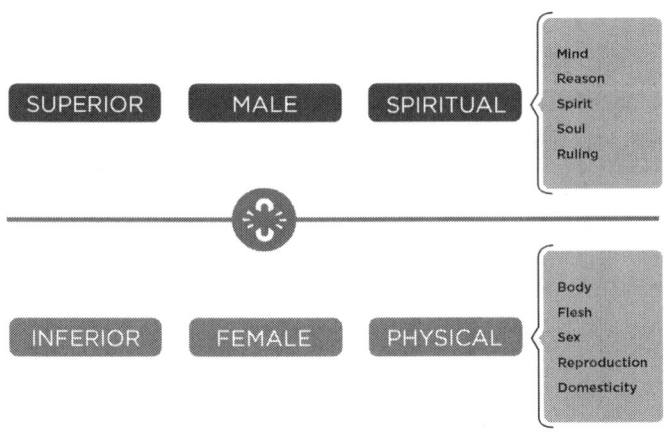

Greek dualism, articulated by Plato and his followers, conceived of the universe as divided into the spiritual and the physical. The spiritual is high and the physical is low. This dualistic thinking was applied to the role of men and women as well. Mardi Keyes writes:

The male was associated with mind, reason, spirit, soul and

ruling; the female was associated with body, flesh, sex, reproduction, domesticity and subordination. The male was superior,
the female inferior. Men were human and male (male=human);
women were female only–defined by sex and reproduction
(whether wives, concubines, slaves or prostitutes).[215]

Dualism, thank God, wasn't the only influence. Middle Eastern Jewish
culture also had a significant role at Jesus' birth. As we have seen, in some
periods of ancient history, the Jews set
the gold standard for family formation, the dignity of men and women,
and the sacredness of human sexuality.
But at Christ's birth, Jewish attitudes
toward women largely mimicked
the Greco-Roman standard. Here is
a prayer the Jewish male recited in
the synagogue: "Thank you God for
not making me a Gentile, a woman
or a slave." Jesus ben Sirach, a Jewish
scholar in Egypt, who penned the
Book of Sirach in 180 B.C., says the
following about women.

> **All that the Scripture
> deems as vice–infidelity,
> homosexuality, bisexuality,
> prostitution (including male
> homosexual prostitution),
> infanticide–was considered
> virtue in Greco-Roman
> culture. Sexual abstinence
> was abnormal.**

- Sirach 22:3: "It is a disgrace to be the father of an undisciplined
  son, and the birth of a daughter is a loss."
- Sirach 42:14: "Better is the wickedness of a man than a woman
  who does good; it is woman who brings shame and disgrace."

Further, Rabbi Eliezer is quoted as saying in the first century, "May
the words of the Torah be burned and not be delivered [rather than be
entrusted] to women!"[216] Elsewhere, he is quoted as saying, "Whoever
teaches his daughter the Torah is like one who teaches her obscenity."[217]

Let's face it: the world into which Jesus was born was hostile to women.
Whether from the smaller Jewish subculture or the larger Greco-Roman
culture, women were considered inferior to men, often as property, and
treated as such.

What was Jesus' attitude to the metanarratives of His day? How did
Jesus view women? Did He accept the status quo, or challenge it?

From everything the New Testament tells us about Jesus, it's crystal clear that He was a revolutionary. He entered a broken world; one He did not accept as normal. "Repent," Jesus proclaimed, "for the kingdom of heaven is at hand" (Matthew 4:17). Jesus honored women for who they were, *imago Dei* humans, and for what they did.

Author Dorothy Sayers said the following about Jesus and women:

> A prophet and teacher who never nagged at them, never flattered or coaxed or patronized; who never made arch jokes about them, never treated them either as "The women, God help us!" or "The ladies, God bless them!"; who rebuked without querulousness and praised without condescension; who took their questions and arguments seriously; . . . who took them as he found them and was completely unself-conscious. There is no act, no sermon, no parable in the whole Gospel that borrows its pungency from female perversity; nobody could possibly guess from the words and deeds of Jesus that there was anything "funny" about woman's nature.[218]

Scripture shows God affirming women's dignity in a world where men seldom recognized it. If you are a man, see what you can learn from Jesus as a man. If you are a woman, be encouraged as you read how the One who designed and created women treated them even in the sexist culture of His day.

First, God affirmed women at the birth of Jesus through the genealogies.

According to *The New Bible Dictionary*, "A genealogy in the OT sense is a list of names indicating the ancestors or descendants of an individual or individuals, or simply a registration of the names of people concerned in some situation."[219]

A Hebrew genealogy passes from father to son, tracing lineage through male ancestry. A kingly genealogy traces royalty. Females were not included, certainly not foreign women. But Matthew's royal line of kings includes four women who certainly were not royalty. In fact, they were all Gentiles. What is more, they were known for their sin.

Tamar is listed in Matthew 1:3. Her story is told in Genesis 38. Despite being twice-widowed and alone, Judah refuses to grant Tamar's right to marry another son in his family. As a result, she deceives her father-in-law and becomes pregnant by him. She was the mother of Perez, David's seventh great-grandfather.

Second is *Rahab*, listed in Matthew 1:5, whose story is told in Joshua 2. She was a prostitute who aided the Hebrew spies. She comes into the royal line as the wife of Salmon and the mother of Boaz.

The third is *Ruth*, who also appears in Matthew 1:5. Her story appears in the book that bears her name. Ruth was not a Jew, but a Moabite. Her people were pagan worshipers of Baal (see Deuteronomy 23:3–5). They had failed to help the Hebrew people in their hour of need and instead had put a curse on them. Because of this, the law of Moses declares that "No Ammonite or Moabite or any of his descendants may enter the assembly of the LORD, even down to the tenth generation" (Deuteronomy 23:3). Yet Ruth entered the royal line as the wife of Boaz, the father of Obed.

Fourth was *Bathsheba*, who is identified but not named in Matthew 1:6. Her story appears in 2 Samuel 11. She was the wife of Uriah, David's loyal commander. David arranged for his murder and brought Bathsheba into his harem. She bore Solomon and became the queen mother during his reign.

These four Gentile "sinners" were grafted into the royal blood line. How fitting that the royal blood of Jesus is shed to make Jew and Gentile into "one new man" (Ephesians 2:11–18). Considering God's husbanding of the harlot Israel (see Hosea), as we saw in an earlier section, it is befitting that from eternity past God ordained that the blood of "sinful" Gentile women was to be part of the royal blood shed on the cross. What an amazing story!

These four were not "holy" women. Each one had a past. Yet God placed them into the royal lineage.

Second, God chose women to announce the birth of Jesus.

The Lord used three common women for an extraordinary purpose, to bring a startling message to the world. Mary, a young Jewess from a backwater village, her older cousin Elizabeth, wife of Zacharias, and Anna, a prophetess.

Mary was likely a young teenager when she responded to the angel Gabriel's startling announcement, "Behold the handmaid of the Lord; be it unto me according to thy word" (Luke 1:38, KJV). Her words reflect another humble response, that of a young Ruth to her mother-in-law, Naomi.

Do not urge me to leave you or to return from following you. For where you go I will go, and where you lodge I will lodge. Your people shall be my people, and your God my God. Where you die I will die, and there will I be buried. May the LORD do so to me and more also if anything but death parts me from you. (Ruth 1:16–17)

Mary's story continues with a visit to her cousin *Elizabeth*, who prophesied about Jesus' birth:

Blessed are you among women, and blessed is the fruit of your womb! And why is this granted to me that the mother of my Lord should come to me? For behold, when the sound of your greeting came to my ears, the baby in my womb leaped for joy. And blessed is she who believed that there would be a fulfillment of what was spoken to her from the Lord. (Luke 1:42–45)

The narrative follows with Mary's beautiful song, the Magnificat, announcing Christ's birth to the world, beautiful poetry that has been read and treasured for over 2,000 years.

Mary of Nazareth is the Everywoman of history, ordinary and obscure. She represents what is possible for us flesh-and-blood women who yield ourselves to God.
Lillian Calles Barger

Finally, we come to the prophetess *Anna*, who was eighty-four years old and had been widowed just seven years after marrying. She likely was destitute, living near the temple grounds. Luke writes, "She never left the temple but worshiped night and day, fasting and praying" (Luke 2:37, NIV). When Mary and Joseph brought the baby Jesus to the temple to be circumcised before the Lord, Anna approached them and prophesied. Luke records the moment: "Coming up to them at that very moment, she gave thanks to God and spoke about the child to all who were looking forward to the redemption of Jerusalem" (Luke 2:38, NIV).

Four women appear in the royal line of Christ, and three "down-to-earth" women were given an uncommon task, to announce the birth of

Jesus to the world. For 2,000 years the world has heard their voices. There is no sexism here in the biblical accounts.

Let's consider what it means for God to choose the womb of an "every-woman" to conceive, gestate, and give birth to the Savior of the world. Some church traditions have "supersized" Mary, elevating her status to that of a "Co-Redemptrix." She is seen as divinely perfect (immaculate from conception) and forever a virgin. While all Christians ought to love and respect Mary for the unique task and the humble way she accepted it, we must not give her honors that are due to God alone. More is at stake than idolatry, as important as that is. Also at stake is our understanding of how God chooses ordinary people to accomplish His extraordinary purposes.

Lillian Calles Barger calls us back to reality in *Eve's Revenge*: "Recovering Mary of Nazareth from perpetual virginity and perfection will allow us to see the possibility that God can and does work through the ordinariness of our flesh."[220]

In choosing Mary of Nazareth to be the mother of Jesus, God is honoring "everywoman." Barger captures this so well.

> Mary of Nazareth is the Everywoman of history, ordinary and
> obscure. She represents what is possible for us flesh-and-blood
> women who yield ourselves to God. Mary recognizes her own
> powerlessness and has no grand vision for herself as the model
> of virtue that she will become. . . . Yet her yes provides hope
> that in our bodies the works of God can be wrought. In her
> we find a sign of God's willingness to use the insignificant,
> even the vulnerability and symbolic nature of our bodies.[221]

Jesus, God incarnate, will live for nine months in the womb He created. He will pass through a human birth canal; He will be nurtured at human breasts. All the things we are loath to talk about—blood, tissue, and fluids—are sanctified by the habitation of the Almighty. The Divine, visiting the ordinary, sanctifies the common. Barger writes, "A holy God enters the bloodiness of the womb, considered unclean under Jewish law, and makes it a temple. In the womb of a woman the eternal and transcendent Word by which the worlds were created becomes flesh."[222]

All that sexism and secular feminism diminishes, God raises up in the womb-life, birth, and breast-nurturing of the Son of God. The One who created the womb inhabited a woman's womb for nine months.

Third, Jesus affirmed a woman's intrinsic worth.

Jesus consistently demonstrated the dignity of women in how He treated and related to them.

First, He regularly communicated with women. In Jesus' day it was considered improper for a woman to speak to a man in public if he was not her husband. The disciples display this attitude after finding Jesus talking with the woman at the well (John 4:27): "Just then his disciples came back. They marveled that he was talking with a woman, but no one said, 'What do you seek?' or, 'Why are you talking with her?'"

Here are some examples of Jesus' communication with women.

1. He talked to the woman at the well (John 4:7–26), a despised Samaritan and an adulteress.
2. He spoke with the woman caught in adultery (John 8:10–11).
3. As he moves toward Golgotha, Jesus pauses to speak to women who are mourning His coming death (Luke 23:27–31).

Second, He treated women as human beings. Jesus did not view women as sex objects but as *imago Dei* humans. Why did women flock to Jesus? He treated them with dignity. Note, Jesus did not *give* women dignity. He recognized their intrinsic dignity as humans created in the image of God.

The One who created the womb inhabited a woman's womb for nine months.

Similarly, men cannot give women dignity. It is not their prerogative. Women already *have* dignity because of who and whose they are. Men can only recognize the dignity inherent in women and treat them with the respect they deserve.

When Jesus addressed women, He spoke tenderly, in a way that would touch their souls, as He identified with them.

- "Daughter" to the woman with a bleeding disorder (Luke 8:48).
- "My child" to Jairus's daughter (Luke 8:54, NIV).
- "Daughter of Abraham" to the woman who was crippled (Luke 13:16). Men were sometimes addressed as "sons of Abraham." But for Jesus to address this woman as a daughter of Abraham was to turn the world upside down.

Third, He treated women, and men, as free and responsible moral agents.

He didn't wink at their sin but lovingly confronted it, as with the adulterous Samaritan woman (John 4:7–26), the woman caught in adultery (John 8:3–11), and the woman who washed His feet (Luke 7:36–50).

The culture of Jesus' day applied a double standard in the matter of lust. Jesus upended that double standard: "But I say to you that everyone who looks at a woman with lustful intent has already committed adultery with her in his heart" (Matthew 5:28). Mardi Keyes notes, "In a culture which blamed woman's very nature for male lust, Jesus put the blame where it belonged—on the men who looked lustfully at women!"[223]

Another double standard existed when it came to sexual sin. We see this clearly in John 8:3–11, where the Jews were ready to stone the woman caught in adultery. There is no mention of the offending man.

As well, a double standard existed when it came to divorce. A man was free to divorce his wife for almost any reason by writing a simple declaration of divorce. There was no judicial process to protect the rights of the wife.

Fourth, Jesus chose women as heroines in His stories.

- The ten virgins exemplified the virtue of readiness (Matthew 25:1–3).
- The widow's plea—perseverance (Luke 18:2–8).
- The Canaanite mother—faith (Matthew 15:28).
- The widow's mite—generosity (Mark 12:41–44).

Fifth, Jesus broke many social customs relative to the sexes. He allowed women to touch Him, and He touched them. This was unheard of in contemporary Jewish life. We see the different attitude of Jesus in His interactions with the ceremonially unclean woman (Mark 5:25–34) and the woman who washed his feet (Luke 7:44–48). In this sense Jesus was a troublemaker. He challenged both Greco-Roman and Jewish culture and customs.

Fourth, Jesus ministered to women.

He met their physical, social, emotional, and spiritual needs. He addressed the needs of men and women whose lives were broken, treating both with equal care. There are numerous examples of His caring for women.

1. He brought inner healing to the woman at the well (John 4:7–26).

2. He healed the woman with a chronic bleeding condition (Luke 8:43–48).
3. He raised Jairus' daughter from the dead (Luke 8:49–56).
4. He healed the woman who had been crippled for eighteen years (Luke 13:10–13).
5. He healed the Canaanite's daughter of demon possession (Matthew 15:22–28).
6. He cared for widows and called for people to support widows (Luke 7:11–15).
7. He taught the Samaritan woman at the well and Mary the sister of Martha (Luke 10:38–42).
8. On the cross, He provided for His mother's care (John 19:25–27).

Fifth, women were part of His ministry task force.

People are always asking, "Can women minister?" Yes, women can and should be involved in ministry. They were actively involved in Jesus' ministry and full-fledged members of His task force.

For three years, Jesus taught and modeled the nature of the Kingdom of God to His ministry team. Women learned the life of the kingdom and became ambassadors for the King. They not only ministered *to* Jesus; they ministered *with* Jesus.

Even more remarkable, this ministry occurred in an age when women were rarely seen in public. Jesus' female team members are not only seen in public, but their names are also recorded in the Gospels. Now the world knows who they are. These women included Mary Magdalene, Mary the mother of James and Jesus, Salome, Joanna the wife of Chuza (manager of Herod's household), Susanna, and the mother of Zebedee's sons.

Women were first at the cradle (Elizabeth, Luke 1:39–44) and the last at the cross (Luke 23:27). Women were part of His traveling team and cared for Jesus' needs. Some helped to financially support the ministry team (Matthew 27:55–56; Mark 15:40–41; Luke 8:1–3).

Some were part of His advance team, securing housing and food in preparation for Jesus and His team before their arrival.

> After this, Jesus traveled about from one town and village to another, proclaiming the good news of the kingdom of God. The Twelve were with him, and also some women who had been cured of evil spirits and diseases: Mary (called Magda-

lene) from whom seven demons had come out; Joanna the wife of Chuza, the manager of Herod's household; Susanna; and many others. These women were helping to support them out of their own means. (Luke 8:1–3, NIV)

Women served Jesus at the end, outstripping their male counterparts for persistence and courage. As Jesus' death approached, the twelve were a pitiful lot. They were not thinking of how they could help Him, but only of how they could save themselves. It was the women who showed courage, love, and care for Jesus. The mother heart of God was manifested through these gritty women.

Women served Jesus at the end, outstripping their male counterparts for persistence and courage.

Many were at the cross, "watching from a distance" (Matthew 27:55–56; Mark 15:40). Some stood at the foot of the cross (John 19:25). All four Gospels acknowledge the women who came to the tomb to do a proper burial anointing (Matthew 28:5–8; Mark 16:5–8; Luke 24:2–9; John 20:1–2). They even announced His resurrection. Barger reminds us,

> From this new beginning God continues the legacy of using women as instruments of grace. Instead of appearing to the powerful Pilate or the Sanhedrin, Jesus appears first to those of lowest status. Instead of calling a press conference, he sends discredited women as messengers into a culture that does not easily believe them. In this way Jesus continues to overturn the power paradigms of the world and establish his true justice.[224]

For all these reasons and more, we see Christ, the first feminist, overturning the ancient tables of sexism. May all who claim to follow Christ in our day do likewise.

STUDY GUIDE

1. Describe the "moral conditions" in the Greco-Roman world that Jesus entered. How are they similar and dissimilar to your own country?

2. What view of women did the Greco-Roman and Jewish worlds hold in the days of Jesus? Did Jesus accept the status quo, or challenge it?

3. What women does the genealogy in Matthew's gospel specifically mention? What did these women have in common?

4. What does the ordinariness of the women God chose to announce Jesus' birth show us about how God works?

5. How did Jesus affirm the intrinsic worth of women? How did He minister to their needs?

6. Did Jesus affirm women in ministry? How did Jesus' female disciples compare to His male disciples?

7. How was Jesus a feminist?

CHAPTER 24

The Perfect Bridegroom and the Ultimate Wedding

YEARS AGO, I was in a very poor community in the Philippines working for a nonprofit organization in a child sponsorship program. Many of the couples there lived together and had children but had never married. The organization led a series of Bible studies on marriage and then held a common wedding ceremony for eight or nine couples, brides and grooms dressed in the best they could find. The women were beaming, the men looked scared, and their children served as flower girls and ring bearers. It was a wonderful celebration.

Weddings are special. Family and friends gather, you wear your finest, and you make a commitment before God and the angels to love and care for one another as husband and wife.

Pastor and author Tim Keller mused about how the best marriages reflect something of the unconditional love of God for his people. "To be loved but not known is comforting but superficial," Keller wrote. "To be known and not loved is our greatest fear. But to be fully known and truly loved is, well, a lot like being loved by God. It is what we need more than anything."[225]

We see this kind of love in Scripture, from beginning to end. In fact, the significance of marriage is highlighted with two weddings marking the beginning and ending of the biblical narrative.

The Bible begins with the wedding of Adam and Eve in the Garden of Eden; this is the prolog of marriage and family formation for all of human history. And it becomes a prophetic foretelling of the "Ultimate Wedding" of Christ and His Church. At the consummation of history, Christ will return as King of Kings and Lord of Lords to marry His Bride—the Eternal Counterpart. The epilogue of history is the marriage supper of the Lamb.

Every earthly wedding pictures an ultimate wedding still to come. In his book, *The Ultimate Wedding*, Bill Risk begins:

> Our God is a God who pays meticulous attention to detail, who fulfills according to what he has established, who was willing to pay an inconceivably high price to secure a bride for his son, and who will not fail to send his son back to reclaim his beloved.[226]

We see this meticulousness when we grasp some of the essentials of Hebrew weddings. There were seven elements.

1. *Shiddukhin*: The Match
2. *Mohar*: The Bride Price
3. *Mattan*: Love Gifts
4. *Shiluhim*: Dowry
5. *Ketabah*: The Marriage Contract—Legal
6. *Kiddushin*: The Betrothal—Time of Preparation
7. *Nissuuin*: The Nuptials—Consummation

In the Hebrew world the commitment to marry came before the courtship and the wedding. The marriage begins with the contract followed by the betrothal, with responsibilities spelled out for the man and the woman. Only then does the nuptial itself, the consummation of the wedding, happen.

There's a parallel to the biblical doctrine of salvation. Salvation, seen as a process, proceeds from justification, to sanctification, and finally to glorification. These correspond with the last three stages of the Hebrew wedding: *ketabah* to *kiddushin*, and finally to *nissuuin*.

All Scripture is nuptial. From Genesis to Revelation, we see God as the husband of Israel and Christ as the Bridegroom of the church. The Hebrew wedding points to the gospel in three ways:

- The key idea
- The Hebrew custom
- The implications for the church today

Let's look closely at the stages of the Hebrew wedding ceremony. It begins with the *match*. The first step in a Jewish marriage was less about love as a feeling and more about a commitment to another person for life. The marriage was arranged: Usually the father of the groom approaches the father of the bride, and they would arrange the match (see Genesis 24:3–6). The marriage of the Lamb will complete what began before the foundation of the world when the Father initiated the match of Christ and the church! "For he chose us in him before the creation of the world to be holy and blameless in his sight" (Ephesians 1:4, NIV).

> **The Bible begins with the wedding of Adam and Eve in the Garden of Eden; this is the prolog of marriage and family formation for all of human history. At the consummation of history, Christ will return as King of Kings and Lord of Lords to marry His Bride—the Eternal Counterpart. The epilogue of history is the marriage supper of the Lamb.**

First, the groom's father gives the *mohar*, the bride price, to the father of the bride. This payment was required by law. By custom the bride price reflected the value of the bride. What *mohar* did the heavenly Father give? The life of His Son. "For God so loved the world, that he gave his only Son" (John 3:16).

Next is the *mattan*, the love gift from the groom to the bride. This was from the heart, a romantic expression. No laws governed this practice. The bride of Christ is the new creation. She receives the gift of eternal life. This incomparable gift comes from the self-sacrificing commitment of the Bridegroom to do anything for his bride.

The final gift is the *dowry*. This is the parting gift from the bride's father to his daughter. The dowry was to equip the bride to begin her new home and life. In the same way, the Father has given gifts to His church: the Holy Spirit and the gifts of the Spirit.

Then you have the marriage contract itself, the *ketubah,* or legal binding of the couple. It's a written document testifying to the *mohar*, the rights of the bride, and the privileges of the groom.

We see this in the Old Testament. The marriage contract with Israel was the Mosaic Covenant. It was established in Exodus 19 and ratified in Exodus 24.

The Old Covenant is a marriage contract between *Ish* and Israel. And the New Covenant, the new contract between Christ and the church, contains the promises of the Groom toward His bride. Here's what the bride can expect from the groom. This is the *ketabah*.

Mary and Joseph were legally married and in the betrothal period when she conceived our Messiah Jesus by the Spirit of God. When Joseph learned she was pregnant, he prepared to divorce her quietly because he knew the child was not his. The law allowed for divorce in the case of adultery, and the breaking of the betrothal was considered adultery just as if the couple were actually married. The marriage was legally binding even before it was consummated.

The *betrothal* was a period of preparation after the signing of the covenant. At some point in Jewish history, the "cup of acceptance" was instituted. In this ceremony, the groom poured a cup of wine for the prospective bride. The cup was blessed, and the bride, if she agreed to the covenant, indicated her acceptance by drinking from the cup with the potential bridegroom. Then the cup was put on the ground and crushed to symbolize, "We have celebrated the contract." This marked the culmination of the *ketubah* and the beginning of the *kiddushin*. Then the preparation for the marriage would begin.

Now the couple is legally bound by the covenant. This created new responsibilities. The man could not go to war for a year (Deuteronomy 24:5). Because Mary had accepted the cup from Joseph and entered into a legal contract, he could divorce her when she was found with child (Matthew 1:18–19).

Here's the implication for the church today as we share communion. Christ says, "Take this cup; it's my blood shed for you. Do this in remembrance of me" (1 Corinthians 11:25, my paraphrase). Until when? "Until I return" (see verse 26).

The *contract* has been agreed to. Jesus will die, will return to heaven, and we await His coming again. And during the waiting, during the preparation for the wedding, both Bride and Groom have responsibilities.

The groom returns home and prepares the *huppah*, the bridal chamber at his father's house. Here the *marriage will be consummated*. As Jesus said, "In my father's house are many mansions. . . . I go to prepare a place for you." (John 14:2, KJV). What is He preparing? The *huppah*, where the marriage will be consummated. The wedding can't take place until the *huppah* is finished.

And who determines when the *huppah* is finished? Not the groom, but his father. When the father decides the *huppah* is ready, only then does the groom return for his bride. As Jesus says, He doesn't know the time of His return. Only the Father knows (Matthew 24:36).

While the groom is carrying out his responsibilities, the bride sets herself apart. She purifies herself to be ready for her groom's return. She would complete a purification bath and wear a veil in public to remind other men that she had been bought with a price.

What price was paid for the church, the bride of the Lamb? The life of the Groom. He bought her with His death. She is set apart so others know she is waiting for her Bridegroom. She doesn't know the exact time, nor does the groom. Only the groom's Father knows. His return will be a surprise. She must have her lamp trimmed and ready and not be caught unprepared.

When the purification and the *huppah* are complete, it's time for the nuptials. First the bride is fetched. Then comes the ceremony, then the wedding feast, and finally the bride and the groom establish their home together. Today the church is waiting for the Bridegroom. The trumpet will sound and the Bridegroom will come to fetch His Bride.

When we lived in Switzerland, some friends got married. The groom and his groomsmen left the church and walked down a hill to the bride's home. Upon the tuxedo-clad groom's arrival, someone announced, "The groom has come!" Upon hearing this, the bride came out in all her beauty and preparation. She took the groom's arm, and he led her to the church, where friends and family were waiting.

Someday the church will hear, "Behold the Bridegroom comes!" We are waiting for that day and that announcement. Christ is coming back to fetch His Bride!

Then we come to the ceremony. The bride has purified and veiled herself. Now the groom takes her to the place he has prepared, the *huppah*, and there they consummate the marriage by becoming one flesh. Meanwhile, a public celebration takes place, away from the *huppah*, for the gathered friends and family.

At the wedding of the Lamb, the woman is dressed in fine linen, bright and clean that was given to her to wear. Then the angel said to John, "Blessed are those who are invited to the wedding supper of the lamb." And he added, "These are the true words of God" (Revelation 19:8–9).

The wedding feast is the public celebration of the two becoming one flesh. The wedding *ceremony* was a tight circle, but the wedding *feast* was a much larger group. The feast could last for days, maybe even a week, while the guests waited for the bride and the groom to come out of the *huppah* to celebrate together.

In Isaiah 25:6–8 (NIV) we read,

> On this mountain the LORD Almighty will prepare
>   a feast of rich food for all peoples,
> a banquet of aged wine—
>   the best of meats and the finest of wines.
> On this mountain he will destroy
>   the shroud that enfolds all peoples,
> the sheet that covers all nations;
>   he will swallow up death forever.
> The Sovereign LORD will wipe away the tears
>   from all faces;
> he will remove his people's disgrace
>   from all the earth.
> The LORD has spoken.

The wedding of the Lamb marks the climax of history, the consummation of God's purposes for His creation. This long-anticipated event was prefigured in the Garden with Adam and Eve and will be manifested in glory when God Himself takes a Bride and the church is with Him for all eternity.

John Piper writes of the age-long preparation of the Bride of Christ:

> . . .[T]he church is finally completed and he takes her arm, as
> it were, and leads her to the table. The marriage supper of the
> Lamb has come. He stands at the head of the table and a great

silence falls over the millions of saints and he says, "This, my beloved, was the meaning of marriage. This is what it all pointed toward. This is why I created you male and female and ordained the covenant of marriage. Henceforth, there will be no more marriage and giving in marriage, for the final reality has come and the shadow can pass away."[227]

While there are always exceptions, as a general rule, God created men and women to form families. Part of the reason that a man and a woman correspond one to the other is to picture the end of history, when the Bridegroom Jesus Christ will fetch His Bride. But before they marry and establish their household, the Bride and Groom will join the wedding feast to receive their gifts.

Revelation 21:23–26 says the kings of the earth will bring the glory of their nations into the city of God. Gifts from the kings of the earth, the glory of nations, will be purified and brought into heaven, given to Christ and His Bride on their wedding day.

> "This, my beloved, was the meaning of marriage. This is what it all pointed toward. This is why I created you male and female and ordained the covenant of marriage."
> **John Piper**

Following the feast, the new couple will establish their household. As we read in 1 Thessalonians 4:17, "After that we who are still alive and are left will be caught up together with them in the clouds to meet the Lord in the air and so we will be with the Lord forever. Therefore, encourage each other with these words" (NIV).

Note also Revelation 21:1–4:

Then I saw a new heaven and a new earth, for the first heaven and the first earth had passed away, and the sea was no more. And I saw the holy city, new Jerusalem, coming down out of heaven from God, prepared as a bride adorned for her husband. And I heard a loud voice from the throne saying, "Behold, the dwelling place of God is with man. He will dwell with them, and they will be his people, and God himself will be with them as their God. He will wipe away every tear from their eyes, and death shall be no more, neither shall there be mourning, nor crying, nor pain anymore, for the former things have passed away."

As *The Divine Romance* by Gene Edwards notes:

> Every angel was now remembering that unforgettable moment when during the creation of Eve, the glory, the light, and the revelation of God overwhelmed all creatures. It was a thing that until now they had never understood. Now they knew. When the Lord created Eve, he had seen someone else and had fashioned Eve in her image.
>
> That someone now stood before them. She had emerged in a vision before their very eyes. . . .
>
> They hardly dared to look upon such terrible beauty, yet they dared not do otherwise. Here was a woman robed in the brightness of God with beauty defying their comprehension. She was like him, yet female. A loveliness, so tender, a countenance so full of love, a creature so pure that angelic eyes shone with awe and terror seeking to take it in. Her hair was black as Ravens. Her mouth had inspired a creating God to fashion springtime. Her features were composed of the highest beauty of every race and tribe and kindred of womanhood from all times past and all times future.
>
> Mercifully, the vision of the glorious woman began to recede. Once more there appeared before the angels, the scene of the *all* of God exhausted. They fell prostrate upon their faces. . . . One of the angels stood still half blinded by glory and uttered aloud the thought of all,
>
> "A counterpart for our Lord,
> The bride of God."[228]

This is the wedding to which all earthly weddings point, however faintly. The Grand Design is assumed, making such a glorious scene possible. As we await the fulfillment of our deepest longings, we join all heaven and earth, the Bride and the Spirit, and cry out, "Come Lord Jesus. Come fetch your Bride.'"

─────────────── **STUDY GUIDE** ───────────────

1. "All scriptural is nuptial! The Bible begins with a wedding and ends with a wedding." What is the significance of this? How might this impact the way we live our lives?
2. How do weddings showcase the love of God and foretell the end of history?
3. What is the parallel between the Hebrew wedding process and the biblical doctrine of salvation? What stage is the church in right now?
4. What is a *huppah*? In Hebrew culture, who determined when the *huppah* was finished? How does this relate to the Second Coming?
5. What should be the prayer of the church until the Lord returns?

Acknowledgments

NO BOOK IS the sole product of one person's efforts. It is always the result of a collaborative effort between friends, advisors, and professional editors. With this in mind, I would like to mention some of the many people who have helped with this project. If I have left anyone out, it is my personal lapse and for that I am deeply sorry.

- Dwight Vogt, a dear friend, and fellow worker for over forty years, has functioned as the project director for the book and without whose guidance and effort the book would have never been finished.
- John Adams, a gifted editor, and researcher whose work has made this book immensely better.
- Naomi Smith a dear friend, a gifted writer, a modern feminist who has morphed into a maternal feminist, has encouraged me throughout this project.
- Tim Williams, friend and member of the Disciple Nations Alliances team whose suggestions and editing has helped shape the outcome of the project.
- Gary Brumbelow, a pastor, writer, and editor who partnered with me in my writing projects for years and was instrumental in the early stages of writing this book.
- In 2019 a group of twenty people, half men and half women, from five continents, gathered in Malaga, Spain, to spend a week together to participate in a week-long video shoot on the theme *The Grand Design*. Thanks each of you for giving me a week of your lives and your insights into this project. You will see your

fingerprints all over this book. This video series is available online at https://disciplenations.org/grand-design/.

- Ana Santos, founder of the ministry Fragile which provides hope for women who are trafficked, for her work in finding and provisioning the venue in Malaga for our gathering and video shoot.
- Joshua Hernandez, a friend and gifted graphic artists from Peru for the cover design and graphics in the interior of the book.
- Karen Guerrero and Lisa Montero, who were of great help in the process of turning a video transcription into the manuscript. They helped to bring both a critical female perspective and a Latin voice to the final manuscript.
- Samuel Felix, a gifted videographer and friend from Brazil, who did the video shoot and then produced the video course on *The Grand Design*. During one of our group discussions in Malaga, Spain, it was Samuel who suggested the title of the video series and the book be *The Grand Design: Rediscovering Male and Female as Imago Dei*. This captured the focus of the book and imagination of the global team.
- Catalina Diaz, the Founder of The Amalos Foundation in South America, who I met many years ago at a regional conference being held in, Lima, Peru for 500 women. I'll never forget hearing Catalina speak on her passion for women and families whose lives were shattered because of sexist culture. She had a similar experience when she listened to my lectures. Her teaching was the application of the principles that I have written about in this book. Catalina thank you for your friendship and the witness of your life for the restoration of *Imago Dei*.
- Viviana Valie, our Spanish publisher, who, before the ink was even dry on one book, was encouraging me to write the next book. Viviana, here is the "next book."
- Scott Allen, my good friend of forty years, the Co-Founder of Disciple Nations Alliance and the President of our organization. Thank you for your support and encouragement over the years.
- Stan Gutherie, an editor, and author in his own right. Stan has partnered with the writers at the Disciple Nations Alliance for over twenty years. Stan worked long and hard with me to turn the manuscript into this book.
- To Tim Beals and the team at Credo House Publishers for their

support and encouragement in getting this book to print. When we told Tim about this book, he wrote back and said: "I've become convinced that the teleological argument from design is our strongest apologetic for this critical issue. We need this book now!"

With a grateful heart, thanks each one of you for your contribution and encouragement to see this book finished.

About the Authors

FOR NEARLY FORTY years, **Darrow Miller** has been a popular speaker on Christianity and culture, apologetics, worldview, poverty, and the dignity of women. He has traveled and lectured in over a hundred countries, and his books and publications have been translated into over a dozen languages.

Darrow's heart beats at the unlikely intersection of worldview and development. He has written hundreds of blogs at Darrow Miller and Friends, numerous articles, Bible studies, and authored or co-authored nineteen books around these themes. These include *Discipling Nations: The Power of Truth to Transform Cultures* (YWAM Publishing, 1998), which relates worldview to poverty and development; *LifeWork: A Biblical Theology for What You Do Every Day* (YWAM Publishing, 2009), which explores biblical worldview and vocation; *Emancipating the World* (YWAM Publishing, 2012), which challenges us to rethink and restore the church's mission—the Great Commission; *Rethinking Social Justice* (YWAM Publishing 2015), which focuses on restoring biblical compassion; *Don't Let Schooling Stand in the Way of Education* (Credo Publishing, 2021), which lays out the need for a biblical theology for education to respond to the crises in public education; and *A Call for Balladeers: Pursuing Art and Beauty for the Discipling of Nations* (Disciple Nations Alliance, 2022).

Darrow has a master's degree in higher and adult education and has pursued graduate studies in philosophy, theology, Christian apologetics, biblical studies, and missions. He and his wife, Marilyn, studied at the Institute for Holy Land Studies in Jerusalem and studied and worked with Francis and Edith Schaeffer at L'Abri Fellowship in Switzerland from 1969 to 1971. Darrow was a student pastor at Northern Arizona University and later pastored an urban church in Denver, Colorado.

For twenty-seven years Darrow served as a vice president of Food for the Hungry International (FHI) in recruiting, staff development, and the creation of curriculum in worldview and development. While at FHI, Darrow, Dr. Bob Moffitt and Scott Allen founded the Disciple Nations Alliance (DNA). The DNA is a nonprofit organization seeking to spread a school of thought—a virus, if you will—through training, publishing, and mentoring. The global DNA network comprises like-minded organizations and people in over sixty countries who are "equipping the church to transform the world."

Darrow and his wife live in Phoenix, Arizona. They have four children and fourteen grandchildren.

Stan Guthrie is Minister of Communications for New Covenant Church, Naperville, Illinois. He is the author or coauthor of seven books, including *Victorious: Corrie ten Boom and The Hiding Place*. Stan is very happily married to Christine. He lives online at stanguthrie.com.

Glossary of Terms

androgyny. State of being androgynous, possessing both male and female sex organs in one individual or organism.

animism. A set of metaphysical assumptions that see the world as ultimately spiritual, in which the physical world is animated by spirits or gods. In some cases, the physical world may be considered an illusion. Man's highest good or goal is to return to spiritual oneness; the physical is denigrated. Folk religions, Buddhism, and Hinduism are examples of highly animistic systems, but animistic beliefs can influence any worldview.

atheism. The disbelief of the existence of a God or Supreme intelligent Being. Confucianism and secularism are atheistic belief systems.

atomism. The belief that everything is diverse without ultimate unity. This concept traces back to Aristotle (ca. 384–322 B.C.). This stands in contrast to Plato's monism.

avocation. An activity taken up in addition to one's regular work or profession, usually for enjoyment; a hobby.

avodah. A Hebrew word עָבַד—translated variously as "work," "worship," and "serve." It indicates that, in the Hebrew mind, there is no separation between work and worship.

Baal. In the Old Testament, a deity in Moab and Philistia. The term *baal* carries the meaning *owner* or *master*; this characterization of a husband is the opposite of the loving, self-sacrificing headship of *Ish*.

beauty. An assemblage of graces or properties in a person or object that pleases the eye. Central to God's act of creation, beauty glorifies goodness and illuminates truth, making beauty a moral necessity. Beauty is found not "in the eye of the beholder," but in its reflection of the glory of God and His creation. Beauty is intrinsic to God's nature.

biblical theism. Synonymous with Judeo-Christian theism. See theism.

binary. Pairs, twofold, double, consisting of two; e.g., male and female.

capital. Resources that can be used toward development. These can be outside of man, such as oil and natural gas, or internal to a human, such as imagination, ideas, and virtue.

chauvinism. Excessive or prejudiced support for one's own cause, group, or sex; in the context of male chauvinism: the belief that men are inherently superior to women.

chrematistics. A word of Greek origin; the process of gaining wealth through any means; the manipulation of property and wealth to maximize short-term value for personal gain. This is in contrast to *oikonomia*.

complementary. Fitting together, fulness, completion, designed to work together.

Complementarianism. The concept that men and women were created equal in dignity and different in design and function to complement each other and form a viable whole.

Communism. Originally a theory of society. The name of a political or economic theory that rests upon the abolition of private property, especially the means of production and distribution, and seeks to overthrow capitalism by revolutions. Attested from 1850, a translation of German *Kommunismus* (itself from French), in Marx and Engels' *Manifesto of the Communist Party*, later, *The Communist Manifesto*.

Confucianism. A belief system based on the teachings of Confucius (551–479 BC). Confucianism believes in nature as ultimate, not God. More a practical philosophy of everyday life than a religion, Confucianism focuses primarily on how to live in the world.

Critical Race Theory (CRT). A set of ideas holding that racial bias is inherent in many parts of Western society, especially in its legal and social institutions, which are asserted to have been primarily designed for and implemented by white people.

critical theory. Any approach to social philosophy that aims to reveal, critique, and challenge power structures in society and culture. Critical theories typically argue that social problems stem more from social structures and cultural assumptions than from individuals.

cultivate: The act of tilling and preparing the earth for crops and the mind and soul for knowledge and virtue.

Cultural Mandate, the. Also known as the First Commission, or the Creation Mandate, founded in Genesis 1:26–28 and expanded in Genesis 1–2. God's instruction to humankind (male and female) to form families and to develop the earth. God's intent is for human beings to take what He has made and do something with it.

Cultural Marxism. Born in the Frankfurt Institute in Germany in the 1920s by a group of Marxist philosophers who realized that economic Marxism would not change the West, and who believed it would take profound cultural change to bring down Western Civilization. This movement is also known as Postmodernism, Critical Theory, or Critical Race Theory. At the heart of Cultural Marxism is the denial of God, revelation, reason, and reality.

culture. Is derived from *cult*-worship and is the manifestation of a people's ethos, creed, or sacred belief system and is related to the term *cultivate*. When a people change the object of worship, their culture changes. Worship is upstream from culture, and culture is upstream from the social, economic, and political institutions of a society.

Darwinism. Also **Evolutionism**; a system of belief originating from the theories of Charles Darwin (1809–1882); assumes that humans are the result of a mindless, thoughtless process of chance, having evolved from the same source as all other living things on Earth. Darwinism asserts that humans are, essentially, mere animals and are not made in the image of God, having no distinct purpose to our existence.

deconstruct. To take apart; to destroy something to replace it with something else.

Difference Feminism. Also known as **Essential Feminism**; form of feminism that acknowledges the biological and physiological differences between men and women, including the idea that women are essentially more nurturing than men. Difference Feminism asserts that both sexes have equal moral status, and their differing functions are complementary and of equal importance.

divine. Pertaining to the true God; as the divine nature; divine perfections.

dualism. The ancient Greek concept of dividing the universe into two fundamental categories: the spiritual and the physical, or the sacred and the secular. The spiritual was considered high and holy; the physical was considered low and dirty. Many Christians have abandoned the biblical worldview for a Greek Gnostic dualism. Also known as the Sacred/Secular Divide.

echad. A Hebrew word meaning "one." In contrast to *yachid,* which means an absolute or indivisible one, this word refers to a compound one ("the two shall become *one* flesh").

Egalitarianism. The concept that men and women are equal in value and thus are "the same"; their abilities and roles are interchangeable.

Equality Feminism. A subset of Second-Wave Feminism that focuses on the basic similarities between men and women. Its ultimate goal is the interchangeability of women and men in all domains of life, including the political and economic arenas. Today, this is also known as egalitarian or modern feminism.

eugenics. A set of beliefs and practices that seek to manipulate the human genetic pool to improve the genetic quality of a human population. It seeks to "weed the garden" of people who have an "inferior" genetic pool and encourage the multiplication of people judged to be of a superior genetic pool.

evangelism. Communication and dissemination of the gospel—the good news of Jesus Christ and His kingdom.

external capital. These are resources of creation that are *external to man* and available for all humanity. Four primary categories exist in external capital: natural (environmental; i.e., sun, water, soil, minerals); social (i.e., other people, religious and civic organizations), physical (infrastructure; i.e., roads, bridges, power grid), and institutional (i.e., libraries, hospitals, schools, government).

ezer. A Hebrew word translated "helper," "act of supplying what is needed for another." In Genesis 2, it refers to a woman's complementary role in relation to man. Far from denoting inferiority, the word is most often used in the Old Testament to refer to God, who comes alongside as a "helper" to His people.

faith. The biblical word *pistis* (moral conviction) comes from *pitheō*, which was a legal term meaning "to be convicted by argument" or "to yield to the evidence." This kind of faith will lead one to expose life, property, and reputation to loss or injury. Risk can be accepted because the evidence is compelling. Today the word *faith* is most often used to mean "a position held despite a lack of evidence" or "believing despite opposing evidence."

fatalism. The doctrine that all things are subject to fate or that they take place by inevitable necessity. The Islamic understanding of Allah's constant, unyielding decrees to creation is an embodiment of the concept—there is only one Creator, one force, that has the ability to determine the course of history. According to fatalism, human creativity is an unnecessary and futile act because one is unable to change or impact the future. Individuals and cultures that have a fatalistic worldview lack hope and take little or no initiative to improve their circumstances.

female genital mutilation (FGM). The partial or total removal of external female genitalia or other injury to the female genital organs for non-medical reasons. Today, genital mutilation is becoming accepted under the guise of "gender affirming surgery" and is a multibillion-dollar industry.

feminism. The advocacy of women's rights on the basis of the equality of the sexes. Feminism has taken many forms; early maternal feminism supported the equal dignity of women through their differences to men, specifically through their unique capacity for caring and nurturing; second-wave feminism shifted the focus to women's holding equal dignity to men through striving to become more *similar* to men; third-wave feminism rejects any difference between men and women.

feticide. the killing of a fetus in the womb.

flourishing. That condition of life—whether an individual, community, or nation—marked by all God's intentions, growth, and abundance.

gender. A social construction, usually used to describe the way an individual wants to present themselves to society. Gender is a fluid concept in contrast to the word sex which is fixed by ones biology to the depth of 6,500 human chromosomes that are marked as either male or female.

gendercide. The systematic murder of a specific gender; in this book the focus of gendercide is on the killing of females simply because they are females.

general revelation. The revelation available to all human beings in all times through God's creation as revealed through reason and reality.

gestation. The process or period of developing inside the womb between conception and birth.

Grand Design, the. God's perfect, intentional design of human nature, of marriage, and of the complementary relationship between men and women, each created in His image, made equal yet gloriously different. The Grand Design for the fulfillment of God's purposes of creating human beings in God's image to fulfill the Cultural Mandate. It looks ahead to the eventual union between Christ and the Church—the ultimate marriage—at the end of history.

Great Exchange, the. The biblical teaching that human beings have exchanged worship of the Creator for worship of His creation and mankind (see Romans 1).

Hinduism. A world religion that originated on the Indian subcontinent around 1500 B.C., Hinduism holds that the universe is ultimately spiritual. Everything in the physical world is seen as a manifestation of the Divine One; all aspects of reality are manifestations of the One. Hinduism has many forms but is generally polytheistic and holds to a belief in karma and reincarnation—the endless cycle of birth and death.

husbandry. The management of a household. A steward of the land and the things that the land produces. Wendell Berry says: "Husbandry is the name of all the practices that sustain life by connecting us conservingly to our places and our world; it is the art of keeping tied all the strands in the living network that sustains us." This would include, for the man, the care for his wife, "as Christ loves the church," and his family.

Imago Dei. Latin phrase meaning "in the image of God"; refers to the characteristic of human beings made in God's image. Found in Gen. 1:27: "So God created man in his own image, in the image of God created he him; male and female created he them" (KJV).

individualism. Focus only on self, personal fulfillment, and gratification. This is distinct from the term "individual," which means the uniqueness of the individual human being.

internal capital. The potential God has placed within each human being (resources for success, prosperity, and fruitfulness). These include six major aspects: physical (i.e., eyes to see, ears to hear, limbs to walk and carry, tongue to taste); intellectual (i.e., mind to think critically, reason to solve problems, analyzing to name the animals and designating phylum; emotional (i.e., to feel, enjoy, cry, passion to create); moral (i.e., to distinguish right from wrong, to make moral judgments); spiritual (i.e. the breath in the body, human soul, the indwelling Holy Spirit in believers, fruits of the Spirit, spiritual gifts); volitional (i.e., ability to distinguish good from evil and to make choices that not only change one's life, but impact the community and affect eternity).

intersectionality. The study of the framework between systems of oppression and domination. People are no longer identified as unique individuals but as being members of "intersectional" communities defined by such things as race, gender, religion, disability, and social-economic class. The more oppressed communities a person belongs to, the greater his or her status of oppression. Intersectionality is a tool of Cultural Marxism that leads to neo-tribalism.

Ish. Old Testament word for "husband"; capitalized, God Himself as a husband. As *Ish,* God is the archetype of a husband: a loving, self-sacrificing servant in His headship of Israel and Christ's headship of the Church.

Islam. Founded in 622 by Muhammad, a monotheistic religion holding that God is wholly other and unknowable. The role of man is to submit to the revealed will of Allah (in Arabic, in the Qur'an, through the prophet Muhammad). Muslims reject the Christian doctrine of the Trinity, believing that God is absolutely one. Islam, like Catholicism, is often found mixed with local animistic beliefs—the syncretism is known as Folk Islam.

Judeo-Christian theism. The historical worldview of Christendom (the West), theism assumes the existence of a God who created the universe, both animate and inanimate, spiritual and physical, separate from Himself but not independent of Him. God is both transcendent (outside His creation) and immanent (present within it). He is everywhere present and involved. The universe is open to God's purpose and intervention. God has revealed Himself through special revelation, both through the written Word, the Bible, and through the living Word, Jesus Christ. At the same time, man can use his God-given reason to discover truth about God and the universe because God has revealed Himself to all people through creation (general revelation) and in making man in His image.

marriage. The holy covenant between one man and one woman, made before God, and part of His Grand Design. Marriage is a complementary and other-centered relationship; complementary because the man and the woman bring different contributions to the partnership, and other-centered because each spouse places the other's needs first. All marriages point toward the end of time, when Christ will come and consummate the ultimate marriage between Himself and the Church.

maternal feminism. Also known as **first-wave feminism**; the idea that women are significant in both their being and function, specifically their nurturing, maternal nature, and are equal to men. Maternal feminism was embraced by most men and women in nineteenth century Western society, and it led to the women's suffrage movement in the early twentieth century.

metanarrative. An overarching account or interpretation of events and circumstances that provides a pattern or structure for people's beliefs and gives meaning to their experiences. Another word for worldview or paradigm.

Metaphysical Capital. Literally meta-physical, beyond the physical. This is transcendent or spiritual capital, from the head, from the mind. Also called worldview. In Genesis 1, God reveals that He spoke creation into existence. Here is the archetypical example of capital. Before the physical universe existed, the eternal God existed. It was the community of the invisible Intelligent Designer who brought the visible universe and life into existence from the heart of His transcendent existence by *conceiving* (forming an intention), *speaking* (articulating the intention), and *willing* (actualizing the intention). The greatest resource for human flourishing is metaphysical capital that matches reality.

metaphysics. The branch of philosophy concerned with the fundamental nature of reality and being.

misogyny. Hatred of women.

monism. Belief in the absolute oneness of all things. Hinduism and Buddhism are monistic religions. Monism is a word used in philosophy and metaphysics of systems of thought that deduce all phenomena from a single principle. Plato (ca. 428–348 BC) was an early proponent. Monism stands in contrast to atomism.

namjon-yeobi. A Korean saying: "Men are honored; women are abased."

neo-tribalism. A term first used by French sociologist Michel Maffesoli in his book *The Time of the Tribes* (1988); the sociological concept that humans naturally form themselves into tribal societies rather than mass society, and therefore will form tribal social networks called neo-tribes, "sources of informal, often emotionally driven, cultural expression" (Oxford Reference).

nuptial. Pertaining to marriage; done at a wedding; as nuptial rites and ceremonies; nuptial torch.

oikodespoteo. A Greek word meaning the act of ruling a house and managing family affairs. *Oikodespoteo* is the role of the woman in the home, to guide the house, to manage and rule over it virtuously, as seen in Proverbs 31.

overpopulation, theory of. First articulated in *The Principle of Overpopulation* (1798) by Thomas Malthus, this evolutionary perspective fears ecological catastrophe because food production is said to increase arithmetically, while population increases exponentially. The theory states that there are not enough resources to provide for everyone. Events of the twentieth century have discredited the theory, which nevertheless has many prominent proponents in academia and public policy today.

paganism. Heathenism: the worship of false gods, or the system of religious opinions and worship maintained by pagans.

paradigm. An example, a model; from Late Latin *paradigma* "pattern, example," especially in grammar and science.

postmodernism. Defined by Terry Eagleton as "the contemporary movement of thought which rejects . . . the possibility of objective knowledge" and is therefore "skeptical of truth, unity, and progress" [*After Theory*, 2003]. A denial of revelation, reason, and reality.

psychology. The study of man's psyche (soul, spirit, inner self).

Sanger, Margaret (1883–1966). A leader of the eugenics movement in the United States and the Founder of the American Birth Control League (now Planned Parenthood) and an advocate of population control, particularly of the poor.

second-wave feminism. Also known as **modern feminism**; movement gaining public attention beginning in 1966 as it rightly challenged the sexist lie that men are superior to women. However, unlike maternal feminism, second-wave feminism placed little value in the nurturing capacity of a mother, in either family or society, and operated from a secular humanistic worldview rather than a biblical one, placing the self as its ultimate focus. Women of second-wave feminism sought to obtain equality with men by becoming more *like* men, seeking sexual freedom and non-pregnancy through abortion.

science. The thinking of God's thoughts after Him. A rational evaluation of empirical evidence, combined with a willingness to follow that evidence wherever it leads.

servant-leadership. The biblical concept that those in leadership have a greater responsibility than anyone else to serve others.

sexism. Prejudice, stereotyping, or discrimination on the basis of sex, predominantly against women.

spirituality. Quality of being spiritual; essence distinct from matter; immateriality.

stewardship. A steward is someone who is responsible to care for or govern something for someone else. The word "stewardship" is generally used to convey the idea that one should manage or steward resources so that they are both conserved and maximized for the benefit of all.

Submission. Derived from *mission*: sending or being sent, delegated by authority, with certain powers for transacting business; a co-mission as sent on a foreign mission. To be on a mission with another and under his or her authority

succorer. One who leads by providing support and comfort for another, especially in times of need.

syncretism. The amalgamation of different religions, cultures, or schools of thought; reconciliation of different beliefs, often to bring an illusion of agreement rather than clarity. Term commonly used when describing the process by which unbiblical beliefs are grafted onto biblical truths.

Teleonomic. The "character of living organisms, to admit that in their structure and performance they act projectively—realize and pursue a purpose."

theism. The belief or system of belief in one God; sees the universe as ultimately personal.

theology. The study of God.

third-wave feminism. A form of postmodern feminism following the second wave, which dismisses the idea that there are inherent differences between men and women. Third-wave feminism seeks the end of binary sexuality, advocating instead for gender identity, and sacrifices absolute truth for personal feeling and opinion.

transcendent. Beyond or outside the natural realm. Often thought of as the spiritual realm. Beyond space and time.

truth. The principle that there is objective truth that can be known and applied, the moral foundation for freedom, and the assumption behind knowledge. Anything that claims to be true can be subjected to four tests: Is it reasonable? Does it match reality? Does it explain all of life? Is it livable?

vice-regent. Someone who rules in the place of another. Human beings are delegated, by God, to rule in His stead. This is the role of *Imago Dei* as articulated in Genesis 1–2 in the Cultural Mandate.

vocation. One's calling. Work is a call of God on an individual's life. It becomes the sphere *through* which, not merely *in* which, a Christian serves Christ and His kingdom. It is the occupation—the principal business of one's life—through which one occupies territory or a sphere of influence (Luke 19:13) *for* Jesus Christ.

volition. The act of willing, determining choice, or forming a purpose; the power of willing or determining.

wisdom. The moral application of truth.

worldview. A set of assumptions, held consciously or unconsciously in faith, about the basic makeup of the world and how the world works. Synonyms would include mindset, paradigm, meta-narrative. Worldview functions as the software behind the hardware of a computer.

Subject Index

Wright, Colin, 95
Wright, N. T., 85

Y
Youmans, Elizabeth, 105,
   197, 214

Z
zoophilia, 51

Scripture Index

301

Endnotes

Prologue
[1] https://www.crossroadsinitiative.com/media/articles/ourheartisrestlessuntilitrestsinyou/

Introduction: The Deadliest Lie
[2] Ashley Carnahan, "Detransitioned teen wants to hold 'gender-affirming' surgeons accountable: 'What happened to me is horrible,'" Fox News, November 11, 2022, https://www.msn.com/en-us/health/other/detransitioned-teen-wants-to-hold-gender-affirming-surgeons-accountable-what-happened-to-me-is-horrible/ar-AA13ZH2a.

Chapter 1: The War Against Women
[3] Amartya Sen, "More than 100 Million Women Are Missing," *The New York Review of Books*, December 20, 1990, https://www.nybooks.com/articles/1990/12/20/more-than-100-million-women-are-missing/.

[4] Lydia Howard Sigourney, *Letters to Young Ladies,* 2nd ed. (London: Jackson and Walford, 1841), 6.

[5] See José Luis and Silvia Cinalli, *La Iglesa Al Desnudo: Escalofriantes Cifras Del Comportamiento Sexual* (Argentina: Placeres Perfectos, 2012).

[6] Lilian Calles Barger, *Eve's Revenge: Women and a Spirituality of the Body* (Grand Rapids, MI: Brazos Press, 2003), 109.

[7] Mary Stewart Van Leeuwen, "The Christian Mind and the Challenge of Gender Relations," *The Reformed Journal*, vol. 37 (September 1987): 22.

[8] World Health Organization, "Violence Against Women," March 9, 2021, https://www.who.int/news-room/fact-sheets/detail/violence-against-women.

[9] Jack Stubbs, "Child Abuse Revelations Divide 'Most Shameful Town in Britain,'" *Reuters*, September 2, 2014, https://www.reuters.com/article/uk-britain-abuse-rotherham/child-abuse-revelations-divide-most-shameful-town-in-britain-idUKKBN0GX1DN20140902.

[10] E Ward, "Rape of Girl-Children by Male Family Members," abstract, *Australian and New Zealand Journal of Criminology* 15, no. 2 (1982): 90–99, https://www.ojp.gov/ncjrs/virtual-library/abstracts/rape-girl-children-male-family-members.

[11] "Nigeria Chibok Abductions: What We Know," BBC, May 8, 2017, https://www.bbc.com/news/world-africa-32299943; Helen Gavin, "Violent Crime as Old as the Bible:

Boko Haram Uses Rape as a Weapon of War," The Conversation, May 11, 2015, https://theconversation.com/violent-crime-as-old-as-the-bible-boko-haram-uses-rape-as-a-weapon-of-war-41470.

[12] Divorce Statistics, "Divorce Statistics and Divorce Rate in the USA," https://www.divorcestatistics.info/divorce-statistics-and-divorce-rate-in-the-usa.html.

[13] Guinness World Records, "Highest Divorce Rate," https://www.guinnessworldrecords.com/world-records/highest-divorce-rate.

[14] Ross Benes, "Porn could have a bigger economic influence on the US than Netflix," Quartz, June 20, 2018, https://qz.com/1309527/porn-could-have-a-bigger-economic-influence-on-the-us-than-netflix.

[15] Charles Colson, "A Job No Woman Would Choose," Breakpoint, December 13, 2002, https://www.breakpoint.org/job-no-woman-choose/.

[16] Heather Bar, "China's Bride Trafficking Problem," The Diplomat, October 30, 2019, https://thediplomat.com/2019/10/chinas-bride-trafficking-problem/.

[17] Damien Ma, "Chinese Workers in Africa Who Marry Locals Face Puzzled Reception at Home," The Atlantic, June 20, 2011, https://www.theatlantic.com/international/archive/2011/06/chinese-workers-in-africa-who-marry-locals-face-puzzled-reception-at-home/240662/.

[18] Africa-China Reporting Project, "Uncertain fate of children fathered by Chinese men left behind in Uganda," April 4, 2022, https://africachinareporting.com/uncertain-fate-of-children-fathered-by-chinese-men-left-behind-in-uganda/.

[19] International Labour Organization, "Global Estimates of Modern Slavery: Forced Labour and Forced Marriage," September 12, 2022, https://www.ilo.org/global/topics/forced-labour/publications/WCMS_854733/lang--en/index.htm; International Labour Organization, "Profits and Poverty: The Economics of Forced Labour," May 20, 2014, https://www.ilo.org/global/about-the-ilo/newsroom/news/WCMS_243201/lang--en/index.htm.

[20] Judicial Watch, Inc., v. U.S. Department of Health and Human Services. Case No. 1:19-cv-00876-TNM (2021). https://www.judicialwatch.org/wp-content/uploads/2021/03/JW-v-HHS-memorandum-opinion-00876.pdf.

[21] Madeline Osburn, "New Unsealed Documents Show Planned Parenthood Profited From Aborted Baby Body Parts," The Federalist, April 15, 2020, https://thefederalist.com/2020/04/15/new-unsealed-documents-show-planned-parenthood-profited-from-aborted-baby-body-parts/.

[22] Bob Unruh, "Organs 'harvested' from unborn babies target of new lawsuit," WND, January 15, 2023, https://www.wnd.com/2023/01/organs-harvested-unborn-babies-target-new-lawsuit/.

[23] Ñusta Carranza Ko, "Peru's government forcibly sterilized Indigenous women from 1996 to 2001, the women say. Why?", Washington Post, February 19, 2021, https://www.washingtonpost.com/politics/2021/02/19/perus-government-forcibly-sterilized-indigenous-women-1996-2001-why/.

[24] Jane Lawrence, "The Indian Health Service and the Sterilization of Native American Women," American Indian Quarterly 24, no. 3 (2000): 400–419. http://www.jstor.org/stable/1185911.

[25] "Unintended Pregnancy and Abortion Worldwide: Fact Sheet," Guttmacher Institute, March 2022, https://www.guttmacher.org/fact-sheet/induced-abortion-worldwide.

[26] Susheela Singh et al., "Abortion Worldwide 2017: Uneven Progress and Unequal Access," Guttmacher Institute, March 2018, https://www.guttmacher.org/report/abortion-world-wide-2017#incidence-of-induced-abortion-current-levels-and-recent-trends.

[27] Suzanne Venker and Phyllis Schlafly, *The Flip Side of Feminism*, (Washington, DC: WND Books, 2011), 137.

[28] "Female genital mutilation," World Health Organization, January 21, 2022, https://www.who.int/news-room/fact-sheets/detail/female-genital-mutilation.

[29] Eva Ontiveros, "What is FGM, where does it happen and why?", *BBC*, February 6, 2019, https://www.bbc.com/news/world-47131052.

[30] Howard Goldberg et al., "Female Genital Mutilation/Cutting in the United States: Updated Estimates of Women and Girls at Risk, 2012," *Public Health Reports* 131 (March-April 2016): 1–8, https://www.uscis.gov/sites/default/files/document/reports/fgmutilation.pdf.

[31] "U.S. Sex Reassignment Surgery Market Size, Share & Trends Analysis Report By Gender Transition (Male To Female, Female To Male), And Segment Forecasts, 2022—2030," Grand View Research, accessed February 25, 2023, https://www.grandviewresearch.com/industry-analysis/us-sex-reassignment-surgery-market.

[32] Yunping Tong, "India's Sex Ratio at Birth Begins To Normalize," Pew Research Center, August 23, 2022, https://www.pewresearch.org/religion/2022/08/23/indias-sex-ratio-at-birth-begins-to-normalize/.

[33] Lori Heise, "The Global War Against Women," *Washington Post,* April 9, 1989, https://www.washingtonpost.com/archive/opinions/1989/04/09/the-global-war-against-women/85a23676-1ba4-43b4-93c4-e01cd1d780ce/.

[34] "Feticide," accessed April 28, 2023, https://invisiblegirlproject.org/about-female-gendercide/feticide/.

[35] John Gittings, "Growing sex imbalance shocks China," *The Guardian,* May 12, 2002, https://www.theguardian.com/world/2002/may/13/gender.china.

[36] R.J. Rummel, *Death By Government (*New Brunswick, NJ: Transaction Publishers, 1994), 65–66.

[37] Kallie Szczepanski, "Female Infanticide in Asia," ThoughtCo., accessed December 12, 2022, https://www.thoughtco.com/female-infanticide-in-asia-195450.

[38] See Journeyman Pictures' documentary film, *Girl Killers* (2012).

[39] Tahira Shahid Khan, "Chained to Custom," *The Review*, 4–10 March 1999, 9.

[40] Khan, "Chained to Custom."

[41] Tim Sullivan, "For Indian Brides, Dowries Are Deadly," *Washington Post,* October 3, 2004, https://www.washingtonpost.com/archive/politics/2004/10/03/for-indian-brides-dowries-are-deadly/b162e147-9f4c-42b6-8b03-5c166cc20bd5/.

[42] "State of World Population 2020," United Nations Population Fund, https://www.unfpa.org/sites/default/files/pub-pdf/UNFPA_PUB_2020_EN_State_of_World_Population.pdf.

[43] *It's a Girl: The Three Deadliest Words in the World*, directed by Evan Grae Davis (Shadowline Films, 2012). Learn more at https://itsagirlmovie.com.

[44] Barger, *Eve's Revenge*, 68.

Chapter 2: The Spiritual Root of Sexist Culture (Hosea)

[45] Mardi Keyes, "The Mystery of Gender" (unpublished paper delivered at L'Abri, Southborough, MA, July 20, 2001).

[46] Nahum M. Sarna, *The JPS Torah Commentary: Genesis* (Philadelphia: Jewish Publication Society, 2001), 21.

[47] Bruce K. Waltke, *The Dance Between God and Man: Reading the Bible Today as the People of God* (Grand Rapids: William B. Eerdmans Publishing Co., 2013), 466.

[48] John Angell James, *Female Piety, or the Young Woman's Guide through Life to Immortality* (New York: Robert Carter & Bros., 1853), 69.

Chapter 3: Servanthood: The Divine Pattern of Leadership

[49] Dictionary of Biblical Languages with Semantic Domains - LOGOS Bible study software.

[50] Moffitt, Robert Emailed to Darrow Miller, 24 January 2023 confirming that this was his quote.

[51] Jonathan Edwards, "The Excellency of Christ," *Christian Classics Ethereal Library*, accessed December 15, 2022, https://www.ccel.org/ccel/edwards/sermons.excellency.html.

[52] Henry Krabbendam, *Sovereignty and Responsibility: The Pelagian-Augustinian Controversy in Philosophical and Global Perspective* (Bonn: Verlag fur Kultur und Wissenschaft, 2002), 52.

Chapter 4: Servant-Leadership Modeled in Marriage

[53] Moffitt, Robert Emailed to Darrow Miller, 24 January 2023 confirming that this was his quote.

[54] Ian Oxnevad, "Professor's Redefinition of Pedophilia could Help Offenders Demand Rights," NY Post, January 1, 2022, accessed March 11, 2023, https://nypost.com/2022/01/01/professors-redefinition-of-pedophilia-could-help-offenders-demand-rights/; Susan Berry, "American Psychiatric Association Reclassifies Pedophilia, Backtracks," Breitbart, November 2, 2013, accessed March 11, 2023, https://www.breitbart.com/politics/2013/11/02/american-psychiatric-association-reclassifies-pedophilia/.

[55] "Bestiality is much, much more common than you think," news24, February 18, 2015, accessed March 11, 2023, https://www.news24.com/health24/Sex/Sexual-diversity/Bestiality-is-much-much-more-common-than-you-think-20150218; M. Jenny Edwards, "Bestiality: The Best Kept Secret in America," Veterinary Wellness and Social Work Summit, November 2015, accessed March 11, 2023, https://www.researchgate.net/publication/298976988_Bestiality_The_best_kept_secret_in_America.

[56] S. Michael Craven, "In Defense of Marriage," *Crosswalk,* July 8, 2008, https://www.crosswalk.com/family/marriage/in-defense-of-marriage-11578872.html.

[57] John Piper, "Husbands Who Love Like Christ and the Wives Who Submit to Them," *Desiring God*, June 11, 1989, https://www.desiringgod.org/messages/husbands-who-love-like-christ-and-the-wives-who-submit-to-them.

[58] C.S. Lewis, *The Four Loves* (1960; Harcourt Brace: 1991), 105.

[59] Piper, "Husbands Who Love Like Christ."

[60] "G2776—kephalē—Strong's Greek Lexicon," Blue Letter Bible, accessed December 15, 2022, https://www.blueletterbible.org/lexicon/g2776/kjv/tr/0-1/.

[61] Wayne Grudem, "The Meaning of 'Head' in the Bible: A Simple Question No Egalitarian Can Answer." *CBMW News* 1, no. 3 (June 1996), 8.

[62] "G1984—episkopē—Strong's Greek Lexicon," Blue Letter Bible, accessed December 15, 2022, https://www.blueletterbible.org/lexicon/g1984/kjv/tr/0-1/.

[63] Susah T. Foh, *Women and the Word of God: A Response to Biblical Feminism* (Philipsburg, NJ: Presbyterian & Reformed Publishing Co., 1979), 208.

Part 2: Unity and Diversity

Chapter 5: The Trinity: A Pattern for Humankind

[64] William Shakespeare, *Macbeth*, ed. George Lyman Kittredge (Waltham, MA: Blaisdell Publishing Co., 1966), 5.5.24–28.

[65] Steve Rudd, "Trinity: Oneness in Unity Not in Number: Yachid vs. Echad," The Interactive Bible, accessed April 29, 2023, https://www.bible.ca/trinity/trinity-oneness-unity-yachid-vs-echad.htm.

[66] Usman D. Ali and Garba S. Yahaya, "Ethnic Conflict in Nigeria: Causes and Consequences," *International Journal of Scientific Research in Multidisciplinary Studies* 5, no. 1 (January 2019): 70–77, https://www.isroset.org/pub_paper/IJSRMS/9-IJSRMS-01607.pdf.

[67] Akila Muthukumar, "Casteism Camouflaged as Culture," *Harvard Political Review*, September 30, 2020, https://harvardpolitics.com/casteism-camouflaged-as-culture/.

[68] Ben Zeisloft, "'Expressive Individualism': Theologian Carl Trueman Explains Why Public High Schools Keep Hosting Drag Shows," The Daily Wire, May 26, 2022, accessed March 13, 2023, https://www.dailywire.com/news/expressive-individualism-theologian-carl-trueman-explains-why-public-high-schools-keep-hosting-drag-shows.

Chapter 6: The Framework: Examining the Assumptions Behind Our View of Male and Female

[69] Gilbert Keith Chesterton, *Orthodoxy* (New York: John Lane Company, 1908), 174.

[70] Chesterton, Orthodoxy,173.

[71] Chesterton, *Orthodoxy,* 179.

[72] Chesterton, *Orthodoxy,* 173.

[73] Chesterton, *Orthodoxy,* 174.

[74] Chesterton, *Orthodoxy,* 174.

[75] Chesterton, *Orthodoxy,* 175.

[76] "N.T. Wright on Same-Sex Marriage," YouTube, video, 5:00, March 25, 2014, https://youtu.be/xKxvOMOmHeI.

[77] Dennis Prager, *The Rational Bible: Genesis: God, Creation, and Destruction* (Washington, D.C.: Regnery Faith, 2019), 35.

[78] Sigourney, *Letters to Young Ladies*, 6.

[79] Ivy George, "The Past Interrupted," *Sojourners*, June 2004, https://sojo.net/magazine/june-2004/past-interrupted.

Chapter 7: Transcendent Sexuality: The Root of Our Biological Differences

[80] "Jordan B. Peterson | Full interview | SVT/TV 2/Skavlan," YouTube, video, 38:39, https://www.youtube.com/watch?v=_iudkPi4_sY. (The quoted portions are at 10:00 and 22:44, respectively.)

[81] Elisabeth Elliot, *Let Me Be a Woman* (Carol Stream, IL: Tyndale House Publishers, 1999), 83.

[82] Elliot, *Let Me Be a Woman,* 4.

[83] Jacques Monod, *Chance and Necessity* (New York: Vintage, 1971), 9.

[84] Monod, *Chance and Necessity,* 22.

[85] Alan Snyder, *If the Foundations Are Destroyed* (Maitland, FL: Xulon Press, 2010), 32.

[86] "Masculine and Feminine: What Is the Difference?", *New Covenant,* February 1982, 20.

[87] Prager, *The Rational Bible: Genesis*, 78.

[88] Karl Stern, *The Flight from Woman* (New York: Farrar, Strauss, & Giroux, 1965), 10.

[89] Nicholas Wade, "Y Chromosome Depends on Itself to Survive," *New York Times,* June 19, 2003, https://www.nytimes.com/2003/06/19/us/y-chromosome-depends-on-itself-to-survive.html.

[90] Colin M. Wright and Emma N. Hilton, "The Dangerous Denial of Sex," *Wall Street Journal*, February 13, 2020, https://www.wsj.com/articles/the-dangerous-denial-of-sex-11581638089.

[91] Erica Komisar, *Being There: Why Prioritizing Motherhood in the First Three Years Matters* (New York: TarcherPerigee, 2017), 37.

[92] Anna Machin, *The Life of Dad: The Making of the Modern Father* (London: Simon & Schuster, 2018), 24.

Part 3: Imago Dei

Chapter 8: Made in God's Likeness: The Structural View

[93] https://disciplenations.org/wp-content/uploads/2020/04/Christian-View-of-Children_Elizabeth-Youmans.pdf

[94] C.S. Lewis, *The Weight of Glory and Other Addresses* (San Francisco: HarperOne, 2001), 45.

[95] Nick Givas, "Man With Down Syndrome Who Spoke About Sanctity of Life Says He Wants to Make Abortion 'Unthinkable,'" *The Daily Signal*, February 1, 2019, https://www.dailysignal.com/2019/02/01/man-with-down-syndrome-who-spoke-about-sanctity-of-life-says-he-wants-to-make-abortion-unthinkable/.

[96] Ryan Scott Bomberger, "Courage: The Remedy for the Violence of Abortion," Radiance Foundation, April 4, 2019, https://radiancefoundation.org/courage-the-remedy-for-the-violence-of-abortion/.

[97] Denise Leipold, Right to Life of Northeast Ohio newsletter, March 7, 2017, https://myemail.constantcontact.com/Rebecca-Kiessling----Conceived-In-Rape.html?soid=1102570619078&aid=ZEmEV8KvfxU.

[98] Nina Golgowski, "Miss Pennsylvania Valerie Gatto opens up about being 'a product of rape,'" *New York Daily News,* June 5, 2014, https://www.nydailynews.com/news/national/pennsylvania-opens-product-rape-article-1.1819104.

Chapter 9: Made for Relationship: The Relational View

[99] Walt Heyer, "Hormones, surgery, regret: I was a transgender woman for 8 years — time I can't get back," *USA Today,* February 11, 2019, https://www.usatoday.com/story/opinion/voices/2019/02/11/transgender-debate-transitioning-sex-gender-column/1894076002/.

[100] Sex Change Regret, accessed December 15, 2022, sexchangeregret.com.

[101] Jonathan Edwards, "An Unpublished Essay on the Trinity," Christian Classics Ethereal Library, accessed December 15, 2022, https://ccel.org/ccel/edwards/trinity/trinity.i.html.

[102] https://www.songfacts.com/lyrics/simon-garfunkel/i-am-a-rock

[103] Stern, *The Flight from Woman,* 273–274.

[104] Elisabeth Elliot, *The Mark of a Man* (Grand Rapids, MI: Baker Publishing Group, 2021), 25.

[105] Michael Ferrebee Sadler, "Sermon XXV: The Deep Things of God," in *Parish Sermons* (London: Bell & Daldy, 1862), 376.

Chapter 10: Made Kings and Queens to Govern Creation: The Functional View

[106] Herman Bavinck, "The Origin, Essence, and Purpose of Man," *Grace Online Library,* accessed December 16, 2022, http://graceonlinelibrary.org/doctrine-theology/doctrine-of-man/the-origin-essence-and-purpose-of-man-by-herman-bavinck/.

[107] Vishal Mangalwadi, Lecture at Mercy Ship's Foundation in Community Development School, Tyler, TX, lecture notes, delivered May 1995.

[108] James A. Swanson, *A Dictionary of Biblical Languages with Semantic Domains: Hebrew (Old Testament),* s.v. "עָבַד," (Bellingham, WA: Faithlife, 1997).

[109] *The Imperial Dictionary, English, Technological, and Scientific,* s.v., "cult," "culture," and "cultivate," (Glasgow, Edinburgh, and London: Blackie and Son, 1859).

[110] https://www.ligonier.org/learn/articles/westminster-shorter-catechism

[111] Russell Kirk, "Civilization Without Religion?," "*Touchstone*, Winter 1993.

[112] Thomas Carlyle, *Past and Present*, 1843, accessed December 16, 2022, http://www.online-literature.com/thomas-carlyle/past-and-present/35/.

[113] The Avodah Institute, as quoted in "Avodah: The One Act of Work and Worship,"

Avodah Ministries, accessed May 5, 2023, https://avodahministries.wordpress.com/the-meaning-of-avodah/.

Part 4: The Glorious Eve

Chapter 11: Woman, the Crescendo of Creation

[114] Swanson, J. (1997). Dictionary of Biblical Languages with Semantic Domains : Hebrew (Old Testament) (electronic ed.). Oak Harbor: Logos Research Systems, Inc..

[115] Swanson, J. (1997). Dictionary of Biblical Languages with Semantic Domains : Hebrew (Old Testament) (electronic ed.). Oak Harbor: Logos Research Systems, Inc.

[116] Swanson, J. (1997). Dictionary of Biblical Languages with Semantic Domains : Hebrew (Old Testament) (electronic ed.). Oak Harbor: Logos Research Systems, Inc.

[117] Gene Edwards, *The Divine Romance Copyright* ©*1984,1992,33–34.*

Chapter 12: The Maternal Heart of God

[118] Henri Nouwen, *The Return of the Prodigal Son: A Story of Homecoming* (New York: Image Books, 1992), 99.

[119] John Piper, "Making Room for Atheism: The Supremacy of God in a Pluralistic World," Desiring God, August 10, 2005, https://www.desiringgod.org/articles/making-room-for-atheism.

[120] https://www.littleflower.org/st-therese-daily-devotional/heart-mother/

[121] *New Bible Dictionary*, 3rd ed., s.v. "mercy, merciful," (Downers Grove, IL: InterVarsity Press, 1996), 751.

[122] Komisar, *Being There*, 17.

[123] Komisar, *Being There,* 45.

[124] J.I. Packer, *Knowing God* (Downers Grove, IL: InterVarsity Press, 1974), 31.

[125] Komisar, *Being There,* 24.

[126] Rebekah Holsapple, "Scars of Love," 2005, unpublished manuscript.

Chapter 13: Eve, the Life Giver

[127] Elliot, *Let Me Be a Woman*, 4.

[128] https://darrowmillerandfriends.com/2014/12/18/divine-dignity-pregnancy/

[129] https://darrowmillerandfriends.com/2014/12/18/divine-dignity-pregnancy/

[130] Carl Friedrich Keil and Franz Delitzsch, in vol. 1, "The Pentateuch," of the *Biblical Commentary on the Old Testament*, accessed December 16, 2022, https://biblehub.com/commentaries/kad/deuteronomy/32.htm.

[131] Prager, *The Rational Bible: Genesis,* 58.

Chapter 14: Nurturer of the Nations

132 Wendell Berry, "Renewing Husbandry," *Orion,* September/October 2005, https://orion-magazine.org/article/renewing-husbandry/.

133 R. Laird Harris, Gleason L. Archer, Jr., & Bruce K. Waltke, *Theological Wordbook of the Old Testament, s.v. "adam"* (Chicago: Moody Press, 1980), 11,

134 James, *Female Piety*, 77.

135 Sigourney, *Letters to Young Ladies*, 15.

136 Ann Crittenden, *The Price of Motherhood: Why the Most Important Job in the World Is Still the Least Valued*, (New York: Henry Holt and Company, 2001), 72.

Part 5: Nurturing the Nations

Chapter 15: The Hand That Rocks the Cradle

137 https://en.wikisource.org/wiki/The_Hand_That_Rocks_the_Cradle.

138 Dennis Prager, "Judaism's Sexual Revolution: Why Judaism (and then Christianity) Rejected Homosexuality," *Crisis* 11, no. 8 (September 1993).

139 Prager, "Judaism's Sexual Revolution."

140 George F. Gilder, *Men and Marriage* (Gretna, LA: Pelican Publishing, 1986), 5.

141 Komisar, *Being There*, 52.

142 Mary Pride, *The Way Home* (Wheaton, IL: Crossway Books, 1985), xiii.

143 Pride, *The Way Home,* xii.

144 Daniel Webster, "'Self-Government the Cause of American Prosperity,' Address delivered in Faneuil Hall, May 22, 1852," in *The Writings and Speeches of Daniel Webster,* vol. xiii, (Cambridge, MA: Little, Brown, & Co., 1903), 518–19.

145 Nellie McClung, cited at "TimeLinks: Maternal Feminism," Manitoba Historical Society, accessed December 20, 2022, http://www.mhs.mb.ca/docs/features/timelinks/reference/db0015.shtml.

146 Sigourney, *Letters to Young Ladies*, 9.

147 Sigourney, *Letters to Young Ladies*, 10.

148 Sigourney, *Letters to Young Ladies*, 11.

149 Sigourney, *Letters to Young Ladies*, 11.

150 Sigourney, *Letters to Young Ladies*, 11.

151 Sigourney, *Letters to Young Ladies*, 12.

152 Sigourney, *Letters to Young Ladies*, 12.

Chapter 16: The Maternal Nature: Essential for Free Societies and Flourishing Economies

153 "Richest Countries in the World 2022," World Population Review, https://worldpopulationreview.com/country-rankings/richest-countries-in-the-world.

154 Crittenden, *The Price of Motherhood*, 4.

[155] "How Much Is a Mom Really Worth? The Amount May Surprise You," salary.com, accessed April 8, 2023, https://www.salary.com/articles/how-much-is-a-mom-really-worth-the-amount-may-surprise-you/.

[156] Juergen Voegele, "We can no longer grow our economies by degrading our natural capital," WorldBank.org, October 27, 2021, https://blogs.worldbank.org/voices/we-can-no-longer-grow-our-economies-degrading-our-natural-capital.

[157] Glenn-Marie Lange, Quentin Wodon, & Kevin Carey, eds., *The Changing Wealth of Nations 2018* (Washington, DC: World Bank Group, 2018), 47.

[158] World Bank, *Monitoring Environmental Progress* (Washington DC: World Bank Group, 1995) https://doi.org/10.1596/0-8213-3365-8.

[159] Crittenden, *The Price of Motherhood*, 68.

[160] Crittenden, *The Price of Motherhood*, 73–74.

[161] Robert C. Winthrop, "The Bible: An Address Delivered at the Annual Meeting of the Massachusetts Bible Society in Boston, May 28, 1849," in *Addresses and Speeches on Various Occasions* (Boston: Little, Brown & Co., 1852), 172.

[162] Ben Carson, *The Big Picture: Getting Perspective on What's Really Important* (Grand Rapids, MI: Zondervan, 1999), 107.

[163] Elizabeth Youmans, "The Christian Principle of Self-Government," unpublished manuscript.

[164] Rosalie Slater, *Teaching and Learning America's Christian History: The Principle Approach* (Chesapeake, VA: Foundation for American Christian Education, 1965), 188.

[165] *The Federalist* (Hallowell, ME: Glazier, Masters & Company, 1831), 187–188.

[166] Edmund Burke, "A Letter from Mr. Burke to a Member of the National Assembly, 1791," in *The Works of the Right Honorable Edmund Burke,* vol. I (London: Holdsworth & Ball, 1834), 490.

[167] Daniel Webster, "Remarks to the Ladies of Richmond, Oct. 5, 1840," in *The Wisdom and Eloquence of Daniel Webster* (New York: John B. Alden, 1886), 71.

[168] "TENET 5: WE ARE EMPOWERED BY OUR FEMININE NATURE AND BIOLOGY, AND WE HONOR OUR PROCREATIVE POWER," Big Ocean Women, accessed December 18, 2022, https://www.bigoceanwomen.org/resources/articles/tenet-5-we-are-empowered-by-our-feminine-nature-and-biology-2/.

[169] Webster, "Remarks to the Ladies of Richmond," 71.

Chapter 17: Making a House a Home

[170] Venker & Schlafly, *The Flip Side of Feminism*, 113.

[171] Linda Hirshman, "Homeward Bound," *The American Prospect*, November 20, 2005, https://prospect.org/features/homeward-bound/.

[172] Betty Friedan, *The Feminine Mystique* (New York: W. W. Norton, 1963), 83.

[173] Sigourney, *Letters to Young Ladies*, 10.

[174] "Jordan Peterson on Cleaning Your Room—The Joe Rogan Experience," YouTube, video, 4:26, accessed December 18, 2022, https://www.youtube.com/watch?v=Z8_gUmt-0k8o.

[175] Friedan, *The Feminine Mystique,* 83.

[176] Sigourney, *Letters to Young Ladies*, 11.

[177] Sigourney, *Letters to Young Ladies*, 12.

Chapter 18: The Home: Where Nations Are Nurtured

[178] "Women's rights; and the duties of both men and women," Theodore Roosevelt Collection, MS Am 1454.50 (161), Harvard College Library, https://www.theodorerooseveltcenter.org/Research/Digital-Library/Record?libID=o285268.

[179] I served as General Editor for a full-length book that deals with issues of education. Look for *Don't Let Schooling Stand in the Way of Education: A Biblical Response to the Crisis in Public Education.* You can also find resources on my blog, https://darrowmillerandfriends.com. Consider taking a look at Dr. Elizabeth Youmans' enriched curriculum for children and Christian worldview courses for the adults who disciple them (https://AMOprogram.com). You can learn more and find resources about the principle approach to education from The Foundation for American Christian Education (F.A.C.E. at https://face.net/why-the-principle-approach/) and from Classical Christian Education (https://classicalchristian.org). Charter schools are governed by parents and not the state. See Great Hearts as one model (https://www.greatheartsamerica.org).

[180] Madame Steinberg, *Lecture on Female Education* (Paris: E. Brière and Co., 1855).

[181] Sigourney, *Letters to Young Ladies*, 13.

[182] J.A. Comenius, *The Great Didactic* (London: Adam & Charles Black, 1896), 157.

[183] "Finding Our Voice," *Essence*, May 1, 1995.

[184] Sigourney, *Letters to Young Ladies*, 14.

[185] Sigourney, *Letters to Young Ladies*, 14.

[186] Venker & Schlafly, *The Flip Side of Feminism*, 89.

[187] Sigourney, *Letters to Young Ladies*, 15.

[188] Sigourney, *Letters to Young Ladies*, 15.

[189] Sigourney, *Letters to Young Ladies*, 75.

Part 6: Recovering a Biblical Feminism

Chapter 20: The First Wave: Maternal Feminism

[190] Alexis de Tocqueville, *Democracy in America* (Auckland, NZ: The Floating Press, 2009), 1158–1159.

[191] Manitoba Historical Society, "Maternal Feminism."

[192] Venker & Schlafly, *The Flip Side of Feminism*, 52.

Chapter 21: The Second Wave: Modern Feminism

[193] Tommaso Marinetti, "Manifeste du futurisme," *Le Figaro*, February 20, 1909.

[194] Mary Pride, *The Way Home: Beyond Feminism, Back to Reality* (Wheaton, IL: Crossway Books, 1985), xii–xiii.

195 Camille Paglia, *Free Women, Free Men: Sex, Gender, Feminism* (New York: Pantheon Books, 2017), 132.

196 Paglia, *Free Women, Free Men*, 205.

197 Paglia, *Free Women, Free Men*, 259.

198 Hirshman, "Homeward Bound."

199 Paglia, *Free Women, Free Men*, 273.

200 Kathleen Parker, *Save the Males: Why Men Matter, Why Women Should Care* (New York: Random House, 2008), 196.

201 Venker & Schlafly, *The Flip Side of Feminism*, 31.

202 Komisar, *Being There*, 186.

203 Barger, *Eve's Revenge*, 74.

204 Maureen Ferguson, "Why Abortion Is Antithetical to Women's Empowerment," Real-Clear Politics, January 18, 2020, https://www.realclearpolitics.com/articles/2020/01/18/why_abortion_is_antithetical_to_womens_empowerment_142182.html.

Chapter 22: The Third Wave: Postmodern Feminism and the Death of Binary Sexuality

205 Laura Perrins, "The Laura Perrins Interview: Feminists specialise in generating conflict, says leading US critic Suzanne Venker," *The Conservative Woman*, June 30, 2016, https://www.conservativewoman.co.uk/the-laura-perrins-interview-feminists-specialise-in-generating-conflict-says-leading-us-critic-suzanne-venker/.

206 *Wikipedia*, s.v. "John Money," accessed May 2, 2023, https://en.wikipedia.org/wiki/John_Money.

207 Riki Wilchins, "We'll Win the Bathroom Battle When the Binary Burns," *Advocate*, April 29, 2016, https://www.advocate.com/commentary/2016/4/29/well-win-bathroom-battle-when-binary-burns.

208 Masha Gessen, on a panel discussion for the Sydney Writers Festival, "Why get married when you could be happy?", Australian Broadcasting Corporation, 06:31, June 10, 2012, https://www.abc.net.au/radionational/programs/lifematters/why-get-married/4058506.

Chapter 23: Christ, the First Feminist

209 Alvin J. Schmidt, *How Christianity Changed the World* (Grand Rapids, MI: Zondervan, 2001), 102.

210 Naphtali Lewis, *Life in Egypt under Roman Rule* (Oxford: Clarendon, 1985), 54.

211 Plato, *Plato in Twelve Volumes, Vol. 9,* translated by W.R.M. Lamb (Cambridge, MA, Harvard University Press; London, William Heinemann Ltd. 1925) accessed December 19, 2022, http://data.perseus.org/citations/urn:cts:greekLit:tlg0059.tlg031.perseus-eng1:90e. [sections 90e-f, 91d].

212 Aristotle, *Generation of Animals,* trans. A.L. Peck (London: William Heinemann, 1943), 401.

213 Aristotle, *Generation of Animals,* 175.

214 Aristotle, *Politics,* 1.1254b, accessed December 19, 2022, http://data.perseus.org/citations/urn:cts:greekLit:tlg0086.tlg035.perseus-eng1:1.1254b.

215 Mardi Keyes, "The Mystery of Gender" (unpublished paper delivered at L'Abri, Southborough, MA, July 20, 2001), 6.

216 Jerusalem Talmud *Sotah* 3:4:7, 120a, accessed December 19, 2022, https://www.sefaria.org/Jerusalem_Talmud_Sotah.3.4.7?ven=The_Jerusalem_Talmud,_translation_and_commentary_by_Heinrich_W._Guggenheimer._Berlin,_De_Gruyter,_1999-2015&lang=en&with=all&lang2=en.

217 Babylonian Talmud *Sotah* 3:4, 21b, accessed December 19, 2022, https://halakhah.com/sotah/sotah_21.html.

218 Dorothy L. Sayers, *Are Women Human? Astute and Witty Essays on the Role of Women in Society* (Edinburgh: Alban Books, 1971), 47.

219 J. D. Douglas, *The New Bible Dictionary,* s.v. "Genealogy" (Wheaton, IL: Tyndale House, 1962).

220 Barger, *Eve's Revenge,* 53.

221 Barger, *Eve's Revenge,* 146.

222 Barger, *Eve's Revenge,* 154.

223 Keyes, 11.

224 Barger, *Eve's Revenge,* 175.

Chapter 24: The Perfect Bridegroom and the Ultimate Wedding

225 Timothy Keller, *The Meaning of Marriage: Facing the Complexities of Commitment with the Wisdom of God* (New York: Penguin, 2011), 101.

226 I am very grateful to Bill Risk for the inspiration for this chapter and much of the basic content. It took my breath away when I read his book. Having been a Christian for many years, I had never seen the relationship between the element of the Jewish wedding ceremony, the Wedding of the Lamb, and the significance of the details for the church and our lives today. Bill Risk, *The Ultimate Wedding: Ancient Jewish Marriage Traditions and their Fulfillment in Jesus the Messiah,* accessed December 19, 2022, http://www.ldolphin.org/risk/ult.shtml.

227 John Piper, "Male and Female He Created Them in the Image of God," Desiring God, May 14, 1989, https://www.desiringgod.org/messages/male-and-female-he-created-them-in-the-image-of-god.

228 Edwards, *The Divine Romance,* 190–191.

THE GRAND DESIGN

ONLINE VIDEO COURSE

REDISCOVERING MALE AND FEMALE AS IMAGO DEI

You can also experience this rich content in an online course taught by Darrow Miller. A series of eight lessons with multiple videos and beautiful graphics will take you through all of the main themes of *The Grand Design*.

Join this free course at www.coramdeo.com

We are confident you will benefit.

Disciple Nations Alliance (**www.disciplenations.org**) is an evangelical discipleship ministry whose vision is to train Christ-followers in an empowered, biblical worldview and equip them to be agents of Kingdom transformation, starting in their families, churches, communities, and vocations.

We invite you to explore our array of discipleship and training resources at **www.disciplenations.org**, and join the movement by becoming a "Kingdomizer" **https://disciplenations.org/kingdomizer**

If you'd like more information about any of our resources or opportunities, please contact us!

Disciple Nations Alliance
1110 E. Missouri Ave., Suite 393
Phoenix, AZ 85014
info@disciplenations.org
www.disciplenations.org

Made in the USA
Coppell, TX
28 November 2023

24884398R00186